DIDEROT
THRESHOLDS OF REPRESENTATION

DIDEROT
THRESHOLDS OF REPRESENTATION

JAMES CREECH

OHIO STATE UNIVERSITY PRESS
COLUMBUS

Library of Congress Cataloguing in Publication Data

Creech, James, 1945–
    Diderot: thresholds of representation.

    Bibliography: p.
    Includes index.
    1. Diderot, Denis, 1713–1784—Criticism and interpretation.
2. Representation (Philosophy).
I. Title
PQ1979.C7   1985   848'.509   85-25881
ISBN 0-8142-0393-0

FOR MY FATHER

TABLE OF CONTENTS

PREFACE

THE QUESTION OF REPRESENTATION INHABITS DIDE-
rot's writing. It is legible through its effects more than in propositional discourse about something which he explicitly names "representation." It is the tropism that accounts for a diverse series
of textual turns, like the exorbitant swerves in the journey of
planets that suggest the proximity of another, invisible body. But
the "other body" of representation, unlike celestial bodies, is not
proximate. It is not a body. It is not discourse. Its effects stem from
its alterity. Its only presence is in a certain turn to the other—to
the Other—the opening in Diderot's writing that demands a response, that makes thought, that elicits dialogue. Jean Starobinski
showed that a "parole de l'autre" in Diderot has in fact ordered a
long dialogue between his works and their posterity. This book is
another attempt to listen and answer in the same way, in the same
tradition. But it takes the nature and function of the text's *address*
to this Other as its explicit object.

The same address or dialogue links philosophical and literary
writing in Diderot's texts, each addressing the other—its Other—
in a profoundly dialogical language. It is something of this dialogue that I have sought to suggest in the division of this text into
a first and second part. The first part focuses on aesthetic and
literary texts, the second part on what are usually thought of as
philosophical texts. (Witness, for example, the canonization of
this difference in the indispensable *Classiques Garnier* editions of
Diderot's *Oeuvres Philosophiques, Oeuvres OEsthétiques,* and
Oeuvres Romanesques.) Here, however, the readings of aesthetic
and literary texts are already philosophical; the readings of philosophy in Part Two arise from the aesthetics that emerge in Part
One.

These references take two forms. First, there are many footnotes that are not of the usual scholarly sort. These are responses
and echoes to and from Diderot's texts. And second, there are
postscripts to several chapters. Each postscript is a more or less
lengthy designation of a resonance or an implicit "renvoi" linking

Diderot's writing to a range of other texts. These connections are too marginal to have been included in the main chapters, where the postscript references are indicated, but too important to be consigned to footnotes. More significantly, the point of the entire book is bound up in the notion that representation, despite its "bad press" in modern times, is not just a "closure," but also an "opening." The postscripts indulge that understanding in a very concrete fashion, by underscoring the openings that link a heterogeneous selection of writings to Diderot, even texts that are manifestly not linked by any traditional representational connection.

These postscripts are not intended to be read as one would a footnote, interrupting the reading of the main text. They are better read after reading a chapter, or perhaps better still, in sequence at the end of the book.

And finally, focusing on the problem of representation obviously opens a Pandora's box of difficulties for anyone trying to formulate a theory or discourse representative of its object. The temptation of self-referential excess is great. But self-consciousness is also, in a certain sense, unnecessary. In her lovely new book entitled *Beautiful Theories* (Baltimore: Johns Hopkins University Press, 1982, p. 86), Elizabeth Bruss writes, "Theory does not need, as postmodern novels do, to seek artificial ways of dispelling representational illusion or construct extra pieces of textual machinery to arouse greater self-awareness and a more aggressive role in readers; contentious reading is traditional to theory. . . . Theory is always openly dialogic. . . . " I have tried to ignore the impulse to control by infinite regression into the meta-meta. I have tried to minimize self-reference. And yet, what I have tried to make legible in Diderot's text is, at the same time, an *ars critica* for the activity which is here being practiced.

Some of the chapters here have been published in various forms in reviews and collections of essays. Chapter two is loosely based on an article that appeared in *The Eighteenth Century: Theory and Interpretation*, Vol. 20, No. 2 (1979); chapter five first appeared in *Diderot: Digression and Dispersion*, ed. J. Undank and H. Josephs (Lexington, Ky.: French Forum Press, 1984), pp. 85–92; chapter six was published in the *Stanford French Review*, Fall 1984, pp. 295–308; and chapter nine appeared in *Yale French Studies* 63 (1982). Grateful acknowledgment is made for permission to reprint them here.

ACKNOWLEDGMENTS

SURELY NOBODY IS MORE RICH IN FRIENDS AND COL-leagues than I have been in writing this book. For supportive comments on early drafts, I extend heartfelt gratitude to Jane Gallop, Mitchell Greenberg, Patricia Harkin, Peggy Kamuf, Janet Mercer, Larysa Mykyta, Suzanne Pucci, James Sosnoski, Jack Undank, Marie-Claire Vallois, Nat Wing, and the Oxford Circle on Literary Theory.

DIDEROT

THRESHOLDS OF REPRESENTATION

CHAPTER ONE

Introduction

Analysis of representations leads thought to
the outer limits of the rational, to the area
of the paradoxical, close to the absurd,
and yet distinct from the absurd.
—Henri Lefebvre
La Présence et l'absence

WHAT DOES IT MEAN TO EN-
gage in a study of the vast question of "representation," as
that issue informs the writings of one eighteenth-century
French writer? Does the issue have a specifically eighteenth-
century or a "Diderotian" aspect that would dictate an
intellectual-historical approach in a study such as this? Or,
can one discuss representation per se, more or less eliminating the historical issue or at least shunting it to the background? Anticipating what follows, we could say already that
neither of these alternatives is satisfactory. The necessity of
beginning with this question of history is itself one of the
paradoxical effects of representation. And indeed, one of
the tasks before us will be to show how this question of
method is related to the nature and function of representation in our culture.

Henri Lefebvre has provided the most ambitious historical overview of representation in his recent book, *La Présence et l'absence: contribution à la théorie des représentations.*[1] Lefebvre's approach is different in that, rather than
focusing on one writer, it aims for broad generality—even if
Marx and Nietzsche claim the lion's portion of his atten-

tion. And yet our perspectives converge to the extent that Lefebvre also sees the question of representation both in its historical specificity and as a constant of philosophical discourse, transcending historical specificity, evident already in Thales (p. 100). "In sum, well before the domination of the representational (and well before the concept), myriads of representations were in circulation, with diverse and opposing destinies, not recognized as such but forcefully bringing with them partisanship and action" (p. 59).

There is yet a further point of convergence with Lefebvre's approach. He proceeds with the belief that when one reads philosophy from a perspective defined by the *question* of representation (perhaps *the* question for the Western logos), philosophy appears in a different light. Philosophy remains opaque to this "different light" when one attempts to grasp the truth or falsehood of philosophical pretentions solely in their own terms, implicitly assuming that the problem of representation is moot for the particular philosophical system or enunciation being scrutinized.

> Are we engaged in a new reading, a self-proclaimed new reading, of the philosophers? Yes, if one wants to use that vocabulary. One could also say that as a concept formed by philosophy—deriving from *philosophy in its entirety*, namely from the sequence and the linkage of philosophies—the concept of representation reacts upon the history of philosophy, shows it in a different light. Philosophy circumscribes itself and thus circumscribes and discerns fields within itself as well as beyond itself: representations, meta-philosophy. (P. 136; my emphasis)

When the frame of reading becomes representation as the *question*—how is it posited, what attempts at closure does it generate, what is its relation to history?—texts are opened to each other, to works by historically diverse writers in other centuries. One begins then to sense the infelicity of simply periodizing representation within historical categories.

This tug-of-war, this tension between centrifugal generality and centripetal historicity, is our starting point here. And although the tension will not be resolved, it can be broadly outlined in advance.

One of the most significant examples of the kind of periodization that I am calling into question can be seen in the earlier works of Michel Foucault, particularly in *Les Mots et les choses* where he spends considerable effort to describe representation in the seventeenth and eighteenth centuries. Foucault maintains that representation is the principal feature of this Classical "episteme" because signs are no longer part of the world, a world of infinite resemblances, as they were in the sixteenth century. In the classical age, signs no longer partake of things in their proximity to themselves but are thought rather to "represent" things in a separate but transparent medium whose privileged form is language. Language represents both the particular as well as the general representability of all things. A particular substitution of a word for a thing represents the very substitutability of word for thing, in transparent adequation to the thing's identity.

Unlike the previous episteme in which one made random and endless lists of things in the world, the new system of representation automatically involves "analysis" of what it represents. The inaugural moment representing identity between words and things leads to an ordering of these word-things among themselves according to their characteristic differences from each other. The transparent relationship of identity through which one thing is represented necessarily entails an incremental passage to increasingly different word-things, thus forming what Foucault describes as a "grid" of identities and differences. And coming full circle, the adequation, the transparent correspondence between the whole grid (language) and the totality of things, is the overarching identity upon which particular knowledge rests in this arrangement. To know in the Classical episteme is to represent in this way.

In important ways Foucault has produced a convincing reading of epistemological procedures in the seventeenth and eighteenth centuries. One is struck by the explanatory power of his analysis when "applied" to a variety of significant texts of the period. The *Encyclopedia* provides unusually rich terrain for illustrating the point, in part because it is based on the particular status accorded to language. As Foucault points out, the work's primary organization owes nothing to an order believed to be intrinsic to the world it represents. It is determined instead by the alphabet, which is an arbitrary order existing only within language. The text's order is accommodated within the very "space" opened by words, within the language element itself (p. 88). Through that space language is put into relation with the universal and to being (p. 86). Although modern usage has consecrated the appellation "Encyclopédie," its original name bears witness to a different emphasis that certainly supports Foucault's claims about its relation to language: it was first conceived as a "Dictionnaire Encyclopédique."

In his "Discours préliminaire," many of d'Alembert's formulations resonate with Foucault's analysis in striking ways. "Nature . . . is composed only of entities [*individus*] which are the original objects of our sensations and of our direct perceptions. In fact, we notice in these entities common properties by which we compare them, and dissimilar properties by which we discern them. . . . "[3] So similarity and difference are indeed the bases for the organization of all "word-things" in the *Encyclopedia* into a representational grid or system in a manner that one would not find in the Renaissance or the Middle Ages.

Similar confirmation could be located in other texts of the period, particularly in Descartes, not to mention other *Encyclopedia* articles (especially those on language). Many of these are of course mentioned in *Les Mots et les choses*. But insofar as it is a historical argument that situates representation as the epistemological keystone of a discrete time, I maintain that it is based on a necessary suppression of competing, extrahistorical aspects of the problem. The historically specific protocols and procedures that Foucault has highlighted will be marked by questions and difficulties that will directly link it to broader issues owing nothing to the Classical episteme. Stated succinctly, my question would be this: Can a historical period open and close a relation to "representation"—simply, serenely, unproblematically? Does not the apparent success of Foucault's analysis derive from the fact that it first assumes for itself a closed historical space, the "classical age?" In our tradition, however, the question of representation seems almost to have particular "properties" that make it impossible to appropriate to a particular historical period. It has a tendency to remain the problem that critical and philosophical discourse has to resolve continually, even in the period of the seventeenth and eighteenth centuries when, for Foucault, it attained unquestioned generality. If one could suggest that attempts to resolve the problem in different historical periods bear a certain resemblance to each other because they are grappling with "the same issue"—but what order of similitude?— what would be left of Foucault's historical closure?

Such a demonstration ideally would devote the same attention to all the authors in question as I shall give to Diderot. Having raised the issue, however, I will illustrate the point by briefly conjuring up three different "moments" in representation's "history," using as examples d'Alembert, John Locke, and then Plato. The question will be, What accounts for a certain sameness that emerges beneath the obvious difference and historical specificity of each?

If we look at d'Alembert's "Discours préliminaire" again—indeed, if we go back to the pages quoted above—we discover an emphasis rather different from the one underscored by Foucault.

As we said, the *Encyclopedia* is ordered according to an alphabetical listing of word-things. Each word is followed by an article defining the thing. The whole, however, is ordered according to what Diderot and d'Alembert call, after Bacon, an encyclopedic "tree." (For readers of Foucault, the encyclopedic tree can easily be understood as a version of the grid of differences and similarities mentioned above.) But if we read a bit further, we discover d'Alembert worrying over something that Foucault's analysis does not account for, namely, a sense of impossibility, of obstacle, that this arborescent system brings with it. "Although the philosophical history of the origin of our ideas that we have just given is quite useful in facilitating such a task [as the *Encyclopedia*], one must not think that the encyclopedic tree should or even could be made to *fit this history* in a servile manner. The general system of the sciences and arts is a *kind of labyrinth*, a tortuous path on which the mind sets out without knowing the route it should take" (pp. 43–44; my emphasis). In principle—the principle analyzed by Foucault, no doubt— there is an editorial point of view from which the "labyrinth" is transformed into a "world map [*mappemonde*]," allowing us to perceive at a glance all similarities and differences, to "distinguish the general branches of human knowledge, the points which separate or unite them . . . " (p. 45). But d'Alembert explicitly recognized that such a point of view from which the grid of identities and differences could be discerned is only an unreal "projection," and as such, it is only one of many different projections that could be imagined: "One can imagine therefore as many different systems of human knowledge as world maps projected at different angles" (p. 45). It is a very direct and clear-cut statement expressing both belief in the ideal of representation and, at the same time, recognition of the arbitrariness, and even impossibility, of its precepts. For d'Alembert there "are"—existing in some mode of relationship remaining to be spelled out—both the general and transparent system of the "mappemonde" and the fragmentary and opaque reality of the "labyrinth."

The best point of view from which to "project" the encyclopedic tree is said to be one that allows the greatest number of differences and similarities—of connections—to appear. (Again, Foucault's argument certainly comes to mind: the best encyclopedia would be the one in which the largest "grid" of identities and differences would represented.) But no sooner has it been anticipated than D'Alembert immediately raises a basic question concerning this all-encompassing point of view: "Yes but is there any reason to think we are able to grasp it? [Mais, peut-on se flatter de le saisir?]" (p. 45). He continues with the passage we partially quoted above. Here it is at greater length:

> Nature . . . is composed only of entities [*individus*] which are the original objects of our sensations and of our direct perceptions. In fact, we notice in these entities common properties by which we compare them, and dissimilar properties by which we discern them. . . . But oftentimes some object which, because of one or several of its properties was placed under one classification, belongs under another classification because of other properties, and just as well could have been placed there. Thus there necessarily remains arbitrariness in the general division. (Pp. 45–46)

Clearly, this is an instance in which an unstated but operative epistemological convention calls for representation of differences and similarities in the manner described by Foucault. But even as d'Alembert prescribes it, he in effect recognizes its necessary failure, its impossibility. The "mappemonde" is always contaminated with the labyrinth from which it promised rescue; the classical grid bears within it the labyrinthine arbitrariness of sixteenth-century compendia. This will not be the last time that ideal representational transparency will find itself linked to reminders of the very obstacles that make it impossible.

But this particular obstacle to the all-encompassing representational perspective is not the only one, nor the most serious. From an ideal point of view—only a projection, I repeat—there would be no categorical divisions of the things represented in the *Encyclopedia*. The most natural arrangement (representing things in the *Encyclopedia* just as they are in "nature") would be a chain in which all things would be bound together by incremental links. But the possibility of this ideal system for representing reality is also ruled out, and once more ruled out in terms that we shall have occasion to see again.

> The most natural arrangement would be one in which objects would follow one upon the other by means of *imperceptible* nuances that serve *both to separate them and to unite them*. But the small number of entities [*êtres*] known to us does not allow us to mark these nuances. The universe is but a vast ocean on the surface of which we perceive a few islands, of diverse scale, whose link to the continent is hidden to us. (P. 46; my emphasis)

Earlier d'Alembert began by insisting that the "object" to be represented—reality, "nature"—is composed of entities "qui sont l'objet primitif de nos sensations et de nos perceptions directes." We see similarities and differences in these objects that are to be represented in the linguistic element of the *Encyclopedia*. But that which unites and separates these objects of our direct perception cannot be perceived. If one cannot perceive these "nuances insensibles" that make unity and difference, then one cannot represent according to Foucault's grid. And this is precisely the *problem* that d'Alembert is underscoring here even as he signals his faith in a representational order that presumes the problem resolved.

If representation is the medium from which the *Encyclopedia* springs, it is also the difficulty that encyclopedists must resolve in order to produce their work. The "Discours préliminaire" expresses the well-known Enlightenment program that for d'Alembert no less than for us was the "true nature" of the Encyclopedic project. But it also writes large the impossibility of these founding ideological a prioris that constitute its "true nature" (its identity as *Encyclopedia*), thus undermining itself to a remarkable degree. I would even say that part of the text's mode of being is *not* to be "itself," *not* to be what it is idealogically programmed to be.

Representation is the name of the theoretical problem around which this diacritical identity is organized. It is the issue that the text would have had to resolve in order to be itself, if by *Encyclopédie* we mean a triumphant indulgence in language's power to represent. And it is my contention that the "Discours" opens to, "refers" to, its "others," other texts, other historical periods, precisely to the extent that it is not itself, in this sense—that it marks its deviation from what it is presumed to be.

Let us then turn to another text to which "Discours préliminaire" can be said to refer through this internal textual disjunction that occurs around the issue of representation. There is a similar moment of anxiety in John Locke, one of the philosophical patriarchs of the *Encyclopedia* from the preceding century, but still within Foucault's Classical episteme. Locke's is an epistemology based on the capacity of the senses accurately to represent what he calls primary and secondary ideas to the mind. If one looks for some clue as to the precise nature of the mechanism by which such representational connections work in the Lockean system, one comes upon a very curious explanation in the *Essay concerning Human Understanding*. For Locke there is no intrinsic link, or basis for an intrinsic link, between the phenomenal world and the ideas that represent it in the mind. It is specifically in this that he is, in fact, anti-platonistic (in ordinary, intellectual-historical terms). And yet he, like Plato, must find some means to account for the representational links between things and other things, between things and the ideas we have of them in the mind. Here is the passage, from book two of the *Essay*:

> The next thing is to consider how bodies produce ideas in us; and that is manifestly by impulse [i.e., motion]. . . . If then external objects be not united to

our minds and yet we perceive these *original* qualities in them . . . it is evident that some motion must be thence continued by our nerves . . . to the brains or seat of sensation, there to produce in our minds the particular ideas we have of them. And since the extension, figure, number and motion of bodies . . . may be perceived at a distance by the sight, it is evident [that] some singly *imperceptible* bodies [my emphasis] must come from them to the eyes, and thereby convey to the brain some motion which produces these ideas we have of them in us.[4]

A similar logic explains how we derive our ideas of secondary qualities as well. We perceive secondary qualities thanks to "the operation of *insensible* particles on our senses" (my emphasis). These particles cannot themselves be perceived, but they cause perceptions of an object to occur in the sense organs, and from these, to become ideas in the brain. They mediate, in other words, between perceptible object and brain, but are themselves imperceptible. Locke's entire sensationalist epistemology, where nothing is in the mind that was not first in the senses, hinges on this copula function performed by "*insensible* particles."

But Locke does not, cannot, really explain them. The particles are an aberrancy in the system, as are d'Alembert's equally imperceptible "nuances" in the Encyclopedic system. Locke is, according to his own precepts, speaking of something of which he has no "idea." That is, he cannot perceive these particles by any of the five senses, no more than he could have an "idea" of those abstract "substances" so cherished by Aristotelean scholasticism and which he discards as abstractions for just that reason: they cannot be perceived. What the particles do for Locke's representational epistemology (and the reason he posits them) is to guarantee two contradictory relations of representation and represented: first, guaranteeing that the object be represented accurately in the senses, that the representation be a return to presence of what he emphasizes are "*original* qualities" (thus a function of mimetic identity); and second, guaranteeing that the object remain different from the mind's perception, extrinsic and thus re-producible, available to the mind *only* as a representation (a function of mimetic difference and a bulwark against all sorts of theologically based arguments). There is an intriguing similarity between this double function and the double function performed by d'Alembert's imperceptible nuances, both separating and uniting things in the all-encompassing representional point of view.

But Locke seems to have difficulty with his own argument. A sign of that difficulty is his turning to God at this juncture as a means of legitimating the representational "equality" of otherwise different, unconnected things and ideas.

> Let us suppose, at present that the different motions and figures, bulk and number of such particles, affecting the several organs of our senses, produce in us those different sensations which we have from the colors and smells of bodies . . . it being no more impossible to conceive that *God* should annex such ideas to such motions, with which they *have no similitude*, than that he should annex the idea of pain to the motion of a piece of steel dividing our flesh, with which that idea hath no resemblance."[5]

The particles are essential to Locke's representational epistemology because they provide a nonidealistic, protomaterialistic explanation of just how sense representations are connected to the objects they represent. Yet at the same time, they radically contradict the empiricism on which Locke's notion of a simple, transparent representation was based. Even as they are supposed to overcome such difficulties, they in fact exemplify the most basic problem that his philosophical discourse, like that of d'Alembert, is setting out to resolve: representational transparency finds itself faced with the necessity to posit both identity and difference, transparency and opacity, between its terms—and at the same time. The text unseats itself from itself, and implicitly "refers" to this same knotted problem of representational identity and difference in other texts, in other historical periods.

(It should be mentioned, in passing, that Locke's posterity in the tradition of Anglo-American language philosophy has inherited the same problem. To cite one typical example, in the recent *Representations* by Jerry Fodor we read: "If representational theory of the mind is true, then we know what propositional attitudes are. But the net total of philosophical problems is surely not decreased thereby. We must now face what has always been *the* problem for representational theories to solve: what relates internal representations to the world? I take it that this problem is now the main content of philosophy of mind."[6] One wonders whether we really had to wait until now for that central problem to declare itself.)

We will end this schematic survey by returning to the "orginal" classical episteme. Plato saw the world of appearances as falling short of ideal reality, as "striving" or "longing" for the ideal identity that appearances represent imperfectly. (I am using the verb "represent" very loosely for the moment. This is not a Platonic concept.)

In the "Phaedo" Socrates argues, as he does elsewhere (e.g., the "Meno"), that all knowledge is recollection of knowledge that we previously possessed, but which we have forgotten. Learning—thus acquisition of knowledge—does take place when we experience or perceive things in the phenomenal world through our senses. What we learn from such experiences, however, is ultimately derived from an ideal source other than the ostensible objects of our perception and knowledge. What we learn from the world of shadows is only a recollection of this ideal world. Thus, although we learn from the phenomena, what we learn is different from the phenomena. This whole issue of knowledge as recollection, in other words, replays the issue of representation that we saw above. The ideas in our minds are in some paradoxical fashion both new and old, both in us and outside us, joined to us and separated from us, identical and different. The nature of these connections is the basic question that Socrates is laboring to overcome.

> *Socrates*: The knowledge of a lyre is not the same as the knowledge of a man?
>
> *Simmias*: True.
>
> *Soc*: And yet what is the feeling of lovers when they recognize a lyre, or a garment, or anything else which the beloved has been in the habit of using? Do not they, from knowing the lyre, form in the mind's eye an image of the youth to whom the lyre belongs? And this is recollection. In like manner anyone who sees Simmias may remember Cebes; and there are endless examples of the same thing.
>
> *Sim*: Endless, indeed.
>
> *Soc*: And recollection is most commonly a process of recovering that which has been already forgotten through time and inattention.
>
> *Sim*: Yes it is.
>
> *Soc*: And in all these cases, the recollection may be derived from things either like or unlike?
>
> *Sim*: It may be.
>
> *Soc*: And when the recollection is derived from like things, then another consideration is sure to arise, which is—whether or not the likeness in any degree falls short of that which is recollected?
>
> *Sim*: Very true.
>
> *Soc*: And shall we proceed a step further, and affirm that there is such a thing as equality, not of one piece of wood or stone with another, but that, over and above this there is absolute equality? Shall we say so?
>
> *Sim*: Say so, yes, replied Simmias, and swear to it, with all the confidence in life.[7]

The outcome of this involved argument is expressed in an assertion by Socrates: "Whenever from seeing one thing you conceived another, whether like or unlike, there must surely have been an act of recollection."[8]

Beneath the apparent self-evidence of this arguement lies a challenging paradox. When perceiving one thing causes us to recollect another thing, we experience a kind of equality of those two things, even if it is only by metonymy (as when "knowledge" of a lover's lyre equals "knowledge" of the lover or causes us to represent the lover to our mind's eye). But we also know, at the same moment, that those things are not the same. A lyre is not a man. Even when the two objects are connected metaphorically through resemblance (as when a painting or statue resembles its object), we see both similarity and difference at the same time.

Socrates is quite explicit. He is faced with a problem—and it is a problem that is certain to come up because, I maintain, it is the problem that is integral to representation: "When the recollection is derived from like things, then another consideration is sure to arise, which is—whether or not the likeness in any degree falls short of that which is recollected?" Here then is the question of difference, its nature, scope, function and most important of all, its controllability. And in order even to ask that question, some difference already has to be instated. Whatever the figuration, by whatever trope, when one thing figures another two cognitive operations occur simultaneously: we know at the same time that X equals Y, and that X is different from Y.

From this equality of two things that are different, we are led to recollect another equality according to Socrates. This second order of equality is not the same as the first representational connection of different things. Rather, it is a relation of things that are absolutely equal, conjoined in an absolute and indivisible presence. (This will be Socrates' qualification of the realm of ideal essences.) In a Kantian vocabulary, we could say that the representational connection of things in the phenomenal realm gives us to know another order of connection in the noumenal realm. In other words, ordinary representational connection itself represents a different kind of connection. Earthly connectedness of different things (in which the question of difference remains) represents another kind of connectedness in which difference vanishes completely. But even as the one represents the other, there persists once again a difference between the first, profane sort of connection and the second, ideal connection. Just as lyre strives fully to represent lover (but fails because it remains different from him), phenomenal representation of X by Y strives to represent ideal and undifferentiated representation, but fails because it can never really transcend the difference between the profane and ideal. This is the meaning of Socrates' conclusion that, "from the senses then, is derived the knowledge that all sensible things aim at an absolute equality of which they fall short."[9]

Of course, Plato's is not strictly speaking an "epistemology" in the modern sense, based on a theory of representation understood as such. I am leaving out many important qualifications, not to mention permutations, of the problem found in Aristotle. I am maintaining, however, that Plato is ultimately involved in a question of representation that does communicate in significant ways with the more modern form of the problem that we saw before.[10] I would echo Lefebvre's formulation mentioned earlier on: "In sum, well before the domination of the representational (and *well before the concept*), myriads of representations were in circulation, with diverse and opposing destinies, not recognized as such but forcefully bringing with them partisanship and action" (my emphasis).

But to return to the present argument, lyre : lover :: phenomenal representation : ideal representation. These associations are produced by a copula that can be understood as performing a function that we think of as representational. The negative "falling short" of terms "coupled" in this way, for Plato, implied a copula of a different and ideal sort in which the joined terms do not fall short but enjoy a relation of absolute identity. Ideality is given to our knowledge then in the representational difference/connection that we can see among the phenomena. In other words, representation in Plato brings with it a certain duplicity: something is made present again, but present in such a fashion as to remind us of something else that remains absent or different, something ideal to which all phenomenal representation remains inadequate. *Adequatio* and *inadequatio*, *mimesis* and *simulacrum*, are conjoined. Knowledge is *in* their conjunction, even knowledge of the ideal. Ideality is then given to us only in difference from ideality. In this sense, difference produces the Undifferentiated.

One thinks of the representational connections that Locke posited between thing and idea that were guaranteed by those imperceptible particles, or of d'Alembert's ideal *Encyclopedia,* so intimately connected to imperceptible nuances. Ideal representational transparency in all three of these systems is grounded in a double function of identity and difference which it is uncomfortable for each discourse to accommodate.

This fundamental and insurmountable difficulty will become familiar as we go along and, I shall argue, accompanies representation as a kind of shadow. The paradox of identity and difference in Plato, far from being resolved at the outset by the presupposition of the Idea, *constitutes* the problem that he, and with him Western philosophical discourse, is setting out to contain. But the question lives on in the very labor to silence it. And it is that question, the question of representation, that unseats these three texts from their place within historical limits, opening them to each other and to other texts in other periods as well.[12]

Before turning to Diderot, a recapitulation of the argument is warranted, and with it, a few preliminary conclusions. The question is: What represents in a representation? That is, what is the mechanism by which representations are connected to their objects, reliably reproducing them while remaining different from them? What status is granted those mechanisms and what effects do they produce? What discursive energies do they mobilize?

Foucault claims that the epistemological protocols of the modern classical age turned to representation, in the mode of language, as a transparent medium by which things could be tightly systematized according to their identities and differences. I have claimed that, omni-historically, representation is a problem that also brings with it certain paradoxes, certain effects of difference. In a summary fashion, I have tried to suggest different historical periods and different views of representation in which an effort to grapple with the trans-historical paradox is legible beneath the epistemological confidence displayed rhetorically in the arguments.

The conclusion that I have been implying up to now is this: representation (in Plato's broad but useful terms, "whenever from seeing one thing you conceive another") brings with it a problem of similarity and difference. This problem fuels epistemological systems. It is what those systems are trying to accommodate, but the effort itself is always incommodious. It generates appeals to divine transcendence, invisible particles and the like, which only serve to instate the problem within the solution. With reference to Foucault's reading of the seventeenth and eighteenth centuries, only a particular and strategic blindness could prompt him to argue for a serene, unproblematic, and transparent representational element— language—even in a past, historic mode. Reading Diderot provides many reasons to question Foucault's strongest qualification of "the total configuration of the Classical episteme" as a *"continuum of representation and being,* an ontology defined negatively as an *absence of nothingness,* a general representability of being, and being as expressed in the presence of representation . . . " (p. 219, my emphasis). An important goal in what follows will be to suggest, through readings of Diderot, some of the reasons to doubt Foucault's conclusions about the historically specific nature of representation in the seventeenth and eighteenth centuries.

One of the many paradoxes in such a project however is that in order to make palpable the trans-historical nature of the issue, very specific readings of Diderot's texts are required, with particular attention to their attachments to the specific discursive universe of the eighteenth century. But what kind of readings and what kind of attachments to "the eighteenth century?" What makes a text "representative" of its historical period or, on the contrary, what allows us to suggest that a text is indicative of a problem that cannot be understood in terms of our usual notions of history and period? Again, these are some of the questions that will emerge, without necessarily finding answers that are altogether satisfying. At least in dealing with these issues one can hope to devise strategies that renew our interest and allow the inquiry to continue.

PART ONE
AESTHETICS

CHAPTER TWO

A Theoretical Fable

If one were to undertake to teach a child
to speak by starting with words that begin with A,
then by proceeding to those that begin with B,
and so forth, half a lifetime could go by
before the child would finish the alphabet.
—Diderot

Whatever may have been the time and the
circumstances of its appearance
on the ladder of animal life, language
could only have occurred all of a sudden. Things
could not have begun to signify progressively.
—Claude Lévi-Strauss

We can think abstractly about the world
only to the degree to which
the world itself has already become abstract.
—Fredric Jameson

*I*N THE DISTANT LAND OF THE
Congo, there lived a rich and powerful sultan named Mangogul.[1] Mangogul had everything: he was a sultan, he had a
harem, a queen, and, most important, he had the fair Mirzoza. The love between the sultan and his favorite was
founded on perfect intimacy. Although he was sultan of a
harem, all his desire was contained within his relationship
to Mirzoza. "Mirzoza had held Mangogul captive for several
years" (p. 6). No cloud of secrecy troubled their ability to
confide in each other absolutely. "Each would have considered it a crime to hide from the other the most minute cir-

cumstance of his or her life" (p. 6). But Mangogul, like many who continue to read this "oriental" tale of his scabrous adventures, was also bored with such perfection. His yawns are symptoms of a malady that Mirzoza diagnoses as "lack of appetite [*dégout*]": "The variety of amusements that pursue you has not been able to ward off a lack of appetite. You relish nothing. That, Prince, is your illness" (p. 7). Mangogul relishes nothing because he has everything. He is sated.[2]

Nor can he any longer be amused by the adventures of others. In the tradition of *Les Mille et Une Nuits*, the favorite is exceptionally skillful at narrating the city's various scandals. But as the story begins, we learn that Mirzoza "had exhausted the history of Banza's scandals" (p. 6). Although this is an unpleasant circumstance for the sultan, it occurs not because of any imperfection in his relationship to Mirzoza but because (as in everything else) Mangogul already has it all.

He would gladly amuse himself by turning from the exhausted adventures of city women to those of court women, but, as he laments, "who knows the history of those lunatics?" (p. 7). When the favorite reiterates her suggestion all the same, Mangogul formulates the problem that brings about the rest of the story: "I shall *imagine* with you, if you like, highly amusing adventures of the women in my court . . . but no matter how entertaining they might be, what difference does it make so long as it remains impossible to *learn* about them?" (p. 7; my emphasis). Recourse to the magic of a genie follows on this initial insistence that knowledge of real sexual adventures is a much more effective cure for "dégout" than the most exciting products of fantasy. "Apprendre" puts one in contact with the real; "imaginer" would leave the sultan in the boring situation that he wishes to escape. But as we shall see, the sultan thinks that knowledge of the real is like the knowledge he already has of/through Mirzoza: unmediated, transparent and absolutely present (the very characteristic that modern psychoanalysis has taught us to attribute to the "imaginary").[3]

The genie, Cucufa, gives the sultan a magic ring. By rubbing the stone (*le chaton*, as it is suggestively called in French), the sultan can force any woman in his presence to recount the true story of her sexual activity, speaking not from her mouth but from those nether parts most directly acquainted with the sort of facts he wishes to learn. Not even the deepest erotic secret can remain inviolate.

But alas, the ring that permits such absolute knowledge—presenting it so absolutely, so transparently—also brings about certain alterations in the initial situation of the exemplary couple that extend beyond the mere entertainment that was anticipated. The diversity of these unexpected side effects is actually the result of one central alteration: something happens to the "perfect" but boring immediacy of the sultan's relationship to his favorite. Despite the fact that their love had been free of the slightest dissimulation up to this moment, "no sooner was Mangogul in possession of Cucufa's mysterious ring, than he felt tempted to try it out on his favorite" (p. 9). Because of the ring, what was extolled as perfect confidence is instantaneously clouded by a possibility of deception, a question of fidelity, a doubt that supplants trust and that will persist throughout the rest of the tale. From the moment he is in possession of the ring, his former experience no longer suffices unto itself. What he experiences now needs supplemental ratification in order to become true. It has to be repeated or doubled in another medium; immediate, carnal knowledge needs to be duplicated and completed by mediate, objective knowledge. It is no longer enough just to know Mirzoza; now he must know *that* he knows her, perfectly, without any cloud of dissimulation. He now requires knowledge, not just of her, but of her fidelity. The once-sated sultan feels a need he never felt before. It is with the ring that doubt and the desire to know erupt between the lovers, and it is also the ring that provides the means to dispel doubt and acquire reliable knowledge.

The gift of the ring is a gift, concomitantly, of difference and of representation. It creates both the possibility and the need to ratify direct knowledge through another, represented version of it. Experience that once was immediate must now enter into a complex relationship with vicariousness, with adequation in a different medium.

The initial effect of the representationality that befalls the happy couple is that Mirzoza becomes less an unqualified presence to the sultan than *a* woman. Although she will be described in increasingly exemplary terms as the novel progresses, her isolatable exemplarity itself results from the new need to insert her into a certain linguistic typology, into a system of categories based on similarities and differences.[4] These extend, for example, from *courtisane* to *femme tendre*. But the shift in Mirzoza's status is already legible at the precise moment that one would expect it, namely, when Mangogul first approaches her with his new ring. Finding her asleep in bed, he says to himself, "Let's turn the stone on this sleeping beauty and awaken her jewel a bit" (p. 10). No longer is she umbilically connected, an undifferentiated extension of himself. She is essentially a tableau, a representation of the topos "belle dormeuse." She is an objective entity that the sultan designates with a demonstrative adjective and an epithet. To name and designate her by means of this label is to recognize the rift of mediation between them where previously there reigned perfect transparency.

Before the ring, Mirzoza was everything for Mangogul. She was the entirety of Woman; beyond her there was no real desiring. Now, however, she is only something, a type, one particular thing in a category of things that by herself, as a categorical instance, she is inadequate entirely to subsume. Her univocal presence to Mangogul is sundered by the space of metaphor: what she represents is no longer the same as what she is. Whereas the sultan, in Mirzoza, previously dwelt in the bosom of a totality—the totality of Woman, of Meaning, where self and Other were in perfect coalescence—he is now confronted with a figural, synecdochal part, signifying a whole only because it no longer *is* the whole. Mirzoza signifies a presence because she is herself struck with a sign of absence that, magically, is a sign of signs, of representationality itself. She is no longer the transparent medium, a "non-language" through which Mangogul knows all—all the gossip in Banza, for example. As a representation, she is now herself the focus of his desire to know, and thus paradoxically, the representation of the absence of knowledge, the lack of immediacy.[5]

It is telling that the sultan's initial "dégout" gives way to voracious and undiscriminating appetite as he acquires, through the ring, both the need and the means to reconstitute something now lost and other: Woman, her Meaning, her willingness to confide that meaning absolutely.

But what precisely is the mechanism by which representation can serve as a tool adequate to retrieve the very loss that it brought about? Mangogul's obsessive relationship to his ring is parallel, it would seem, to Rousseau's obsessive relation to the evil of writing: it operates as both cause of the evil and means of a cure.

It is true that the notoriously untruthful court women leave little to the imagination when consulted by means of the magic ring. The mask of convention and hypocrisy is lifted; no secrets are possible. The sincerity guaranteed by the ring is so absolute that even the separation of the locus of language and the locus of sexual pleasure is obliterated as the jewel itself speaks its own, immediate truth.[6] The terms used are, at least by eighteenth-century standards, unadorned and literal evocations of sexual activity. When the sultan encounters a jewel that speaks in the broken sighs of desire or that tells less than the whole story of its adventures, he rubs the stone of his ring harder until he elicits the kind of narration that he seeks—who, when, where, how, and so forth (e.g., p. 77). Moreover, the mouth is forced to keep silent while the private parts are speaking. Women lie from the mouth. Orally generated speech would impose the problem of contradiction. "When the *bijou* and the mouth of a woman contradict each other, which do you believe? (p. 19). By simply eliminating oral speech from the moment of truth, all duplicity, all hypocrisy, and all rhetoric are banished in favor of literal referentiality. The sultan's ideal language, then—literal, referential, and noncontradictory—is the representational language of empirical science and of the "métaphysique expérimentale" that recurs as a leitmotiv in the novel's philosophical dialogues.[7] When they become the object of the scientific "essai," things themselves render their meaning to the inquiring subject. This is an empiricist's wish dream come true.

Mangogul wants frequently "to conclude" (see especially p. 91), in both senses of the term: both "to end" his search and "to reach a decision" concerning the question of Woman. But unless all women are consulted and known, any conclusion is premature and "all secrets are not known" (p. 91). No conclusion is possible then until the whole is metaphorically repossessed. But all metaphor for the whole is undermined by the synecdochal (metonymic) concatenation of the private parts that propel the sultan's quest. The coincidence of any particular jewel with that which the sultan seeks to know—the status of any one woman as a successful representation of all women—can never be so perfect as to terminate the representationality through which she comes to signify more than she is but less than the whole. Each consultation therefore yields a double result. It provides a satisfying confirmation of the sultan's new potential for knowing the absolute truth, and yet redoubles his need to know all, to move on to the next consultation, the next advance in his journey to the conclusion of his need to know.

Perhaps the clearest sign of the dilemma is in the implicit transformation that occurs once he consults any particular jewel. Although the revelations it affords preoccupy him centrally and insatiably, once they are delivered their significance is minimal. The plenitude of meaning he seeks and expects from each representation arrives in the radically devalued form of empty "prattle [*caquet*]." But the vacuousness of any response, rather than diminishing his curiosity, heightens his need to move on to the next consultation. "I am counting on wresting more important things from the jewels that remain to be consulted" (p. 91).

By a kind of contamination effect, the instrument that the sultan intended to use for mere pleasure alters the matrix within which all pleasure was contained. When she learns of the sultan's "diabolical secret," Mirzoza dreads the consultation itself more than the answers that she might be forced to give. If her jewel were to reveal infidelity, she reasons, Mangogul's confidence in her would be lost. If, on the other hand, it were to reveal complete fidelity, the question itself would formally instate the sultan's lack of confidence in her. It would perpetuate his incapacity to affirm their relationship without the benefit of absolute knowledge, transparently represented. Both the problem and its remedy would become permanent parts of their life together.

The sultan shares these forebodings but is overcome continually by need to satisfy his new desire to know. Referring to Mirzoza's argument against the consultation, he confesses, "That's what I was saying to myself . . . when you woke up. Even so, if you had slept two minutes longer, I don't know what would have happened" (p. 11). In spite of this new lack of self control, he makes a promise not to turn the ring upon Mirzoza.

That Mangogul does manage to resist the temptation until the last part of the text in no way protects his relationship from the effects of the ring. He learns that once there is representation, everything is representational. Everything is linguistic, displaceable, mediate and therefore alien. Although he is deferring the consultation of Mirzoza, Mangogul is always consulting her vicariously. His repeated inquiries of ever more women are clearly tropological attempts to discover what she is by discovering the truth about all those like her. Similarly, Mirzoza is threatened by the sultan's consultations of other women because she too understands them as displacements of his desire to consult her (e.g., p. 5). What she is (for him) is now being mediated through the discourse of other women, and she confesses that she does not care to hear more of it in the future. Mangogul's response to her request is telling: "I'll spare you, if you like, the tedium of their speeches, but as for the account of their dalliance, you'll hear it either from them or from me. That decision is final" (p. 16). The threat is covered by the thinnest of veils: all women consulted are unfaithful; Mirzoza is surely unfaithful too. By forcing her to hear directly or indirectly their scabrous stories, Mangogul is using the representationality and the displaceability of their language to pressure her into allowing the consultation of her own jewel as the only means to prove that she is different. The vexing question of her difference from what she represents is at the heart of their struggle.

Mirzoza sees through him and musters an angry and multifaceted defense of herself. Much of the bickering between them occurs when the sultan attempts to "know" Mirzoza vicariously and Mirzoza attempts to block the equivalences that make representational substitution possible.

> —So in your opinion, this fidelity [of women] is a rather doubtful thing? . . . put in Mirzoza.
> —Beyond anything you imagine, answered Mangogul.
> —Prince, Mirzoza fired back, a hundred times you've pointed to your ministers as the most honest people in the Congo. I've so often received compliments from all your officials, that I'm able to repeat their praise word for word. How strange that the object of your affection should be singled out for exclusion from the high opinion you have of those honored to belong to your inner circle. (P. 123)

When the sultan claims that *women's* virtue is dubious, the favorite counters with evidence that justifies *herself*. She claims a difference between herself and the category she has come to stand for. But in order to exculpate herself in this way, she resorts not to the fact or the essential reality of her virtue but to its representation in the discourse of others. In other words, she has to resort to more of the poison in order to bring about a cure. Her reference to language rather than "fact" is underscored by her insistence that she can repeat the discourse that represents her virtue "word for word." But, of course, that is precisely the problem. Her virtue exists only as representation and is now subject to displacement. What she "is" is no longer inalienably hers alone. This is the radical infidelity that motivated the sultan's quest at the outset, and resorting to representations of her fidelity is like using gasoline to put out a fire. As the dialogue continues, Mangogul's retort is no less effective for being the height of bad faith, and it clearly indicates the battleground that both lovers now occupy.

> —And what makes you think that? replied the Sultan. You should realize, Madam, that you are not implicated in the discourse, true or false, that I get from women—unless it should please you to *represent the sex in general.* . . .
> —I wouldn't advise it, added Sélim, who was present at this conversation. By doing so, Madam could acquire only defects.
> —I do not accept compliments addressed to me at the expense of my fellow women, answered Mirzoza. If anyone wants to praise me, I would not like for it to be at the expense of someone else. (P. 123, my emphasis.)

Mirzoza takes account of her new, rhetorical status. She back-pedals to the far safer position that complimentary evaluations (such as Sélim's) should represent no one else and should have no consequence for other women. This strategy also insures that the sultan's negative evaluations of other women as a category have no metaphorical bearing on herself. She would like very much not to represent anything beyond what she is. But that is no longer possible.

In just this way the subtle Mirzoza demonstrates her own form of naïveté about the true nature of their struggle. To win her battle with the sultan on these grounds would be to prove that she is different from all other—that is, unfaithful —women. But again, the real issue is not infidelity in the minor, sexual mode, but in a far more threatening mode of being "different" or "other" at all. This she is already, fundamentally, by virtue of her fall into representation. To establish fidelity in alterity can only be a contradiction in the terms of their particular problem, and can only be done agonistically.

The real issue staged in this novel is how to resolve the intersubjective dilemma resulting from the intrusion of Cucufa's magic. Thus the content of the Sultan's question (Is Mirzoza faithful?) is ultimately secondary. The primary issue becomes the relationship of representation and difference to truth and presence, and the means to ensure their direct connection.

Paradoxically, the satirical "pirouette" with which this lowbrow farce ends—literally, after the genie comes and takes back his ring, "il partit en pirouettant" (p. 233)—is a rather rigorous response to the issue of representation that has propelled the story. The novel opens with a fall into representationality and continues with Mangogul's tenacious attempt to shut down all difference between what Mirzoza is and what she represents, and thus to restore the transparency of her presence to him. It becomes increasingly obvious, however, that after such a fall, representation provides the only means of returning to presence, and that such a means continuously destroys its end. What is required is for the sultan both to have Mirzoza and to give up the ring, to have Mirzoza and to renounce his impossible question for presence. And indeed, this is precisely the new order that emerges on the final page.

Mirzoza has an attack of "vapors" during an overlong oration, and the sultan believes she is dying. (Indeed she is—dying from a surfeit of language.) He addresses her as, at least potentially, already dead: "If I have lost you, delight of my soul, he cried, your jewel must, just as your mouth, remain eternally silent" (p. 232). Perceiving Mirzoza as dying coincides with a lifting of the interdiction against using his ring to consult her, and the long-deferred consultation takes place. In it Mirzoza represents herself as "faithful even into the night of the grave" (p. 232), which ironically sums up the present situation pretty well since these terms expressing her fidelity are taken to be her dying words. But—this being a fairy tale—Mangogul's noisy response to the news of her faithfulness brings the favorite back to consciousness. She protests his transgression and momentarily returns the situation to one of hostile confrontation. "Ah! Madame," he responds, " . . . do not attribute to a shameful curiosity an impatience that was prompted only by my despair at having lost you: I did not put you through the test of the ring; but I thought I could, without breaking my promise, use a resource that returns you to my wishes, and which assures you of my heart forever" (p. 232). Mirzoza accepts this explanation. At the same time, she asks him to give up the ring, which he gladly does, signifying the advent of a new order.

The final consultation of Mirzoza certainly remains within the same representational protocols that organize the rest of the novel: language restores a lost object to one who has the power to exact a verbal account. The "sleeping beauty" of the first, aborted consultation is forced to reveal that, in fact, she has been sleeping faithfully with her lord and master.

And yet this final consultation is transvalued by the emergence of a major mode of alterity between the two lovers in the guise of death. Until now the sultan remained convinced that he was forever on the verge of satisfaction, not of a major form of desire, but of his "shameful curiosity" and of his need to control through knowing. His quest was fueled by an unfettered certainty that all difference could soon be named and thus restored to being and to presence.

At Mirzoza's "dying," however, his desire is transformed and now proceeds from a recognition—thus an inchoate acceptance—that its object is irretrievably other. It is, as he says, "prompted only by my despair at *having lost* you." The silence of obstinance and resistance is overshadowed by the more radical silence of the tomb. Even after her return to life and to language, death remains as a new potentiality that representation serves only to recall or to repeat, even as it momentarily overcomes it. In this final, desperate use of the ring, the sultan addresses her as *this* other, and thus as an other beyond representation according to the ordinances of his power.[8] With this ending of the tale, representation turns out to be efficacious only when its project of return to presence is already known as, like its object, doomed; and when that negative knowledge becomes the condition of possibility for an affirmation of what one modern theorist calls "the barred possession, pitted against usual literary appetites [which] breeds a tantalizing prolongation of desire, a pain of anticipation so quietly acute and so indefinable that it is quite akin to pleasure."[9]

The problem that opens and continues to motivate *Les Bijoux indiscrets* opens, and never ceases to inhabit, the writing of Denis Diderot in general. The *Encyclopedia*, which is a jarringly different text, suggests something of what that might mean for the way one reads him. It is fully as solemn and serious as *Les Bijoux* is satirical and frivolous. As a project to represent everything, however, it shares certain basic epistemological features with Mangogul's quest. And at moments Diderot is thoroughly sultanesque in his qualification of language through which such a project can be accomplished.

> Each science has its name, so does each notion in the science: everything that is known in nature is desig-
> nated, just as everything invented in the arts, as well
> as phenomena, techniques [*manoeuvres*] and instru-

ments. There are expressions for things outside ourselves, for those inside ourselves. . . . We say "universe"; we say "atom": the universe is everything, the atom is its smallest part. From the general collection of all the causes to the solitary thing, everything has its sign, as does what exceeds all limit either in nature or in our imagination; as does what is possible and what is not. . . . [10]

The supposition that one can represent everything through the transparent medium of language, which for Michel Foucault underlies the episteme of the seventeenth and eighteenth centuries, could hardly be more forcefully expressed.[11] When even the natural or imagined excess "beyond all limits" has its own particular sign, what could possibly be exterior to linguistic representation—and, thus, unavailable to us as knowledge? Language is an all-powerful ring of magic, as is implied by the very project of an alphabetical *Encyclopedia*.[12]

For the Diderot we see in moments such as these, just as for Mangogul, language is not an object but a transparent medium through which all being is given up to representation. In Foucault's formulation,

At the meeting point between representation and being, at the point where nature and human nature intersect . . . what Classical thought reveals is the power of discourse. In other words, language in so far as it represents—language that names, patterns, combines, connects and disconnects things as it makes them visible in the transparency of words. In this role, language transforms the sequence of perceptions into a table, and cuts up the continuum of beings into a pattern of characters. Where there is discourse, representations are laid out and juxtaposed; and things are grouped together and articulated. The profound vocation of Classical language has always been to create a table [*de faire tableau*]—a 'picture': whether it be in the form of natural discourse, the accumulation of truth, descriptions of things, a body of exact knowl-

edge, or an encyclopaedic dictionary. It exists, therefore, only in order to be transparent. . . . (Pp.
310–11)

The description indeed fits Mangogul's empiricist wish-
dream—at least as it first emerges. (For the moment we are
leaving aside the radical alterations brought about by the
novel's ending.) And it is corroborated by his first perception of Mirzoza, after receiving the ring, as a tableau ("Belle
Dormeuse") to be situated taxonomically and categorically
somewhere between "courtisane" and "femme tendre."

Les Bijoux, then, would seem to be leading us into the
question of representation in the eighteenth century as Foucault has conceived it. But in fact the novel exemplifies what
could only be, according to Foucault's analysis, an anachronistic awareness of the limits of taxonomical representation.[13] What is more, the notion of those limits owes nothing to the new epistemic order that Foucault finds in the
nineteenth century, when the properties determining inclu-
sion within a category will change from the visible to the
invisible or internal properties such a function and structure.[14] In other words, there is no basis for claiming, within
a Foucauldian framework, that Diderot anticipates the
nineteenth-century episteme. The interest of the novel as
an opening for the present investigation is greater when we
consider the text from another angle.

At the same time as recognizing the problem of representation in the Classical age, it is important to begin analyzing
certain of its more general characteristics. For it is a peculiar
feature of representation that, in ways that will become
more apparent further on, it becomes confused with the
more modest and restricted project of reference or indication. It is too unruly to be handled from a referential distance. When we describe representation analytically, our
description is always tainted because, being something of a
representation itself, description participates in that which
it seeks to describe. Defining representation is tantamount

to using the word to be defined within the definition. It is at least partly tautological for us to say that "representation" is *this* representation of it. If *Les Bijoux indiscrets* already represents the quest for adequate representation and all its attendant effects, then any attempt to speak critically about the novel proceeds on very treacherous grounds—if "grounds" there are at all.

What is more, the resemblance, the imbrication, is not just a formal one. One must consider, for example, that the desire which the sultan's project attempts to fulfill is a critic's desire, and his experience is an allegory of theoretical activity in general. His project is a forerunner of our own, which is also inevitably structured like a search for the truth about linguistic representations that, as objects of the theoretical enterprise, begin to seem limitless in number and complexity. The texts to be consulted give up their secrets only reluctantly and resist interpretation based on the criterion of "truth." In the light of these more-than-formal similarities, the issue of representation begins to deploy more of its force.

If such is the case, the problem would seem to be one of finding some theory or strategy of reading that would force texts to come across with the kind of true representations we seek. Or, to describe the difficulty in less hermeneutic terms, such a theory would have to prevent the texts in question from saying so much, so easily, so obviously that their truths are delivered in the devalued form of "caquet." For by withholding nothing, they deliver nothing that satisfies our need to know, and we fall prey to the inexorable logic of Mangogul's quest for the whole. As models for our activity, either of these surely gives us pause.

And yet, nothing is more common today than the attempt to seek what one might call, in the terms of Diderot's fable, a second ring, a metalinguistic ring, a theory of criticism or a metahistory that would perhaps provide a self-conscious measure for the "truth" produced by the first ring.[15] But a ring is always a ring, a sign is always a sign, a representation always a representation. Its effects cannot be remedied by more representation, as Rousseau realized with unsurpassed lucidity.[16] Once there is representation, all one's strategies ultimately reduce to attempts at deriving more advantageous or correct representations. Jonathan Culler's recent work is well-titled, for signs do always entail a "pursuit" that theory *per se*, captive to the same logic, cannot halt.[17] And Elizabeth Bruss describes a relation to theory itself that shows all the signs of repeating Mangogul's relation to women.

> At one level, the thrill of reading theory is rather like being confronted with an exotic language or a blueprint drawn to an unknown scale—an overwhelming and undifferentiated confusion that will gradually (for the patient enquirer) resolve itself into perceptible lines and a usable order. There is an intoxication even in the simple passage from obscurity to sense, from helplessness to mastery—or to (increasingly) a mastery just out of reach, always promised but forever postponed. (P. 129.)

On the question of metarepresentation, some of the more visible critics on the current American scene can serve to economize a thousand words. Thus, Stanley Fish's first chapter of *Is There a Text in This Class?* passes in review the list of his own, past metacritical truths, each of which has dissolved and sent him on to the next.[18] The very concatenation itself makes it obvious that there is a logic of theory's relation to its object that theory, "meta" though it be, does not dominate from outside the problem. Fish's experience suggests that the much-sought exteriority, from which propositions "about" texts can be enunciated, behaves very much like the elusive and contradictory linguistic objects it seeks to represent. And yet, the imperative for such an exterior position is such that there are critics who enjoy considerable attention because they write books that do little more than affirm that such a theoretical space exists, and that we all speak from it whether we recognize the fact or not.[19]

So, we are left to wonder what produces the two different but clearly related features that mark such critical projects and that link them to the efforts of Diderot's sultan. The first feature is that we desire and accredit a stable space in which representation occurs, outside of, and uncontaminated by, its objects—be they things, ideas, or other representations. As a second feature, this space is nevertheless compromised by an obscurity, an indeterminacy quite similar to the object it is charged to represent clearly. The tension between these two features of the critical enterprise seems to be irresolvable.

Foucault again provides us with a concrete example of these two incompatible features in his own commentaries on Diderot's novel. In *History of Sexuality*, he begins his own remarks on *Les Bijoux indiscrets* by repeatedly recognizing a metaphoric resemblance that we today share with Mangogul. "For many years, we have all been in the realm of Prince Mangogul: under the spell of an immense curiosity about sex, bent on questioning it, with an insatiable desire to hear it speak. . . . "[20] Cucufa's magic ring is for Foucault the emblem of that curiosity which has lead us "to direct the question of what we are, to sex" (p. 78).

But we must ask of Foucault's text what curiosity lead *him* "to direct the question of what we are," to a literary text about sex. For that is clearly the question he is asking of Diderot's novel.

> Our problem is to know what marvelous ring confers a similar power on us, and on which master's finger it has been placed . . . and how it is that each one of us has become a sort of attentive and impudent sultan with respect to his own sex and that of others. It is this magical ring, this jewel which is so indiscreet when it comes to making others speak, but so untalkative about its own mechansim, that we need to render lo-

quacious in its turn; it is what we have to talk about. We must write the history of this will to truth, this petition to know that for so many centuries has kept us enthralled by sex: the history of an obstinacy and an obsession.

Clearly (if only implicitly), Foucault's posture presupposes an outside from which one can produce a metarepresentation that interrogates the representation of our will to know as Diderot has reflected it. One of the more remarkable features of Foucault's enterprise, however, is the extent to which (like Fish in the previous example, like ourselves here) he seems to fall into imitating that which he is attempting to represent at a critical remove. For, in proposing to carry out a "historical inquiry" (p. 72) that would reveal the nature and function of our "obstinacy" by forcing it at last to speak the truth about itself, Foucault is launching into a highly Mangogulian project: literally, a *History of Sexuality* of which *Will to Knowledge* is only a first volume. In this he is Mangogul's relay, "consulting" at another remove the representations of an "obstinacy," the metaphors of desire, so as "to know" and "to write [its] history." There is a representational link between Foucault's desire to interrogate "this jewel which is so indiscreet," and Mangogul's desire to consult "indiscreet jewels." The history of that desire as recounted in *Les Bijoux* is repeated in Foucault's desire for true history. Like his predecessor he is seeking a history of sexual "obsession [*acharnement*]" that he himself is *bent on* knowing. Like his predecessor he is insisting on "histoires" that deliver "savoir." Historical inquiry is, for him too, a magic ring of representation that promises conclusions. But here again the promise brings with it a feeling of doubt that simultaneously shadows that belief: "Historical inquiry *will* provide answers," he writes at first, but then adds the telling qualification, "or *should* provide answers [Répondra—ou devrait répondre l'enquête historique]" (p. 97, my emphasis).

Foucault's link to Mangogul, our link to the desires and powers represented in *Les Bijoux indiscrets*, is quite close. At the very moment he stands "outside" the realms of Prince Mangogul so as to point to it, to represent it from a critical distance, he in fact reproduces its organization in an uncanny way. With this first volume in the projected series of works entitled *The History of Sexuality*, he sets out "to transcribe into history the fable of *Les Bijoux indiscrets*" (p. 77); but somehow the text has managed to transcribe his history into a repetition of the fable.

But this indeterminacy of critical subject and object is only one aspect of the representational link that needs to be understood here. There is also the second feature of critical activity mentioned above, namely, the tendency to assert and to accredit the existence of an exterior, metarepresentational space in which we can operate unhindered.

Earlier in his career, writing in *The Order of Things* about the Classical episteme founded on representation, Foucault made this claim:

> The entire system of grids which analyzed the sequence of representations . . . all these distinctions created by words and discourse, characters and classifications, equivalences and exchanges, have been so completely abolished that it is difficult today to rediscover how that structure was able to function. . . . When discourse ceased to exist and to function within representation as the first means of ordering it, Classical thought ceased at the same time to be directly accessible to us. (Pp. 303–4)

The episteme that gave rise to the relation of representation and discourse exemplified in *Les Bijoux* has disappeared so thoroughly that it takes all the archeological labor of *The Order of Things* to reconstruct its skeletal remains. Here then is the second feature. The representation produced by the critic is radically different from its object. They belong to two incommensurate worlds.

If this is the case, if the Classical episteme is totally other for us, what does it mean for Foucault to recognize so readily—indeed, with such immediacy—our own reflection in this sultan who frenetically seeks to establish characters and classifications and equivalences in sexual discourse? The point is not to hurl a stone at Foucault for contradicting himself. Having recognized our own critic's image in Mangogul, we live in a glass house. Rather, it is more fruitful to assume that the double relation of similarity and difference binding Foucault and Mangogul can itself tell us something about representation in general and about the role of the critic or philosopher in particular.

It would make little sense to say that representation has no history, for surely it is ordered according to different protocols in different historical moments, by different ideological necessities. But the case of Foucault suggests that historical inquiry is by itself inadequate to account for this double nature of representation. History itself cannot easily explain why we could sustain such contradictory relations to the historical past: an episteme is said to have been abolished, all but unimaginable to us, lost in radical historical difference; and yet the same period is said to have produced our very "emblem" in the sultan's desire to find what one is through sexuality. Something about representation contrives to make it remain the question that one never leaves behind in the historical past, and whose ever-duplicitous effects we undergo even as we set out to put them aside.

Something of what constantly recurs is implied in the word itself.[21] Although it is a commonplace (particularly since the ascendancy of Derrida in contemporary critical theory), it is worth repeating here that representation seeks to be re-*present*ation. Re-*present*ation implies a return to presence of something that once was present but now—at the moment of its representation—is not present in quite the same fashion as it originally was. It is present "again," spatially and temporally, here and now, but remains different from its first presence all the same.

Whatever marks a representational presence as a return to presence—as a second presence of its object—is therefore something like a "negative mark." It is a reminder that the representation is not the object that it strives to represent. It is *only* a representation. Representation "fails," in this sense, because it does not really render its object present, so fully present that its other presence (the so-called original presence) is entirely subsumed or obliterated by its representation. Instead, the representation remains secondary. That is even the condition of possibility for it to represent at all. In order to be efficacious, to succeed, it must fail in just this way. It must remain a concept in mourning for the loss of its "original" object. Such nostalgia—except in fables like *Les Bijoux indiscrets*—is based on a fiction. For the representation was never really one with its object, and came into being only on the condition that its object be originally, already, differentiated from itself.[22] Differentiation is a basic feature in representation, even representation of identity.

This is the paradox that, a-historically, the question of representation brings with it. "History" therefore is not able to dominate the paradox from the outside since history is itself involved in the same logic, evident even in the common usage of the term. In ordinary usage "history" is both representation and object. History is the empirical situation or event that has the capacity to constitute itself as a representation; but history is also process or result of representing significant situations and events. History is that which is—or is subject to being—written down in history books, *and* it is that writing process itself.[23] When we take representation as an issue, as a question in itself, therefore, we are dealing with problems in which history is too embroiled to provide any privileged form of guidance. Thus, as we have seen, Foucault finds himself both remarking and re-creating the resemblances we share with an episteme that, historically speaking, is irretrievably different from our own.[24]

In the end, however, the symmetry of Foucault and Mangogul is broken because Foucault's project remains one of curiosity about our own "curiosity about sex." His quest remains a quest for "histoire(s)" predicated on a tenacious belief that the instrument at his disposal can adequately represent it. In contrast, Mangogul throws his instrument away and finally renounces his desire—insofar as it seeks magisterial knowledge—as "shameful."

Although Foucault has had a great deal to say about the subject of representation that illuminates the issue with remarkable clarity and detail, he has relatively little to say in this context as it is opened (or re-opened) by Diderot. For the latter context, as we shall see, brings with it a necessary juxtaposition of successful and failed retrieval of its "object."[25] Representation, to function, must accept and even advertise its blocked access to presence—thus placing presence in dialogue with that radical alterity which in *Les Bijoux* was named "death."[26]

Let us be clear. Up to its final stage, Mangogul's project does exemplify the epistemological protocols traced by Foucault in *The Order of Things*. At that point, however, it opens onto a quite other order, so that the experience of the magic ring finds its ultimate legibility in the transcendence of the old order. That possibility coexists with and in the Classical order that Diderot inherits and represents anew. What remains, therefore, is to forge an understanding of the possibility of manifesting a different relation to that order, even while representing it. It is again a question of what, in the previous chapter, I described as a mode of being in which is and is not itself, which opens it to other texts and to other "histoires."

Indeed, even in Diderot's most characteristically eighteenth-century texts, there is writing that stages the emergence of a different relation to representation. As we shall see, he often can be found focusing upon the "stage" itself, upon the abstract problematic of representation with which differing ideologies must always negotiate their ties as best they can. In the *Encyclopedia*, no less than in *Les Bijoux*, the clarion affirmation of language's unsurpassed power to name everything will turn out to be a backdrop against which the silhouette of another order, another relation to language, can always emerge.

That other order requires from us a different order of reading as well. Relative to Foucault's archeological schemata, and to traditional intellectual history, the reading so required can only be described as anachronistic and "an-epistemic." Such a qualification necessarily misses the point, however. For it is precisely the passage into a differentiated order, which is staged throughout Diderot's writing, that communicates in turn with the alterity, the difference that is accommodated and suppressed in other epistemological moments, be they Platonic, Cartesian, Lockean, or Foucauldian. It must be in the nature of such a critical reading that is attentive to these openings, to read laterally, to allow and to elaborate the very feature that a notion of epistemic periodicity, taken by itself, necessarily disallows.

The present text, this critical discourse, is attempting to learn from, and respond to, these openings of an other representational order in Diderot's writing. From the perspective of such openings, Diderot's writing is "about" the condition of possibility of doing what here is being done, both allowing and radically compromising the objectivity of this representation. To the extent that it is done well, and representations and differences thicken among all "these" texts, the anachronism of our reading will redeem itself, at least in part—the only part left to one seeking to discourse on language. Diderotian representation will be well represented even though it may refer us backward and forward in time. For that is, in large degree, what Diderot's epistemological dreams are about.

CHAPTER THREE

The Beginning of a Beautiful Relationship

—I would like you to tell me what difference
you see between a man and a statue,
between marble and flesh.
—Rather little. Marble is made with flesh,
and flesh with marble.
—But the one is not the other.
—Diderot
Le Rêve d'Alembert

AS A FIRST CONSULTATION,
what could be more enticing to a sultan-critic than a text
from the *Encyclopedia* that sets out to define the beautiful?
In the article "Beau" (1751), Diderot strives vigorously to
frame a basic aesthetic theory that would claim neither an
innate aesthetic sense nor a preliminary knowledge of ideal
beauty.[1] At the same time, he must not succumb to the aesthetic relativism or Pyrrhonian skepticism that would pre-
vail by default if no aesthetic definition were possible, which
Diderot condemned no less than Kant.[2] The beautiful,
Diderot says, begins in sense experience, specifically in the
perception of "rapports" (relationships).

The perception of "rapports," the experience of things in
their relationship to other things, finds its ultimate source
in natural physical needs. These, in turn, give rise to intellectual operations to meet those needs. These intellectual
operations, in turn, necessarily generate notions of connection, disconnection, pattern, order, proportion, symmetry—
all the forms of "rapport" (p. 417). The attempt to find the

origin of the aesthetic in natural perception stems in part from the polemical context of the argument, but it is also a good example of Diderot's overarching desire to think aesthetic questions in terms compatible with scientific empiricism.[3] It is an argument that like much aesthetic theory of the period is bound up in fundamental epistemological questions. (Cassirer, for example, points to moments in which aesthetic thought entered "the realm of pure epistemology"; and Paul de Man has recently spoken of aesthetics in general as "part of a universal system of philosophy rather than a specific theory.")[4] Thus the article "Beau" can correctly stand as an emblem of mid-century aesthetic and epistemological debate, and for Diderot's place within it.

The significance of the article "Beau" is different in the present context, however, for it offers some of the clearest entries into the problem of representation provided by Diderot's opus. It is a text that leads us to ask what happens, what effects are produced when things come to be perceived in terms of their connections to other things. (Again, Plato's broad but useful terms in the "Phaedo" come to mind: "whenever from seeing one thing you conceive another. . . . ") In Diderot's narrative the advent of "rapports" marks the advent—in rudimentary form—of the same representationality that played havoc with empirical definition in *Les Bijoux indiscrets*.

Foucault again provides us with a propitious place to begin. For, in his qualification of language in the Classical age, the link to aesthetic questions is already implied quite clearly by the various meanings of the word "tableau"—a "picture" or "scene," as well as a "table" or "grid"—in certain of his formulations. "The profound vocation of Classical language has always been to 'faire tableau'."[5] By this he means that Classical language is itself transparent. It is only the agent of representation that makes visible, in the form of a picture or grid, all the similarities and differences by which things are defined. Language makes "tableaux" as it "patterns, combines, connects and disconnects things . . .

in the transparency of words" (p. 311). The particular pertinence of Foucault's argument for us stems from the similarity between the function he ascribes to language, and the function of "rapports" in Diderot's definition of the beautiful. "Rapports" are charged with the same representational mission characteristic of language. That is to say, in Diderot's analysis they are agents that also pattern, combine, connect and disconnect things.

Yet this definition of the beautiful, rather than concluding anything in Diderot's text, seems to inaugurate a complex series of questions. Once there is an abstract copula of "rapport" that can pattern, combine, connect, and disconnect, Diderot, not unlike Mangogul, finds himself launched on something of a quest to determine the nature and the extent of the representational links that it produces. Here is a formulation in which one can sense his dawning intuition of these problems to come: "No sooner had the use of our intellectual faculties, and the necessity to furnish our needs . . . provided our minds with rudimentary notions of order, of relations, of proportion, connection, arrangement and symmetry, than we found ourselves surrounded by things in which the same notions were, so to speak, repeated *ad infinitum*" (p. 417). Once they existed for us, perceptions of ever-new "rapports" entered our mind without cease. Everything that occurred inside or outside ourselves, in the present or in the past "continued to inculcate in us notions of order and of relation . . . " (p. 417).

Whatever we may think about Diderot's analysis of the origins of such notions, the perception of "rapports" does not seem very useful as a basis for a definition of the beautiful (or anything else) since, by his own reckoning, such perceptions are infinite and thus nondiscriminating. If "rapports" can be repeated infinitely, everything can be linked in such "rapports," and thus everything is to some extent "beautiful." Thus the enclosure of the beautiful within meaningful, definitional confines is compromised by the infinite virtuality on which the definition comes to rest.

And yet, Diderot persists, fully cognizant of just this difficulty. For, he reasons, if we say that "an infinity of things" are beautiful (p. 417), either we misuse the term, or there is indeed a specific quality in all these things for which the proper term is "beau." "This quality cannot be among those which constitute their specific difference" because so many disparate things share the same attribute. Thus the quality common to all beautiful things has to be their "rapports," whether in things themselves or in one's perception of them. Perception of "rapports" is concomitant with aesthetic feeling, with pleasure, even if the perception is not of a mathematical or conscious sort. Someone who is not an architect or a musician can nevertheless experience true aesthetic pleasure in seeing a building or hearing music: "It suffices that he perceive and feel [*sente*] that the elements of that architecture and the sounds of that music have relations, either among themselves, or with other objects" (p. 419).

Diderot's next task is, intrepidly, to define the "rapport" that is, in turn, the "specific difference" of the beautiful in itself:[6] "Rapport" in general is an operation of the mind, which considers either a thing [*être*], or a quality, inasmuch as that thing or that quality supposes the existence of another thing or another quality. Example: When I say that Pierre is a good father, I am considering in him a quality which supposes the existence of an other quality, that of son; and likewise with other relations, whatever they might be" (p. 424). The aesthetic and moral quality of "good father" is produced not by relations of similarity that can be drawn between Pierre and other good fathers but rather— and from a psychoanalytic perspective Diderot never produced a more intriguing example—between Pierre's paternity and "une *autre* qualité," a quality of alterity, in this case that of "filiality." The "rapport" of the paternal and the filial is an articulation of differing terms in Pierre. In other words, if we perceive Pierre as morally-ethically "beau," we are considering him in terms of his "rapports" with something he is not. He is "beau" to the extent that he bears this odd, diacritical mark that invites us irresistibly to perceive him as a representation, but as a representation of something from which he differs. Therefore if, as Diderot says, the "specific difference" of the beautiful is "rapport," the specific difference of "rapport" is difference itself.[7]

The rest of the article "Beau" offers twelve reasons to explain why aesthetic judgments disagree, if there is indeed a universal definition of the beautiful. The entire explanation not only fails to explain the discrepancy but in fact has the opposite effect: it demonstrates the inevitability of the very diversity that Diderot—to the degree that he resembles Mangogul—would want to contain.[8] That tenacity can be gauged by his unflinching belief in two propositions that are in effect contradictory. The first, implicit, is that the aesthetic experience is predicated on the representationality (the "rapport") of objects or persons that serves to link them in a stable, if diacritical fashion, to other objects or persons: $X = $ not-Y (father $= $ not-son). The second belief is that once X is related to Y, it can also be—and in fact is—diacritically related to an infinity of other terms, and thereby surpasses all relational or representational specificity.[9] The notion of the "beau réel" is in fact predicated upon an abstraction from the simple, empirical, or real presence of the aesthetic object. To the extent that it is beautiful, the real is de-realized, differentiated from itself, "rapporté," carried over into its other.[10] And again, there is nothing in this definition to contain its infinite extension. The beautiful, which Diderot had set out to "define," turns out to be the infinite virtuality of a definitional "rapport"—of representation—itself. The beautiful is only a copula. But that is no cause for despair.

> Regardless of all these causes of diversity in our judgments, there is no reason for believing that real beauty [*le beau réel*], consisting in the perception of "rapports," is an illusion; the application of this principle *can vary infinitely*, and its *accidental modifica-*

tions can occasion dissertations and scholarly disputes: but the principle is none the less constant. There are perhaps not two men on earth who perceive exactly the same "rapports" in the same object, and who judge it beautiful to the same degree; but if there were a single man who was not affected by "rapports" in any genre whatever, he would be completely senseless [*un stupide parfait*]. (P. 435; my emphasis)

Diderot embraces a principle of diacritical differentiation that promises no ultimate authority to any particular aesthetic response or judgment, but that explains the universal process by which aesthetic experience is always produced. "Will the truth of this definition be local, particular and momentary? or will it encompass all things, all times, all men in all places?" (p. 427). In opting for the latter alternative, he goes so far as to propose that his theory of diacritical "rapports" is the nonhistorical background against which all other, historically specific aesthetics can be gauged. "Choose any other characteristic you please as the differential quality of the beautiful in general, and your notion will immediately be limited to one point in space and time" (p. 428). Diderot's is an aesthetic economy that aspires then to be both general and "constant" (p. 435). To the degree that its explanatory power has any legitimacy, we are, in spite of everything, "far from skepticism" (p. 437).

In his opening list of earlier, unsuccessful definitions of the beautiful, Diderot presents Augustine's position quite vividly by momentarily assuming his role in an imagined dialogue with an architect (pp. 392–93)—so vividly, in fact that at least one recent critic has taken it to be Diderot's own position. The beautiful as defined in this essay, however, represents neither an ideal form nor of any ontological presence. It is representational, but the object of its representation is representationality itself—as an "objective" process that, because it can be described but not mastered, admits of no final authority.[11] Regardless of its empirical effects, he understands that beauty, as difference, has no Being. He knows that its non-being—in some sense at least—should entail aesthetic skepticism. In Diderot's writing, however, it does not.

The epistemological cast in which he has molded his aesthetic problem is as much a departure from the Platonic tradition as possible in an eighteenth-century context. He clearly rejects the Platonism of Augustine, Shaftesbury, and Père André. He is also at the antipodes of Kant's later definition of the beautiful as a principally self-contained experience with no essential referential component. For the theory of "rapports" is a theory of the beautiful based on unfettered reference "outside," to a virtually infinite range of different objects. It supposes an unsuturable breach in the unity that in the Platonic-Augustinian tradition, in Diderot's words, "constitutes . . . the form and the essence of the beautiful in all genres" (p. 394). Yet, the classical aesthetic ideal of unity is not merely rejected or negated. (Diderot explicitly prizes aesthetic unity on more than one occasion.)[12] But it is shown to be *based in* the absolutely ununifiable, in the infinite virtuality of representational links to what the beautiful object is *not*. Unity is diacritically produced in difference, inhabited by difference, which is the specificity of unity experienced aesthetically.

Diderot is clearly miming Classical aesthetics since Plato, a tradition furthered by such contemporaries as Du Bos and Batteux.[13] But he is only miming it. And by miming it in this way, he is deforming it. Yes, like his predecessors, he too reduces the fine arts to a single principle, that of diacritical "rapports."[14] But such a principle deconstructs principial pretensions in aesthetic matters, its own included. It provides the precise and rigorous definition of the "beau réel" as movement beyond the real, beyond the simple, empirical perception on which its argument depends. The trope of "definition" lies at the heart of aesthetic practice of both Plato and Aristotle. For them ideal absolutes provide the ultimate, defining source of an object's beauty: the closer the rhetorical link, the greater the beauty. For Diderot, however, according to the precise terms of the article "Beau," greater beauty would result less from closer, more complete links to an absolute than from a greater quantity of links to a greater number of different things.

Mangogul's was a quest for petty mastery, an attempt to dominate the infinite virtuality of Mirzoza's "rapports," to stabilize her representationality with an ultimate definition. In the article "Beau," Diderot, at least for the moment, has parted company with his sultan. He manifests a striking capacity for affirming both the desire to know the ideal of beauty in definitional terms and the difference that makes beauty irreducibly ideal—and desirable. What is perhaps most striking for a modern reader accustomed to a certain rhetoric of irony and despair is that Diderot's affirmation is most powerful at the very moment that a certain logic expires, spending its last explanatory energy only to find that it has grasped an impossibility. It is a process that we shall have occasion to witness again and that is, I believe, one of the most important reasons for us to read Diderot today.

CHAPTER FOUR

"Je Ne Saurais Resister"

What therefore is truth? A mobile army of metaphors,
metonymies, anthropomorphisms . . . illusions of which
one has forgotten that they are illusions;
worn-out metaphors which have become powerless
to affect the senses. . . . For between
two utterly different spheres, as between subject
and object, there is no causality,
no accuracy, no expression, but at the
utmost an esthetical relation, I mean a
suggestive metamorphosis, a stammering translation
into quite a distinct foreign language,
for which purpose, however, there is needed
at any rate an intermediate sphere, an intermediate
force, freely composing and freely inventing.
—Nietzsche
The Dawn of the Day (No. 507)

DIDEROT'S AESTHETIC WRIT-
ing returns frequently to problems of representation in various
guises (implicitly to imitation, for example).[1] He always
attempts to treat them in materialist, non-idealist
terms. But Cucufa's magic ring continues to haunt his texts
just as in the article "Beau," skewing the empirical materiality
of his references, imprinting upon them all the effects of
rapport-as-difference. The issue is opened still further in
the *Essais sur la peinture* (1765), especially "Essay IV" entitled,
"What Everybody Knows about Expression and
Something that Everybody Does Not Know."
Artistic "expression" is inserted into the classical mi-

metic tradition by the definition that introduces the essay: "Expression is in general the image of a sentiment."[2] The initial focus of the argument is on physiognomy and other transparent signs of "sentiment" and, by extension, of character. "Each station in life has its own character and its own expression" (p. 65), and "in society, each order of citizen has its character and its expression; the artisan, the noble, the commoner, the man of letters . . ." (p. 66). Some expressions are part of a universal language that we carry within us. "If an individual has a face suggesting benevolence, justice and liberty, you will perceive it, because you bear within yourself images of these virtues and you will welcome whoever signals them to you. Such a face is a letter of recommendation written in a language common to all men" (p. 65). Socrates could not have said it better. Du Bos and Batteux would feel quite at home. If one were to stop reading the essay at this point, the conclusion would have to be that physiognomy and "body language" detailed in these early pages are transparent and universal, perfectly adequate to their referents. The task of the artist therefore would be to observe and then to represent mimetically the human exterior. Human character would be automatically represented in the process. This is no doubt the part of the essay that corresponds to the first clause of the title—"What Everybody Knows about Expression"—and is characteristic of the kind of things Shaftesbury, Du Bos, and Batteux had been writing in Diderot's own age.

In other words, the essay on expression opens with a belief in—an expression of—the possibility of simple and transparent mimesis. The condition of possibility for the *adequatio* of expression to character, however, is the magic copula of representationality that in *Les Bijoux* undermined all simple expression of "caractère propre." In the article "Beau," it functioned again to make an infinite virtually out of the definition of beauty that Diderot set out to nail down once and for all. Similar effects intrude into the essay on expression in the form of a lengthy digression that he finds irresistible: "I cannot resist . . ." (p. 169). In it, Diderot intends to account for the historical beginnings of art's influence upon nature, of nature's influence upon art, and the various arts upon each other. It is this segment that corresponds to the second clause of the title, "Something that Everybody Does Not Know."

The argument goes like this. When the poets described the physical attributes of the gods, they created orthodox expectations that subsequent visual representations were obliged to respect. Because of poetic description, Jupiter's dark brow, Venus' breasts, Apollo's shoulders, all existed, but they only existed as belief—"de foi" (p. 70). Sculptors were in an impossible situation when they carved such divine images. The pious Greeks doubtless would have ridiculed a statue of Hercules with slack shoulders, but no one knew what a proper statue of a god should resemble positively. There was no visual model of divinity, for "after all, the poet had revealed nothing, nor had he created belief; the painter and the sculptor had represented nothing except qualities borrowed from nature" (p. 70). The feet, bosom, and shoulders with which the artist represented the gods were copied "mimetically" from profane, human features that manifested no intrinsic divinity. Precisely insofar as such statuary was mimetic, it was *un*representative of the divinity that it was supposed to express.

At this point of the explanation, the artist has completed his work, and the faithful have seen it in the temple. In a realm of mimetic transparency, that should be the end of it. But in Diderot's analysis, the artist's work has not yet "expressed" the character of orthodox divinity that the viewers had anticipated. That is still for a future moment. It poses a question, a problem, that aesthetic analysis will have to resolve.

The text continues:

> So, when, at the threshold of the temple [*au sortir du temple*] the people came to recognize those qualities

in several individuals, they were much more strongly affected by them [*il en était bien autrement touché*]. Womankind had lent her feet to Thetis, her bosom to Venus; the goddess returned them to her, but returned them sanctified, deified. Man had provided Apollo with shoulders . . . [but Apollo] returned them sanctified, deified. When some permanent or even fleeting circumstance has associated certain ideas in the minds of people, those ideas never separate again. And if it happened that a libertine discovered his mistress on the altar of Venus, because indeed it was she, a pious man was no less led to revere the shoulders of his god on the back of a mortal—whoever he might have been [*quel qu'il fût*]. (P. 70)

When, at the exit of the temple, people recognized those qualities in the bodies of their fellow citizens, they were affected by them in quite an other fashion ("il en était bien autrement touché"). At that moment, there was the reciprocal imprint of art upon nature and of nature upon art that Diderot mentions at the outset of his digression. The libertine finds himself just as apt to revere the religious image of his mistress on the sacred altar as is a pious believer to revere the image of a god that he now finds represented in a mortal. In nude competitions, as Diderot goes on to explain, "there was in the tribute of admiration that they paid to beauty, without their suspecting it, a blend of sacred and profane colors, some bizarre mixture of debauchery and devotion" (p. 71). The lover who, while embracing his mistress addressed her as a goddess, spoke truly. "For in effect, he was in the heavens, among the gods; he was indeed pleasuring himself with the object of both his own and of popular adoration" (p. 71).[3]

Once one tries to understand it clearly, the simplicity of this clever, mythical etiology disappears.[4] Diderot is, in a sense, miming the Platonic tradition once again, and radically deforming it at the same time. As in Plato, when we see a work of art, a statue, it moves us and is beautiful to us because through it we are given to recollect the ideal of beauty (here, of divinity) that it represents phenomenally. But in the present text, there is no unidirectional "expression" of divine character, from model to representation, if for no other reason than that its "imprint" (p. 70) marks both the natural body (the natural model) and its artistic representation simultaneously and at a particular moment. Diderot is not describing an instance of nature imitating art, or any other simple reversal of traditional mimetic priorities. Rather, he is analyzing a "bizarre mixture" of antithetical qualities: the sacred and the profane, devotion and debauchery. When the people, at the threshold of the temple, saw the features of the gods in their fellow citizens, "il en était bien *autre*-ment touché," we should read. They are touched by the alterity that is now perceptible both in the human model and in the statue on the altar. Each now bears upon itself the imprint, not only of mimetic similarity— which was never in question—but of a liminal differentiation.[5] Both have entered general representationality. They can diacritically signify many gods, any person ("quel qu'il fût"), and mark them as beautiful or divine—as ideal. The threshold of the temple, the "sortir" defining the sacred and the secular world in opposition to each other, has now opened within representation and model as well.[6] Both are now *reft* by metaphor, meaning: "robbed" of simple presence, "split" between presence and representation of divinity. "My queen, my sovereign, my goddess!" (p. 71), one now says to mortal women. And, moreover, it is "true" (p. 71).[7]

Classical literature is replete with comparisons between objects of passion and objects of worship. Their relationship, however, can no longer be understood as one object imitating another, with absolute priority going to the original over the (necessarily inferior) copy. " 'Go to Delphi, and you will see my Bathyllus,' " mimes Diderot before concluding: "They failed only to tell us more often where the living original of the god they were caressing was to be seen; but nations who read their poetry have not been deprived of that knowledge" (p. 71). Anacreon's statue and the (ironic) "living original" are, in the logic of his analysis, simultaneously originals and copies of each other. It still remains, however, to situate the poetic text in relation to the generalized representationality that Diderot has found so irresistible.

When Homer says (*Iliad*, 1. 5. 528–30) that Jupiter causes all Olympus to tremble with a single movement of his dark brow, that brow exists "de foi," which is to say that it exists already in the anticipation of whoever reads such "theological" poetry. "The people expected to recognize [*retrouver*] in their gods and goddesses on the altars the charms characteristic of their catechism" (p. 70).

In naming poetry a source, Diderot explicitly rules out any understanding of that origin as a phenomenal presence or religious belief that subsequently gives rise to simple, unidirectional mimesis in a secondary medium. "For, after all, the poet had revealed nothing, nor had he created belief." The poetic text is only an anticipation of representation. The "divine imprint," the liminal difference of statues on the altar and mortals outside the temple, is predicated on that expectation thanks to which representationality in general exists before there is any particular representation.[8] (In the idiom of *Les Bijoux indiscrets*, there is a ring before there is a specific consultation; but it is the general, meta phorical promise of the ring that anticipates the specific synecdochal representation by any one jewel, statue, or body.)

This is not the last time that generalized representationality will find something close to its definition in the notion of anticipatory expectation.[9] The two are in fact inseparable. Neither can be prior to the other. To anticipate is to represent; to represent is to anticipate. The relationship seems to be governed by prolepsis—since that is the rhetorical figure in which an epithet depicts either a future or a past state as if it were present.[10] Anticipation represents a future moment in the present; in representation something present conjures up something that is absent, situated either in the past or the future relative to the moment of its representation. The temporality of Diderot's narration is such that "those epithets indivisibly attached to the heroes and the gods" (p. 72) refer to religious fervor or erotic fervor that is always past or future relative to the moment in which it is expressed. The lover's cries of "ma souveraine, ma déesse" were true ("c'est qu'ils étaient vrais" [p. 71]); but the "divinity" that they "express" as if it were present, in fact finds its source in either a past or a future experience inside the temple. And likewise the religious passion of the faithful kneeling before the altar is linked to experience in another time, in the profane world outside the temple. The emotion experienced by each is a concomitant of the anticipatory interruption that converts presence into representation. And strong affect, in turn, will always be the sign, almost the definition, of true mimetic efficacity in Diderot's writing.

Here, despite formal similarities, Diderot again diverges sharply from the classical ideology to which reflection on mimesis has been traditionally bound. For Plato, the logos is itself, already, essentially representational, pictoral, eidetic. In addition to the writer within us (see below), Socrates describes a second "workman" that dwells within the soul.

> Protarchus: What workman?
> Socrates: A painter, who paints in our souls pictures to illustrate the words the writer has written.
> Protarchus: But how do we say he does this, and when?
> Socrates: When a man receives from sight or some other sense the opinions and utterances of the moment and afterward beholds in his own mind the images of those opinions and utterances. That happens to us often enough, does it not?
> Protarchus: It certainly does. (Philebus, 39, b-c)[11]

Formally speaking, Diderot's etiology of divine representation follows the Platonic prototype remarkably. The artist works both after, and according to, a "writer" (Homer) who is the "source" of the primary image to be represented. "The sculptor fired up his brain, and picked up his clay and roughing chisel only when he had conceived the orthodox image" (p. 70). But the resulting visual representation is unrelated to the divine ideality indicated in the primary, written text. The visual and the scriptural—neither of these prior terms is transparently eidetic as they are for Plato. They are "adequately" represented, as we have seen, only when a representational (differential) space is circumstantially produced, effecting a generalized representationality. "Once some permanent, or sometimes even a fleeting *circumstance* has associated certain ideas in the mind of a people, they remain inseparable" (p. 70; my emphasis).[12] The artist's work lays bare no preexisting essence; it is no longer accountable to any "noumenal" authority other than that which produced in the same representational process as art itself; it is only an instance of the continuing process, already under way in the anticipation awaiting any representation.

In this later essay "Expression," Diderot thereby reveals a remarkable degree of consistency with the article "Beau." The discovery of a "rapport" between statues on the altars and any number of bodies outside the temple is a perception of a diacritical link that produces the aesthetic (erotic, religious) experience. The experience, as we saw in "Beau," "can vary infinitely." No absolute ontological authority obtains. But we are still "far from skepticism." By unleashing representation from its grounds while at the same time adhering to representation's traditional claim to re-present, Diderot has suggested a response to the problem without lapsing into solipsism or authoritarianism.

CHAPTER FIVE

The Ideal Model

Let us leave open the question of this
energy-carrying absence, this mysterious book,
that is, this gap which creates stories and scenes.
—Jacques Derrida
"White Mythology"

A CURRENT OF SCHOLARSHIP
(recent exponents being Jacques Chouillet in France and
Lester Crocker in the United States)[1] seems to view Diderot's manifest interest in a unifying epistemological principle partially as a response to the chaotic multiplicity of reality viewed from a materialist perspective. Diderot's theory of an ideal model responds directly to this preoccupation with the important question of unity, and will serve as a bridge to the other forms of its insistence that we shall encounter in his writing. He develops the concept of a "modèle idéal" in two texts most notably, first in *De la poésie dramatique* and later in the introduction to the *Salon de 1767.* We shall discuss both these instances.

As in the article "Beau," Diderot again seeks to avoid the equally unattractive alternatives of an aesthetics founded either on innate ideas or on skeptical relativism. He seems to be seeking a unifying aesthetic principle based on an external model more reliable than the vagaries of individual taste and belief, more substantial than passing fashion. In addition to providing grounds for aesthetic judgment, the theory of the ideal model is intended to guide artistic production as well. Ideal models for sculptural representation, for painting, for dramatic roles, theoretically would allow for a unity and objectivity otherwise impossible in such productions. Models admittedly would be created by individuals, but would be created according to explicit criteria, subject to perfection and revision. No production, no judgment would ever represent the model perfectly, but each would seek to approximate it as closely as possible. The artist, the actor, and even the philosopher, in echoing their ideal models through their work, would derive an authority that otherwise would be denied individuals working solely in their own right.

This ideal model was not a theory that originated with Diderot. In addition to its obvious Platonic antecedents,[2] the concept enjoyed general currency in the 1750s and, at first, was more associated with the Abbé Batteux.[3] The significance of Diderot's reformulation, however, extends beyond the place it grants him in the intellectual history of the decade.

For one thing, it has recently been recognized by Jacques Chouillet that Diderot's ideal model is the first instance in the eighteenth century of an aesthetic theory in which the sterile opposition of natural versus artistic truth is surpassed. Chouillet makes a strong case for considering it the most significant synthesis in aesthetic theory before Kant's *Critique of Judgment*. It is predicated on what Diderot called "the necessity for the painter to alter the natural state and to reduce it to an artificial state."[4] In Chouillet's analysis, "sensate material delivered to us by nature must be 'reduced' to the status of idea, and that idea will serve as a model for the painter. The path which leads from object to representation passes through the idea."[5] Chouillet insists that this alteration of the natural object, its transformation into an idea, "does not modify the *rapports* intrinsic to the object, it is in reality only a 'reduction.' It does not lose the quality of a *true representation*" (p. 479; my emphasis).

It must be said, however, that the "idea" and the etymologically related "ideal model" as understood by Chouillet offer no real escape from the impasse of sterile oppositions such as nature versus representation, truth versus falsehood. "Idea" is itself a representational concept—especially in an age so indebted to Locke—and thus can hardly be set against or between "object" and "representation." Both are inextricably imbedded within the Platonic tradition that depends upon and perpetuates just such "sterile oppositions" as original and copy, and with them, the inevitable privilege of one over the other. (As Derrida has made clear, if Diderot's contribution is only to prescribe that the artist first reduce the natural to the artificial, the real to the represented idea, he would be in keeping with the Platonic tradition, rather than in fundamental opposition to it.)[6] To insist on the fidelity of the ideal model to nature—on the model as "true representation"—is to place Diderot's theory well within the sphere of the most classical mimetic protocols in which "representation" can at best hope to be nothing more than a conduit leading reliably back to some "original."

If it is not just an eighteenth-century version of the overarching Platonic tradition, what then is this "modèle idéal?" What is its nature? What are its effects? How can it invoke classical notions of ideality without simply perpetuating the classical mimetic tradition? How can it have this double relation—both perpetuating and rupturing—such a long history?

Such queries call for several initial remarks. The question of the ideal model is a major vehicle for reflection on the problem of representation in Diderot's writings, a reflection that tends to unleash many of the effects that we have seen shadowing the issue all along. Perhaps most significantly, these effects are particularly intense around the question of unity, and the question of authority that the problem of aesthetic or philosophical unity tends to bring with it. What is more, the question recurs in different guises in different texts. (It is fundamental to the reading of *Le Fils naturel* that follows in the next chapter, for example.) And yet, commentators have not generally been willing or able to recognize its status as a nodal point through which many larger issues are linked.

The place of the ideal model in the text of *De la poésie dramatique* is a case in point, and will be occupying our attention in the present chapter. Although Diderot's first full-blown elaboration of it comes at the end of that text, critics have often suggested that it was tacked on almost as an afterthought. The intrinsic connection between the theory and the treatise that precedes it has proved very elusive. (Chouillet, for example, thinks it may have been "inserted into the last chapter in a rather artificial manner" [p. 482].) It is my belief, however, that the ideal model is the most telling outcropping of the logic that propels Diderot's dramatic theory, and that an examination of the whole text will show that it's placement at the end of *De la poésie dramatique* is not arbitrary. A successful analysis of these links will go some way toward recognizing the place of the ideal model in Diderot's writing, and through it, the insistence of representation as an all-pervasive question.

De la poésie dramatique (1758) first appeared as a companion piece to the play *Le Père de famille*. Its goal is to account for, and prescribe means whereby, a dramatist can achieve the greatest success, which for Diderot means the maximum possible impact upon the spectator. "It is not words that I want to bring back from the theater, but impressions. . . . The excellent poet is one whose effect lasts within me a long time" (p. 197).[7] Although Diderot links good theater to a wide spectrum of techniques, it is this specific kind of strong, long-lasting theatrical impact that seems to be the aim of his most insistent prescriptions. He is both explaining and promulgating a loosely conceived "system." But whatever system there is cannot be discerned in his elaboration of the techniques themselves. The only systemacity in this treatise is that which can be intuited in the common thread running through his qualifications of this peculiar effect on the audience which the various techniques are designed to achieve.

"Violence" is the word that seems best to cover the common denominator underlying his various qualifications (e.g., pp. 228, 229). Diderot wants the audience to be left "uneasy [*à la gène*]" (p. 197), "troubled, uncertain, floating, bewildered" (p. 198), like witnesses of an earthquake who see their houses shake "and [who] feel the earth vanish beneath their feet" (p. 198). Although not always metaphorized as physical violence, the effect of dramatic poetry is always powerfully disruptive.

The text is difficult to read because, in typical fashion, it scatters its attention in many different directions. Instead of reading it as a text, commentators usually tend to raid it, freely looting its better lines for use elsewhere. And yet, there is a certain coherence to be found. Consider, for example, both the arbitrariness of the following list of dramatic concepts and the common denominator of differential violence or disruption that underlies their heterogeneity:

Dramatic Illusion. For Diderot, disbelief is not willingly suspended but must be overcome independently of the spectator's will. "Illusion is not voluntary" (p. 215); it is wrested from the audience by a certain force. Success in creating illusion depends on careful manipulation of the plot according to a quasi-mathematical formula that is variable but that must always be in balance. The "negative terms" consist in the kind of extraordinary circumstances that occur only rarely in reality. The positive terms in the equation are common and banal circumstances that occur daily. The negatives are also called "mensonges" (p. 216), or fictions; the positives are called "vérités." "They must redeem each other, mutually" (pp. 215, 216). If the balance is kept constant, illusion overcomes the spectator and with it an unsettling sense of "merveilleux": "The important point [for the dramatist] would have been to be *merveilleux*, without forgoing verisimilitude: that is what he would have achieved by conforming to nature's order, when it takes a notion to combine extraordinary incidents, and to redeem these extraordinary incidents with commonplace circumstances" (p. 217).

The "merveilleux" effect of theatrical illusion, therefore, is not just the commonplace circumstance, nor is it the "coup de théâtre." It is the differential of positive and negative values in an infinitely variable equation—"a sum of terms, some positive, the others negative" (p. 215)—constituting thereby "the general system [*toute la poétique*] in which truth is constantly being placed in parallel with fiction" (p. 223).[8] The force of illusion is a concomitant of their difference.[9]

Imagination. Playwrights need lots of it. Diderot defines imagination (at least in this context) as the capacity to conjure up images from signs, to combine them in different arrangements.[10] It is the capacity to return from language back to the perceptual reality from which language presumably emerged.

But notice how he illustrates the point. He chooses the abstract word *justice* to illustrate the move from a sign to a "sensate representation [*représentation sensible*]" that is the task of imagination. "Justice" will be fully understood only when represented concretely by images ("signs" or "symptoms" [p. 218]) of an unjust man's fear of his victim and the victim's resentment of his oppressor. No matter how many variations may be possible in the definition of justice, it is necessarily differential in nature. "There will perhaps be as many different images as there are people; but all will represent two men experiencing *contrary impressions at the same moment*, producing *opposite movements*; or sounding inarticulate and savage cries which, translated in time into the language of civilized man signify, now and forever: justice, injustice" (p. 219; my emphasis).[11]

Character. Diderot's theory of dramatic character is related to his example of imagination's differential representation of images. Like the two "characters" in his image of justice, characters in a play should be placed in situations that contrast with their nature. "True contrast is contrast between characters and situations, of interests with interests. If you make a lover out of Alceste, let him be in love with a coquette; Harpagon with a girl who is poor" (p. 234). Diderot goes to some lengths to discourage the explicit, heavy-handed contrasting of dramatic characters with each other, alleging that it creates simple antitheses that have a petty effect. It is as if violent dramatic effect required an experience of "contrast" of aspects related to the very identity of the character, such that the character's identity becomes fundamentally diacritical. Harpagon loves a poor girl; miserly wealth is drawn into a differential conjunction with poverty.[12]

Dialogue. The difficulty in the art of dialogue is in creating a sense of struggle, not just between two discursive positions, but between two forces in real opposition. Corneille is the consummate master because in his dialogues, "a repartee is not just hooked onto the one last spoken; it goes to the very heart of the argument at hand. Stop wherever you choose; it is always the present speaker who seems to be in the right" (p. 253). In Corneille's dialogue real opposition is made palpable.

Virtue. At this nexus we return to familiar terrain and look ahead to important issues to come. As a playwright Diderot is often criticized for his scenes of intrusive moralism. But if we believe *De la poésie dramatique*, the semantic content of moralistic scenes counts less for him than their purely dramatic value. In a dramatic context, they make an impression on the audience that moral sententiousness in itself can never achieve. "If such a scene is necessary, if it goes to the heart of the issue, if the way for it is well paved and the audience desires it, they will pay full attention and will be much more moved [*bien autrement affecté*] than by those pretty little phrases that decorate our modern works" (p. 197). One can indeed represent virtue on the stage, "without hindering the *violent* and rapid course of dramatic action" (my emphasis), because virtue for Diderot is the stage of a "violent" confrontation of opposites.

But what exactly does that mean? If moralism enjoys a privileged status in Diderot's dramaturgy, that priority is not determined on ethical or theological grounds. Rather, the conflictual difference of virtue and vice is a matrix in which the most potent theatrical effects can be achieved. "If there is something moving, it is the *spectacle* of a man rendered guilty and miserable *in spite of* himself" (p. 214; my empahsis). Or: "If you must depict vice, first be aware of just how *contrary* it is to the general order of things, and to the happiness of public and individual alike, and you will depict it *forcefully*" (p. 282; my emphasis).

The principal doctrine that Diderot promotes therefore would be predicated on the emotive force inherent in the confrontation of virtue and vice. In other words, it is less an ethics than it is an aesthetics whose logic parallels the essentially dramatic "mixture of sacred and profane" that marked Greek statuary and Greek bodies in their differential relations to each other. And because it is a matter of difference, *both* vice and virtue are essential ingredients for "la poésic dramatique." It is not surprising, therefore, that in the same text Diderot can make essentially opposite claims. "Let me repeat then: the virtuous, the virtuous [*l'honnête, l'honnête*]. It moves us in a manner more intimate and sweet than those things which excite our disgust and derision" (p. 195). But later, referring to the poet's obligation to depict the passions and interests of his characters, we find this: "Hence, at every point, the necessity of trampling underfoot the most sacred things and of sanctioning the most atrocious actions. There is nothing sacred for the poet, *not even virtue* upon which he will heap ridicule if the character and the situation demand it" (p. 252; my emphasis). Virtue is necessary, but it is just as necessary for vice to trample on virtue.

Diderot wrote *De la poésie dramatique* as Rousseau was writing his *Lettre à d'Alembert*. They were published only a month apart. (Rousseau's text in October, Diderot's in November, of 1758.) The oppositions that link these two texts are telling. Rousseau fundamentally mistrusted dramatic representation because it is always a lesson in false appearance that necessarily incites its audience to perpetrate the same vice. Diderot's was the apparently opposite assumption, that "the pit of the theater is the only place where tears of the just and tears of the wicked are commingled [*confondues*]" (p. 196). The theater is the only place, in other words, where the wicked and the virtuous person are one: wicked in actual character, virtuous by identification with the virtuous charcters on stage. What then is at stake in this disagreement between the two?

The spectator's tears in Diderot's analysis spring from yet another mode of the "bizarre mixture." "[In the theater] the wicked man rebels against injustices that he himself would have committed, feels pity in the face of evils that he would have occasioned, and takes offense at a man with a character like his own. But *the impression is struck*: it indures within us, in spite of ourselves; and the wicked man leaves his box less apt to do evil . . . " (p. 196; my emphasis). The imprint struck upon the mind of the wicked is that of a differential value of vice and virtue, a duplicity, a dialogue that has the effect of opening a new space in his monologically wicked character. (It is another instance of the "divine imprint" that, in the essay on expression, will open a "dialogue" between the sacred and the profane in both the human body and its divine image on the alter.)[13]

Concomitant with this theatrical "impression" is indignation "against a man of his own character," which posits self against represented self. Once the wicked man experiences the difference, Diderot, unlike Rousseau, seems convinced that he will opt for virtue. In its specificity, however, virtue is always spectacle, always a role. It is always linked to the "theatricality" of self-reflexivity, the duplicity of consciousness out of which theater emerges, and upon which it depends. As such, it is first an effect of the difference that defines duplicity and representation.

Rousseau's position does not differ so simply or radically as it may seem, however, in part because neither position is entrusted to monological propositions, and thus neither position is subject to simple contradiction.[14] Yet, in the *Second Discourse* (1754), Rousseau does write that pity or commiseration is a form of identification—that prompts us to project ourselves into the place of those who suffer, "a pure movement of nature, anterior to any reflection."[15] Even animals feel pity (p. 154). He uses the same paradox invoked by Diderot of a wicked man identifying with stage victims that in real life he would not hesitate to injure: "Such is the pure movement of nature, anterior to any reflection: such is the force of natural pity, which the most depraved morals have difficulty destroying, since those who would not hesitate to augment the torments of their enemies if they were in the place of the tyrant, are the same people we see every day at the theater, becoming emotional and crying over the miseries of an unfortunate" (p. 155).

For Diderot, as I have said, the tears of such a person are a sign of the differential mark that is imprinted upon the soul circumstantially. Rousseau, beginning with the same example, moves in a different direction when he insists that pity—putting oneself in the place of another—is a natural given. (At one point he calls animals "spectators" in the natural theater of pity [p. 155].) But the representational magic or the tropological indeterminacy that makes it possible for another's misfortune momentarily to become one's own cannot be controlled with any certainty. Natural though it may be, the representationality on which pity is based is also the wedge that can separate the natural self from itself and divert it into the artificiality that Rousseau consistently laments. In view of that danger, identification with the feelings of others whom we perceive as "spectacle" —when not naturalized as in the first part of the *Second Discourse*—will always be rejected as evil by Rousseau, as in the *Lettre à d'Alembert* or the *Contrat social.*[16]

Here we can get a close look at Diderot's different approach to the same problem. If he writes differently about the issue, it is in large part because of a different relation to "nature." For the Rousseau of the *Lettre à d'Alembert*, nature cannot be difference. Rather, it is an untouched origin preceding the representational, tropological process. (This is reversed in the *Essai sur l'origine des langues*, as both Derrida and de Man have pointed out.) For Diderot, on the other hand, this so-called natural virtue is always theatrical from the outset—as is identity itself. For Diderot, "virtue," like "nature," presents itself as one of the most powerful effects that representation can achieve, but it is nevertheless an effect of representation. For Rousseau, however, representation is the cause and the very sign of virtue's demise and nature's perversion, even though it is itself "natural."

The same point could be made concerning an entire constellation of other terms treated by both writers, such as—to take only one—"justice."[17] "There is within our soul an innate principle of justice and virtue," writes Rousseau in his *Profession de foi,* "by which, in spite of our maxims, we judge our acts and those of others as good or bad, and it is this principle that I call conscience."[18] For Diderot, as we have just seen (under the above entry on "Imagination"), justice is a product of differential representation, an idea that we create only when we "represent two men experiencing contrary emotions at the same moment."

Diderot's various prescriptions in *De la poésie dramatique* follow consistently from this understanding of a natural connection of representation and virtue. Notice the telling confusion of theatrical, natural, and ethical terms invoked in his prescriptions for becoming an author: in order to become an author or a critic, "begin by becoming a good man. What can be expected of someone who cannot be deeply moved [he peut s'affecter profondément]; and what would move me deeply, if not truth and virtue, the two *most powerful things* in nature?" (p. 281; my emphasis). "Truth and virtue," as for Rousseau, are "the two most powerful things in nature." But for Diderot their power is, naturally, a moving theatrical spectacle rather than an internal presence. Virtue's aesthetic value comes not from the privileged status granted it by ehtics or nature, but rather from the abundance of its differential energy.

Confirmation comes in the form of a counter example. The miser will never be a great author. He strives to remain impervious to the theater of virtue—and the genitive here is double—which means that he remains impervious to a certain duplicity of self and other. "Bent over his strongbox" and "concentrated within himself . . . the happiness of his fellow man is nothing in his eyes, compared to that little piece of yellow metal" (p. 192). No identification, no virtue, no theater.

Consequently, Diderot's program for becoming an author or a critic includes also leaving society for a period of time. "Go study yourself. How will the instrument render a proper harmony if it is out of tune?" And finally, "upon returning to the society of men, listen a lot to those who speak well, and talk frequently to yourself" (p. 282). The writer's apprenticeship in this recipe repeats the same interiorized dramatization that reformed the wicked man in the theater. The self must be split into both subject and object, spectator and actor, such that listening to others who speak well is on the same continuum as listening to oneself speak. The interiorized "limen," the proscenium of internal representation, is the space of self-awareness and self-judgment that makes it possible to bring one's doubled selves "in tune" with each other, to be virtuous. There is a quasi-equivalence of writing, of being moved reflexively (*"s'affecter profondément"*), of truth and of virtue; and perhaps also an equivalence between the extraordinary "puissance" of truth and virtue in this context, and the "violence" that Diderot has been claiming for theatrical experience throughout the essay.

Again, virtue is defined in a fashion that clearly borrows from the traditional Platonic imperative to know oneself, to bring oneself into harmony with, and to be governed by, the forms of Ideality. But for Diderot, virtue is a product of the same structure of "rapport," a perceived relationship ontologically grounded in nothing beyond its own differential effects. (See "Postscript A to Chapter V" for further development of the connections, between reflexivity, identification and virtue, with reference to Leo Bersani's reading of Sade.)

After his lengthy analysis of all these various aspects of dramatic poetry, Diderot formulates the theory of an "ideal model" for the first time. It is his *Discours de la méthode*.

Now, one might well suppose that a treatise on theatrical aesthetics would in and of itself claim to represent a model for artistic creation. (Clearly, *De la poésie dramatique* does just that.) The addition of an abstract discussion of models in general may seem then to be either redundant to the model we have just been given or off the point. What one finds here has less to do with dramatic art than with an ideal model for the artist, for the philosopher and for all other "états [stations in life]" in general.

The link that I believe it is important to grasp is the differential threshold around which both segments of the text are similarly articulated. It is as if the instances of (often violent) difference that mark the analysis of theater in general are only prologues to this final development concerning an ideal model that, contrary to all expectations, inscribes difference in a still more radical fashion.

This rather complex and condensed last segment begins immediately after the prescription for becoming an author. (One must leave society, talk to oneself, get the instrument in tune with itself, then return.) After urging the would-be writer to talk to himself often, Diderot *stages a scene* in which his alter-ego, Ariste, "performs" just such a dialogue. It is a clear organic link between Diderot's notions of theater and the ideal model that Ariste will conceive while talking to himself.

There are even virtual stage directions in which the text describes the circumstances that led to this prescribed interior dialogue. Ariste pays a visit to his friends (who call him "le philosophe") "in order to converse [*s'entretenir*] about literature and ethics" (p. 283). The reflexivity of "*s'entretenir*" that Ariste expected to be mutual, among different discussants, winds up having to be internalized because "[his friends] were absent, and he decided to take a walk by himself. . . . Daydreaming as he went, here is what he said *to himself* [*voilà ce qu'il se disait*]" (p. 283; my emphasis). We know from the preceding pages of the treatise that from this moment when, in the absence of his friends, he speaks to himself, Ariste is effectively carrying out Diderot's earlier prescription for becoming a dramatist. His friends' absence becomes a liminal gap within himself, rendering possible a dialogue between himself and his self-as-other (-as-represented).[19]

The beginning point of Ariste's musings is the same as Diderot's in the article "Beau." Recognizing the same physical and mental "vicissitude perpetuelle" of all people, he maintains that no two individuals are alike and that each person is constantly changing.[20] Judgments and actions are only private and relative expressions of an isolated moment, bearing no relation to a transcendent truth or beauty. No stable model of judgment or action stands free from human vicissitude.

Recognition of the absence of such a model is synonymous with feeling its need. "That suffices, it seems to me, to feel the necessity of seeking a measure, a module outside of me" (p. 284). His interior dialogue turns therefore to the question how to procure an exterior model that would grant some degree of authority to actions and judgments that in reality enjoy none whatsoever: "But where to obtain the unvarying measure that I seek and which I lack? . . . In an ideal man that I shall create for myself, to whom I shall present things, who will judge, and whom I shall restrict myself to echoing faithfully? . . . But that man will be my handiwork. . . . What does it matter, if I create him according to constant elements? . . . " (pp. 284–85).

This line of reasoning will falter with Ariste's realization that one would have to have divine capacities to create an ideal man: "It is impossible to form a general ideal model, unless the gods grant me their intelligence and their immortality" (p. 285). Although a general ideal model of man is impossible, an ideal model of one's own particular role ("*état*") is not. Therefore, "Let the scholar make for himself an ideal model of the most accomplished scholar," concludes Ariste, "and let all judgments of his own work, and of others' work, pass through the mouth of that model." In the end Ariste will retire to his library for fifteen years of study before emerging as a great author and an excellent critic.

It seems strange that the search for an external and objective model should occur in the mode of an internal, subjective discourse. Accordingly, one must connect the absence (and resulting need) of an objective philosophical model, and the absence of the *other*, the friends who call Ariste "philosopher." Ariste now internalizes this alterity, replacing the intersubjective with an intrasubjective dialogue that can in turn produce a final, authoritative correlation between original and representation, of subject and "ideal man . . . whom I shall limit myself to echoing faithfully."

But very quickly this program goes awry, for the objective authority of the proposed model is only the mirror opposite of Ariste's subjective relativity. Subjective relativity and lack of unity thus serve as a negative model. That is to say, because of his subjective relativity, Ariste knows his inadequacy as a philosopher, determines to embark on an autodidactic project, and knows where to search and what to study in order to create the "ideal model that is appropriate

[*propre*] for my *role* as philosopher" (p. 286; my emphasis). (In this context the theatrical terminology should not
pass by unnoticed.) The model for this role that was granted
him at the outset, and that served so well in the constitution
of his ideal, was himself—himself as "lack," as other. "Let
the scholar make *himself* a model of the most accomplished
scholar," one could read literally. Ariste's felt "lack" in fact
defines the shape of the model required to fill it, which is to
say, "lack" (and its cognates) is the model of the ideal
model.[21]

The effects of this relationship will not be negligible as,
more and more, the model will come to resemble the very
lack and "vicissitude" that it arose to rectify.

The ideal that Ariste actually derives is never spelled out
in detail, nor will it ever be in any of Diderot's writings on
the matter. He is even at pains to underscore its absolute
virtuality, which is to say, its truly ideal and utopian nature,
always opening (within) the real to its other. References to
it are in the future tense ("whatever seems [*semblera*] beautiful to the model will be beautiful" [p. 285]), and the model
itself will be in constant evolution as the artist's experience
and knowledge expand. "The more one expands one's
knowledge, the greater and more rigorous the ideal model
will become" (p. 286). Diderot's ideal shares a basic feature
with the utopias described by Louis Marin, among others.
For Marin, "the critical impact of utopia is not the fact of the
model itself, but the differences between the model and reality; these differences being exhibited by the utopian
picture."[22]

Man makes the model as the model makes the man; both
are inscribed in the same "becoming" that renders moot any
question of either's being. For, once there "is" an ideal
model, its destiny is to be constantly changed. "But once I
have it . . . what use shall I make of this ideal model? . . .
I shall modify it according to circumstances. That is the second project to which I shall have to dedicate myself" (p.
286). Furthermore, constant alteration of the model leads

Ariste confidently to predict, in a telling formulation—heavy with scrambled Platonic references—that, "thus from a single simulacrum there will emanate an infinite variety of different representations" (p. 286). The experience of lack and "vicissitude perpetuelle" that provoked the search for an ideal of stability thus issues in a model whose major feature is perpetual vicissitude. The scholar has indeed made *himself* the model of the scholar, constantly "remodeled" by the difference that makes him. The theory of the ideal model is an attempt to name the differential space of representationality itself and to show its power to create roles for us, to give us a unified identity—but identity that enjoys all the power and cogency of theatrical identity, of roles on a stage. It is a theory that inscribes our unified identity within theory—theory that always has that theatrical quality of striving to encompass and represent unity, identity, right there before our eyes. It is an adumbration of a lesson that Elizabeth Bruss has recently formulated in language close to our own here: "The great theories are great not only because they answer questions successfully but because they initiate them. . . . It is tricky business this, to insinuate a need even as one tries to fill it, yet this is what theory as a literary form must accomplish. . . . "[23]

The ideal model is then, as Diderot calls it, "a single simulacrum" that produces "an infinite variety" of representations, just as the "rapports" that grounded beauty in the article "Beau" produced an infinity of beautiful objects. In both cases the "model" enjoys status as a theoretical model that answers our questions successfully, a model that one copies as in the traditional ideology of mimesis. And yet, it is a radical departure from traditional mimesis because it grounds or authorizes no particular, preordained mimetic act. Rather than arming a particular mimetic act with ontological authority, it causes a plurality of mimetic acts to proliferate. It is a copula. In this sense it is the same model that was elaborated in the preceding treatise, a model for differentiation and representation that affects us when we are spectators in the theater, giving us an image of ourselves that is at variance with ourselves, inviting us irresistibly into a theatrical fluidity of identities. The model is an agency of identity, a go-between that converts monologue into dialogue, single being into changeable re-presentation.

In conclusion, let us look briefly at the introduction to the *Salon de 1767*, which is the other important instance of Diderot's reflections on the ideal model.[24] Its resonances with the essay on "Expression" are striking, all the more so because of the repetition of vocabulary from one text to the other. Not part of Diderot's standard lexicon is the notion of a "ligne de foi"—a plastic form dictated by the expectations of faith—and an explanation of the project to "lift man above his condition, and to *imprint a divine character* upon him" (p. 12; my emphasis). But more significant is Diderot's explicit refusal of a theory of art based on classical mimesis. The logic of that refusal coincides with the earlier perception that mimetic, anthropomorphic representations of the gods were not marked by the essential quality of divinity. Here the point is that strict, mimetic fidelity to natural models does not represent beauty, the true object of artistic representation. Even the painter who copies the most beautiful woman in the world is only creating what Diderot consistently calls an individual "portrait," as distinct from an image of beauty itself. To copy any natural model is to remain in a tertiary position, after the beautiful woman who is in a secondary position to Beauty, the primal ideal. In another classical formulation, to paint a "portrait" is to copy a copy.

Clearly, Plato looms large, perhaps all the larger because the reference is so obvious as to not require mentioning.[25] But it soon becomes clear that although Diderot implicitly invokes prototypical Platonic constructs, he again inscribes them within his argument in a deconstructive manner. For, he continues, all truly great artists in fact ignore a thousand details that would have to be copied in order to represent their models with perfect fidelity. They do not paint every hair. They practice a selective violation of mimetic perfection; that stems not from technical necessity, but from fidelity to another model, a general idea that is different from the idividual model before them. This seems to be a purely Platonic analysis.[26] But this "other model" turns out in fact not to be Socrates' ideal essence so much as it is the same model/difference that emerged in *De la poésie dramatique*. In a dialogue with an imaginary artist, Diderot puts it like this: "You have perceived [*senti*] the *difference* between the general idea and the individual thing, even in the most minute parts, since you would not go so far as to assure me that, from the moment you first picked up a brush until now, you have accepted the onus of rigorously imitating every hair" (p. 9; my emphasis). The fact that the artist accepts and affirms the discrepancies between his painting and his real model, for Diderot, is proof that there is another "model," but a model that the artist feels in/as the difference between the general idea of beauty and the real exemplar before his eyes. The specificity of the ideal model, its presence, its "reality," is not expressed through the mimetic similarity between a natural model and its representation, but through their very dissimilarity and difference. Diderot rejects even the proposition that the models of ideal beauty come from skillful agglomeration of beautiful parts.[27] He refuses any incremental process that proceeds from a theory of the beautiful as a given or natural presence that can be simply copied.

Every animate and inanimate being is altered by its functional uses, by its experiences, or by the simple passage of time. "With use and time, these functions have had to extend, throughout the entire organization, an alteration that sometimes is so marked that it allows one to guess the function" (p. 10). Alteration of any part entails a network of subtler alterations of the whole. To the degree that he represents mimetically, the artist undertakes to represent the alterations that mark his model. "Would you not agree, once you have faithfully rendered the alteration particular to the whole, and the resulting alteration of each of the parts, that you have created a portrait. There is therefore a thing which is not the thing you have painted, and a thing you have painted which is between the primary model and your copy" (p. 10). (See "Postscript B To Chapter V" for a disagreement with Jacques Derrida on the question of idealism and reversal.)

The "faithful" mimetic copy of the natural model—the "portrait"—is marked by the "presence" of something that is not represented, which is the model in its ideal state before its alteration, a state that never exists in reality. "You must agree therefore that this model is purely ideal and that it is not directly borrowed from any individual image in Nature whose scrupulous copy remains in your imagination, and which you can subsequently call up . . . " (p. 11). Diderot could hardly be more clear, though the radical nature of the text has rarely been fully appreciated. The ideal model exists, it precipitates certain effects, but it "is" only a difference.

CHAPTER SIX

"Who Will Save Me From Myself?"

The Death of the father opens the
reign of violence. In choosing violence
(and that is indeed what it is from the beginning),
and violence against the father, the son—
or patricidal writing—cannot avoid exposing itself.
—Jacques Derrida
"La Pharmacie de Platon"

MADAME DE STAEL NOTWITH-
standing, Diderot's contribution to reform of the theater
was by any standard major. There is no want of names, such
as Beaumarchais, Sedaine, Mercier, Schiller, and Lessing,
that spring to mind when one raises the question of whether or not Diderot's dramatic theories had significant impact.[1] The difficult question has been how such energetic
theory could issue in such dreadful plays by Diderot himself.
It was as a dramatist that he most wanted to make his mark.
It was there that he was most personally committed. Critical
reaction has all the same been mostly negative regarding his
overall dramatic output, and outright condemnation of *Le
Fils naturel* has persisted since its publication in 1757. The
tradition has been perpetuated even by Diderot's most
sympathetic contemporary readers. (Jacques Chouillet's
critical vocabulary expands to include terms such as "un-
bearable" and "disastrous" when faced with *Le Fils naturel*.)[2] Most agree that the death blow is dealt by Diderot's
irrepressible tendency to moralize in a sentimental fashion.
Dorval's apostrophes to virtue—"Oh virtue, have I still not

done enough for thee!"[3]—no less than Constance's homilies, convert the stage into something between a pastry shop and a pulpit. But the disgust that the play seems to call forth from its readers may be the sign of a more interesting textual and theatrical dynamic than such expressions of aesthetic disapproval would suggest.

When we consider Diderot's insistence on violent effect, on naturalness, and on situational rather than discursive conflict in his theoretical writings (in *De la poésie dramatique*, as we saw in the last chapter), it may well seem that an overriding impulse forced him simply to sacrifice such precepts when he wrote *Le Fils naturel*. But if some legibility could be discovered linking the theory and practice that seem to be so much at odds in this case, we might gain an increased understanding of Diderot's overall writing economy. If we could discover such a "legibility," it would provide a means to hinge together and to articulate the theory and practice which, as things now stand, are simply incommensurate and disconnected.[4]

As a first basic point, *Le Fils naturel* is bracketed by a brief introduction and a theoretical dialogue entitled "Dorval et moi" in which theory's relation to praxis is itself the subject of discussion, is itself "dramatized." As a result, the traditional categories "theory and practice" are from the start inadequate and misleading. But we are anticipating on what the following analysis will be trying to demonstrate.

In the "Introduction," the narrator tells of his encounter with Dorval. Dorval's true "histoire" is going to be the subject of a play (the one that follows in the text), which is soon to be performed in quite peculiar circumstances: the same Dorval who actually lived through the events recounted in the play, along with other friends and family members who were participants in these events with him, will all "play" themselves in the upcoming representation. The play that is to follow will be as much a ritual repetition as a theatrical representation.

The fictional context thus established in the "Introduction" links the play, *Le Fils naturel,* to an entire series of issues that Diderot will discuss in later, theoretical texts. Most important, the logic of the performance that is described here diametrically opposes each of the most salient arguments that will be put forth in *De la poésie dramatique* and *Le Paradoxe sur le comédien.* According to the precepts of *Le Paradoxe,* the actor should remain at the greatest possible distance from his or her role. According to the fictional setting of Diderot's first play, however, people become actors in order to play themselves and to replicate exactly their own experiences and feelings. The fictional "actors" of *Le Fils naturel*—if they can be considered actors at all—are meant to function at a zero degree of "representationality." Even when they perform their roles, they remain themselves, for they are not marked by the usual difference between what they are and what they represent, between being and appearance. If one thinks of Rousseau's *Lettre à d'Alembert,* perhaps the best point of comparison here, the introduction to *Le Fils naturel* presents us with a situation in which an actor can both "se donner en spectacle," as Rousseau calls it, while paradoxically remaining "à sa place": literally at home in the salon, but also present to himself, to his own being, uncontaminated by the evil of representation. Here, in other words, is an effective confusion of Rousseau's categorical opposition between an orator and an actor. Dorval and his family are actors, but as in the case of Rousseau's orator, "the man and the role are the same being."[5]

Before returning for a full-scale treatment of this incompatibility, let us look at the other major preoccupation that surfaces in *Le Fils naturel,* that of the ideal model. It is safe to assume that Diderot's personal inflection of the notion of an ideal model emerged contemporaneously with his first plays. As we saw in the preceding chapter, its earliest full-blown formulation comes at the end of *De la poésie dramatique,* a text that is itself appended to his second play, *Le Père de famille* (November 1758). The question therefore is whether or not the chronological proximity of the "modèle idéal" to the first plays covers a more essential relationship and, if so, what light does it shed on the broader issue of theory and praxis that we raised at the outset.

The ideal model appears in everything but name within the text of *Le Fils naturel* (February 1757), almost two years before *De la poésie dramatique*. The context is, to say the least, puzzling. And fascinating. Rosalie is engaged to marry Clairville, but by the beginning of the play, she has fallen in love with his devoted friend Dorval. Dorval loves Rosalie in return, and both are deeply torn between love and loyalty because of their imminent betrayal of Clairville. Rosalie confesses her love to Dorval, referring to him coyly in the third person:

> *Rosalie*: The features, the mind, the glance, the sound of the voice, everything in this sweet and awe-inspiring object seemed to correspond to some unknown image that nature had engraved in my heart. I saw him [i.e., you, Dorval]. I thought I recognized in him the truth of all those fantasies of perfection that I had dreamed up, and he had my confidence from the start. . . . Whatever he said, I had always thought. He never failed to condemn whatever would displease me. Sometimes I praised what he was going to approve before he did so. If he expressed a sentiment, I thought he had divined my own . . . What can I say then? I saw myself hardly at all in others; . . . but in him I met myself constantly. . . .
>
> *Dorval*: If you are in love, you are no doubt loved in return?
>
> *Rosalie*: Dorval, you know it is true.
>
> *Dorval*: Yes, I know, and my heart feels it. . . . What have I heard? . . . What have I said? . . . Who will save me from myself? . . . (Pp. 32–33)

Rosalie had created for herself ideas of perfection that she had assumed to be only "fantasies [*chimères*]" because they seemed not to exist in reality. When Dorval appears, he seems to correspond to the image that she bore within her. Above her own contingency and uncertainty, there is now an ideal source of mirroring and comparison that serves to ratify her discourse, her judgments, and her sentiments—a triad that will have quite a future in this play. In 1758, in *De la poésie dramatique*, Ariste will seek little else from his own ideal model: "Let the scholar make himself an ideal model of the most accomplished scholar, and let all judgments of his own work, and other's work, pass through the mouth of the model. Let the philosopher follow the same plan. . . . Everything that seems good and beautiful to that model will be good and beautiful."[6]

The differences between Rosalie's inchoate version of the ideal model and its subsequent elaborations are, however, far more important. Dorval, for Rosalie, *is* an ideal rather than the intellectual anticipation of something that can never be phenomenally present. And more important, he is ideal for Rosalie insofar as he is *like* her. Whereas she felt different from all other people, "in him I met myself constantly." Recognizing the ideality of that image is all the more narcissistically satisfying because it is engraved on her own heart by nature itself. In *De la poésie dramatique*, an irreducibly prospective model will be described as something like a fulcrum that affords leverage from outside oneself, a kind of accountability according to external criteria. Far from being granted by nature, it will be described as the product of lengthy, if not interminable, effort.[7]

All these contrasts between the later, fully elaborated theory and its shadowy presence in *Le Fils naturel* are in fact only extrapolations from another metaphor. The ideality of the later model is indissociable from its difference, whereas here it is the very figure of indifferentiation, which is to say, of incest. For when Lysimond returns from America in act 5, he identifies both Rosalie and Dorval as his children.[8] The scene of Dorval's lament to his enamored sister looms larger in retrospect. Dorval might well ask, "Who will save *me* from *myself?*"—which is to say from indifferentiation, from incest. And in the scene of her declaration of love,

Rosalie gave proof of a similar perception when she said of Dorval that "in him I met *myself* constantly."

(Clearly, what is being figured in this earlier reflection on the question of ideality is the *absence* of the internalized limen, the difference that will both ground and destabilize identity, self-reflexivity, and our relation to models in *De la posésie dramatique*.)

As it turns out though, at the time of Lysimond's arrival these problems have already been resolved. Dorval has decided that he will marry Clairville's sister Constance, and Rosalie has chosen the equally virtuous path of reaffirming her original promise to marry Clairville. The return of Lysimond, therefore, is not what one would anticipate in an anthropological or psychoanalytic scenario of oedipal conflict, since the menace of incest seems to have been effectively circumvented already, without the intervention of a symbolic, paternal presence. We are thereby denied any theory of the later ideal model as some "oedipalization" of the present version, or an acculturation of the "natural" son. What one finds instead is a different version of the drama's teleology. During the play itself, Lysimond is never told of the romance between his children, but his subsequent reactions to it are recorded in the introduction. Hardly the oedipal father, he responds by empathizing with his son's incestuous desire; in effect he even amplifies it by giving expression to his own. "Ah! my son, I never looked upon Rosalie without quaking at the danger that you [*tu*] have skirted. The more I see her, the more I find her modest and beautiful, and the more the danger seems great" (p. 15). Great for whom, one has to wonder?

So Dorval's ability to resist the temptation does not result from respect for a father in whose name incest is a crime that the virtuous avoid as if instinctively. In Lysimond's view Dorval was spared by mere chance: "But the Heavens that watch over us today can abandon us tomorrow. No one knows his fate. All we know is that as life advances we escape the evil which pursues us. Those are the thoughts I have every time I recall your experience" (pp. 15–16). There is no guilt, and evil is an entirely exterior force. If Heaven abandons us, as it can at any moment, we may well end up in incestuous love affairs.[9] Because incest is not prohibited by any differentiating principle more certain than the vagaries of fate, Lysimond's position is tantamount to passively allowing it. That this attitude echoes a classical model of fatalism is clear.[10] ("No one knows his fate.") The surprise is that it should be a precise echo of a *mother's* attempt to discourage the revelation of incest, and thus to *forestall* its effective prohibition. Jocasta to Oedipus: "Why should anyone in this world be afraid / Since Fate rules us and nothing can be foreseen? / A man should live only for the present day. / Have no more fear of sleeping with your mother. . . . "[11] Within a cultural code ubiquitously patterned on oedipal triangulation, this play constitutes an unmistakable message or instance of incest's ratification.

It is at this juncture that Lysimond calls for the repetition of events surrounding his return, a repetition in the form of "a play whose subject will be an important part of our life, and that we shall represent among ourselves" (p. 16). The same words would be spoken annually, in the same salon by the same people; Lysimond and his servant André would even wear the same clothes. The elaborate repetition of the same that is thus launched, on the face of it, corresponds to Diderot's cherished dream of theater as quasi-religious ritual. But the project as conceived by Lysimond is hardly destined, through identificatory catharsis, to guarantee a postoedipal symbolic order on the model of Greek tragedy.

The arrival of Lysimond, toward which the play moves from the beginning, does signal the advent of difference. Dorval and Rosalie are identified as brother and sister, their love is (implicitly) named incestuous, their actions become retroactively illicit, and their marriage unthinkable. But since they no longer plan to marry each other by the time Lysimond arrives, the paternal office in the oedipal structure has been usurped by another agent. Its law has been preempted and circumvented painlessly, nonviolently, by

Virtue. Virtue in the play is not the product of the incest prohibition but rather, if anything, its cause. If *Le Fils natural* is designed perfectly to repeat the family's formative experience, then its subtitle—"The Trials of Virtue"—points to virtue as prior to the genesis. What is being celebrated is the survival of a preexisting, familial order of virtue, a bizarre kind of virtue based on pre-oedipal undifferentiation.

Virtue speaks through Constance.[12] In act 1 she boldly admits to Dorval that she loves him, at a time when he is still absorbed by his secret passion for Rosalie, his half-sister. Part of Constance's confession is a completely accurate prediction of the role virtue will play in sorting out the plot's four-part muddle of love and friendship: "I never doubted that virtue would give birth to love when the time for it arrived."[13] The "time" comes in act 4 in a scene that shows Constance successfully carrying out a seduction of Dorval. But the means by which she seduces him—that is, gets him to give up Rosalie for her—is a discourse of virtue. More precisely, of virtue-as-sublimation. (The *Oxford English Dictionary* defines sublimation as "the process of . . . converting a solid substance by means of heat into vapor. . . .") Here is Constance's speech: "Woe to whoever has not sacrificed enough [to virtue] to prefer it above everything, to live and breathe it above all else, to live intoxicated by its sweet vapor and reach the end of his days in its rapture" (p. 66).

Virtue does entail renunciation of unmediated, incestuous desire. (The "sacrifice" referred to by Constance is nothing else.) And yet, through its vapors, Dorval can retrieve with one hand the full value of what he discards with the other: not Rosalie, but something equally inebriating. His is the hedged sacrifice in which all loss is more than compensated by the delicious, undifferentiated omnipresence of ideal virtue. "As we have learnt," writes Freud in his essay on narcissism, "the formation of an ideal heightens the demands of the ego and is the most powerful factor in favouring repression; sublimation is a way out, a way by which those demands can be met without involving repression."[14]

Dorval's severance speech to Rosalie is predicated entirely on the demands of virtue. But the danger that it depicts, the principal risk of ignoring the dictates of virtue, is not the horror of incest so much as the loss of ideality. This "virtue" of Dorval's turns out to be a bulwark against the real: "That fateful word [the marriage vow] would have stamped a seal of permanence on our injustice and our misfortune. Yes, Mademoiselle: forever. Rapture passes. *People see each other as they really are.* They despise one another. They accuse one another, and misery begins" (p. 75; my emphasis).

Still more revealing is Dorval's reaffirmation of the same ideal mirror relationship by which they had originally fallen in love. According to Rosalie's act 2 declaration of love to Dorval (p. 33), his discourse gave expression to thoughts and sentiments that Rosalie herself had always harbored. And now, in the moment of "rupture," it is his turn to assure her of precisely the same correspondence of sentiment, thought, and discourse on which their incestuous love was based in the first place. He even refers to her in the same third-person address that marked her original declaration of love to him.

> But what have I executed [by breaking off] that Rosalie could not have done a thousand times more easily! Her heart is made for *feeling*, her mind for *thinking*, her mouth for *speaking* everything that is virtuous. Had I deferred an instant, I would have heard from Rosalie everything that she just heard from me. I would have listened to her. I would have regarded her as a benevolent divinity who held out her hand to reassure my halting steps. At the sound of her voice, virtue would have been rekindled in my heart. (P. 76; my emphasis)

The perfect narcissism of the virtue bond only replicates the bond of incest that it pretends to supplant. The perfect identity of feeling, thought, and word constitutes a union as undifferentiated and as erotically charged as the incest bond that preceded it. Sweet tears are never forbidden, and they are never in short supply.

The return of Lysimond only adds a paternal blessing to the entire, unholy brew. His dream of an annual ritual in which the familial drama would be celebrated is not an insurance against future incest but a sublimated indulgence in its pleasures. If there is in this play a proto-Freudian anthropology, as has recently been suggested, it is written in the neologistic idiom of a Totem without Taboo.[15] The play projected by Lysimond would not be a "portrait"[16] of the new order, its symbolic representation, so much as a repetition of the same trio of "ideas," "sentiments," and "discourse" that has been the hallmark of undifferentiation all along. Here is Lysimond's speech in which he proposes the annual play:

> And I would survive myself, and I would go on to converse from age to age with all my descendants. Dorval, do you think that a work that would transmit to them our own *ideas*, our true *sentiments* and the *discourse* that we have spoken in one of the most important occasions of our life would not be worth more than family *portraits* which only show what our faces looked like in an isolated moment? (P. 16; my emphasis.)

From the perspective of *De la poésie dramatique*, the *Salon de 1767*, or *Le Paradoxe sur le comédien*, *Le Fils naturel* so far appears to have no relation to the theory of representation-as-difference in those texts.[17] It would seem to signal a theory of theater as a privileged locus of a mimetic/incestuous epiphany. The ideality of its model is as present and as real as Dorval is to Rosalie. Its actors would be acceptable to "Le Premier" of *Le Paradoxe*, or even to Rousseau, because their roles are (oxymoronically) sincere and remain "entre nous," in Lysimond's words. In Rousseau's terms, we could say that, according to this scheme, each family member will both represent a role and remain "à sa place" at the same time.

The principial distinction of "le salon" and "le théâtre" in later texts is here collapsed entirely. In the appended dialogue between Dorval and a "Moi" (who, in part at least, represents Diderot), Dorval is able to counter each aesthetic criticism of the play's verisimilitude by the simple claim that almost everything in the representation happened in reality. In effect, another basic distinction in the later texts is sacrificed here as the difference between the "vrai" and the "vraisemblable" vanishes.

Not only would the "us" of the play be a repetition of the "us" of experience, but the same replication would be perpetuated in generations to come. Repeatedly, Dorval's children are announced as his fac-similes, not by virtue of a genetic principle of consanguinity, but by an aesthetic principle of mimesis. Constance: "Dorval, your children . . . will learn from you to think as you do. Your passions, your tastes, your ideas will pass into them. . . . It will depend on you alone whether they have a consciousness exactly resembling yours" (p. 63). When Dorval persists in his fears that his children might be "wicked," Constance becomes more explicit still: "But you would not be worried if you realized that the effect of virtue upon our soul is neither less inevitable nor less powerful than the effect of beauty upon our senses . . . [and] that imitation is natural to us, and that there is no example that captivates more powerfully than the example of virtue . . . " (p. 64).[18] Dorval's children will be just like him because they will mime his virtuous nature—naturally. Lysimond concludes the play with a benediction of the same principle: "May heaven which blesses children through their fathers and fathers through their children, grant you offspring that *resemble* you . . ." (p. 81; my emphasis).

The disjunction between this play and the dramatic theory articulated in *De la poésie dramatique* and *Le Paradoxe sur le comédien* seems radical. A kind of Platonic idealism-gone-awry seems to reign in *Le Fils naturel*. Ideal models father representations that strive naturally for undifferentiated and castration-less replication. *Le Fils naturel*, true to its name, does seem to celebrate an imaginary, familial context where nature and culture are seamlessly coextensive. Dialectical and genetic tensions have dissolved into an ideology of mimetic transparency.[19]

It is this aspect of the play that has prompted commentators to view it as example of Diderot's theatrical practice that is simply unrelated to his more forceful theoretical insights. But it may make more sense if the two spheres are understood to be bound together—intimately but diacritically—in a term-to-term relationship. The key to the nature of that linkage can be disengaged if we look at the play's appendages, the "Introduction" and the "Entretiens sur *Le Fils naturel*," which follow the play. Here we must return to our initial remarks about the fictional setting of the first annual performance of the play.

In the "Introduction" the narrator asks Dorval if he might witness the first presentation of the "play" called for by Lysimond, which is scheduled for the next day. Dorval reluctantly agrees and on the day of the performance surreptitiously admits him through a window just prior to the premier performance. "Unbeknownst to anyone, Dorval placed me in a corner from which, without being seen, I saw and heard everything that follows, except for the last scene. Later I shall explain why I did not hear the last scene" (p. 17). What thereby intrudes into the salon is the structural position of audience, whose effects are hardly limited by the spectator's singularity. With him the liminal space of representationality ruptures what was supposed to be repetition of the undifferentiated, "natural," and incestuous family closure that the play, taken by itself, fully indulges.

Moreover, the disrupting and differentiating presence of an audience finds its analogue in a disruption by a true actor within the family salon. We learn this, however, only in the "entretiens" following the text of the play, which offers the following narration:

> I promised to tell why I did not hear the last scene, and here is the reason. Lysimond was no more. One of his friends, with approximately the same age, height and voice, with the same white hair, had been engaged to replace him in the play. This old man entered the salon just as Lysimond himself had first done . . . dressed in the clothes that Lysimond had brought back with him from prison. This segment of the action set before the eyes of the whole family a man they had just lost, such that as soon as he appeared . . . no one could hold back his tears. . . . Spreading from the masters to the servants, grief became universal, and the play was interrupted. (P. 83)

This play was to be the celebration of incestuous ideality within the family and of Lysimond's return in the guise of its monumental capstone. His "murder" in the marginal texts—the lack of any necessity or even advantage in fabulating the character's demise connotes a "patricidal" structure—signals a new order that is strongly differentiated from the incestuous ideal that Lysimond sought to consummate. Death interrupts that ideal by injecting both the possibility and the necessity to *represent* this father—theatrically. When Lysimond originally called for a commemorative play, he explicitly avoided any "properly" theatrical implications. "A play, father!," exclaims Dorval. "Yes, my child. It is not a question of setting up a stage here, but of conserving the memory of an event which is important to us, and of rendering it as it really happened . . ." (p. 16). Death then intervenes in such a fashion that this "father" becomes an actor. With the intrusion of an audience, the "salon" becomes a theater; with the intrusion of a real actor, one is no longer "à sa place," and the whole range of representation's effects slices its way into the fetid familial closure.

What was supposed to be an unproblematic repetition of the same gives way to questions of mimetic adequation indicated by the choice of an actor based on his resemblance to Lysimond—necessarily his *approximate* resemblance, paradoxically instating his difference from Lysimond at the same time. Constance's principle of familial mimesis passing uninterrupted from generation to generation is aborted by the need for an exogamous replacement from outside the family. Furthermore, mimetic adequacy does not require that the replacement be a perfect replication of Lysimond—that he be mistaken for him. Rather, the actor's success can be gauged by the degree to which his similarity impresses upon the family the difference between the actor and his model, between his presence and Lysimond's absence, between life and death. Difference supersedes indifferentiated, incestuous ideality in the moment of the father's "second coming," his return as other, as representation—"[setting] before the eyes of the whole family a man they had just lost." In that moment ideality is the differentiating space we recognize as belonging to later articulations of the "ideal model." Diderot's first play, in this way, finds its place among theoretical developments that seemed simply to contradict it. *Le Fils naturel* offers up a lachrymose ideality to the blade of difference, an ideality already differentiated by the "Introduction," in which Lysimond's death is reported—at the outset. To the degree that we are (like the narrator) voyeurs in the salon, the father who enters in act 5 is already a conjuration of the dead. (And in case the point has been forgotten, the very first pages of the *Entretiens* detail the complete breakdown of the ritual when the "false Lysimond" enters the salon.)

Thus, the differential violence that for Diderot "is" dramatic poetry[20] is produced only when the accompanying dialogues rupture the incestuous ideality figured by the play itself. The relation between the play and the dialogues is itself differential, and with them the whole becomes a play of differences. Our original conviction of a radical incommensurability between Diderot's theoretical texts and his first dramatic effort must be discarded. Any account of their relation in terms of a "disequilibrium" between theory and practice—or surrogate terms such as force and timidity suggested by some critics[20]—substitutes an accidental disparity for the active and necessary differentiation that Diderot's first play undergoes thanks to his theoretical dialogues. Of course, if one attends a presentation of *Le Fils naturel* by itself, the effect is surely quite other. Without the dialogues one is denied the lemon juice necessary to cut the grease of the play. But for Diderot, even—and particularly—in this his most sentimentalized indulgence, there is not the one without the other. The opening of the ideal family closure that is figured in this conjunction of opposites figures the opening of the text, its self-differentiation that makes it legible from another place and time. This rupturing of ideal (incestuous) self-preservation entails one of Diderot's most theoretical moments, opening a communication between closed narcissism and a stage in which the ego no longer derives its only happiness from reproducing itself.

PART TWO

PHILOSOPHY: AN EXCELLENT GO-BETWEEN

On the one hand, it is impossible to dominate philosophical metaphors as such, from outside [philosophy], by using a concept of metaphor which remains a philosophical product. Philosophy alone seems to possess some degree of authority over its metaphorical productions. But on the other hand, for the same reason, philosophy is deprived of what it is granted. Its instruments belong to its own field, and it is thus powerless to dominate its general tropology and metaphorics. They can only be perceived around a blind spot or a threshold of deafness.—Jacques Derrida, "White Mythology"

CHAPTER SEVEN

La Lettre sur les aveugles

Through words and concepts we shall never
reach beyond the wall of relations to some sort
of fabulous primal ground of things.
Even in the pure forms of sense and understanding,
in space, time and causality, we gain nothing
that resembles an eternal verity.
It is absolutely impossible for a subject to see
or have insight into something while leaving itself
out of the picture, so impossible that knowing
and being are the most opposite of all spheres.
—Nietzsche
Philosophy in the Tragic Age of the Greek

*I*T IS A COMMONPLACE TO CHAR-
acterize Enlightenment thought by its overarching interest
in the link between basic philosophical issues and the experience derived from the five senses. When La Mettrie wrote,
referring to the senses, "Voilà mes philosophes,"[1] he
summed up, albeit in its extreme form, a position that philosophers after Locke had to either oppose or adopt to some
extent. "Nothing in the mind that is not first in the senses"
is an old dictum given new meaning by the more serious
empiricists. "Except for mind itself," retort their more cau-
tious adversaries.[2] The point is, however, that both sides in
such arguments about the precise nature of sense experience were opposed in one way or another to the traditional
a priority of theology and metaphysics.[3]

Such wisdom about the eighteenth century before Kant is
traditional, of course, and it is well founded. Empiricism,

materialism, "idéologie"—all must be understood in the context of an important struggle to escape the limitations we associate with traditional theological discourse and with Cartesian rationalism in particular.[4] These are historically "new" terms in philosophical discourse. But the novelty of the Enlightenment thus understood lies in the particular configuration of its philosophical forces more than in the fundamental nature of the arguments themselves. For one could maintain—also in harmony with conventional wisdom—that the problem of sense perception was no less central to Platonic and Aristotelian discourse. Socrates' proteiform meditation on the discontinuity between being and appearance is, in its own fashion, a meditation on what later philosophy was to call the epistemological status of the sense experience through which appearances appear. In this way Platonic idealism and eighteenth-century materialism communicate through the medium of Western philosophy, but more particularly through philosophy's problematic relation to metaphor. As Jacques Derrida writes, the problem of philosophy's relation to metaphor is that philosophy both makes metaphors that are essential to it and pretends to exclude metaphoricity from what is specific to philosophical discourse. Philosophy closes its eyes in a kind of sleep in which it can continue to act as if "the meaning aimed at through these figures is an essence rigorously independent of that which carries it over [i.e., metaphor]. . . ."[5] The separation of independent meaning from the vehicle through which meaning is transported is basic to philosophical definition of metaphor. But Derrida points out that that version of metaphor "is already a philosophical thesis, one might even say the sole thesis of philosophy, the thesis which constitutes the concept of metaphor, the opposition between what is proper and what is not, between essence and accident, between intuition and discourse, between thought and language, between the intelligible and the sensible, and so forth" (p. 29)—and, one could add, between *représentant* and *représenté*.

Derrida's demonstration of the metaphoric cusp producing philosophy's most lasting concepts in metaphor, frequently returns to the visual, and to the appearance/disap-
pearance of the sun which has traditionally grounded it.
With reference to the present context, the eighteenth century's reflection on sense experience shows the same predi-
lection for the visual as did Plato. The division between the
falseness that we can see and the truth to which we are
blinded—or in those most famous of Platonic terms, between the visible shadows in the cave and the ideal reality of
the sun, which, because it blinds the human eye, cannot be
seen—has become a sine qua non of our thought.[6] "White
Mythology" both analyzes and as a modern philosophical
text itself, bears witness to the continued necessity of that
metaphor and, with it, to philosopy's inescapable ties to metaphoricity in general.[7]

So we are far from surprised to find, in the new discourse
particular to eighteenth-century philosophy, the old metaphors of Platonism again pressed into polemical service.
One is even used to finding them underlying the most basic
arguments in materialist, specifically anti-idealist writing.
"I am just as resigned to being ignorant of how inert and
simple matter becomes active and composed of organisms
as I am not to being able to look at the sun without a red
glass; and I feel the same way about the other incomprehen-
sive wonders of nature, about the emergence of feeling and
thought in a being which appeared otherwise to our weak
eyes as a mere bit of dust." The writer is again La Mettrie,
this time in his *L'Homme machine*.[8] Not only do such examples abound, but the visual metaphor, with the host of its
corollary metaphors, seems to be the organizing principle
for large blocks of eighteenth-century writing.[9] (The period
is, after all, called the Enlightenment.) And Diderot is certainly no exception: "Presenting the truth to certain people
is . . . like introducing a ray of light into a nest of owls; it
serves only to hurt their eyes and excite their cries."[10]

In particular and historical terms, the status accorded

sense perceptions in the late seventeenth and early eighteenth centuries derived in part from the Cartesian break with the Aristotelian tradition. For Aristotle the perceptions we have of things in the world are not their "reflections" in the mind (similar to what Locke was to call "impressions"), but are of the same nature as the things themselves. In relation to the idea, perceptions are no more nor less secondary than the physical world that they represent. Descartes inaugurates a break between the perception and an intellect that "inspects entities modeled on retinal images,"[11] the break without which Locke could not have produced his particular mode of empiricism.

The Lockean view, then, is that the world is only represented by sense impressions that are, in themselves, of a different nature than the world they represent. So, in the above quote, La Mettrie is typical of his age in that, like Jacques the fatalist, he is resigned to accepting his "blindness" to whatever essentials, to whatever first or final causes might determine the world he inhabits. Representations of the world, in the form of sense perceptions, are all we have, and all we can do is to attempt to account for them systematically.

But at its most fundamental level, the resulting psychologism and phenomenalism of eighteenth-century epistemology are still only a further elaboration of the Platonic legacy. Locke is, in this narrow sense, only another permutation. Since we cannot gaze directly upon the noumenal sun itself, we must look all the more intently at the phenomenal that we are given to see by the reflections of its rays. (The noumenal is momentarily hidden, a literal meaning behind a temporary veil of metaphor.) Atheism, deism, and faith can all coexist with such an epistemology, and in the eighteenth century they all did. The point remains the same as that made by the atheist La Mettrie, or, in a deistic mode, by d'Alembert in his *Eléments de philosophie*: "The supreme Intelligence has drawn a veil before our feeble vision which we try in vain to remove."[12] As Diderot writes in his article "Encyclopédie," the causal chain is simply so complex that we "lose sight of the links that precede and those that follow."[13] So whether or not any form of ideality is believed actually to exist, we still must be "resigned to being ignorant" or blinded as we seek to gaze on nature. Transcendental metaphysics, it was thought, could be left behind forever. Descartes and Malebranche bow to Newton and Locke.[14] In Cassirer's tidy summation, "The assertion that every idea that we find in our minds is based on a previous [sense] impression and can only be explained on this basis, is now exalted to the rank of an indubitable principle."[15] But philosophy's link to metaphor remains and subtends these shifts in philosophical discourse. And furthermore, the effects of that linkage continue to be legible.

For what Cassirer rightly called the "indubitable" in the eighteenth century—that our ideas are all derived from the senses—is only the positive side of the principle. In fact, this positive value is closely doubled by its obverse, expressed by the old questions: How can one be assured that these interior representations of exterior phenomena are accurate?[16] Or: What is the relation of the world perceived by one sense to the world perceived by another sense? Or: Is there a *sensorum commune* that coordinates these different sense data? How is it different from the same notion proposed by Aristotle? Could it be called a soul? How can it be accounted for without recourse to idealism? And so on.

The "indubitable principle," in other words, is purchased by a doubt. It is just this doubt that is systematized in the skepticism of Berkeley and gives rise to what would be recognized, after Kant, as "epistemology." "To think of knowledge which presents a 'problem,' and about which we ought to have a 'theory,' is a product of viewing knowledge as an assemblage of representations. . . . "[17] And Rorty's claim that such a view becomes possible in the seventeenth century with Descartes finds ample support in Foucault's analysis of the determining role of representation in the classical episteme.[18] But "representation" is at this level only another name for metaphor.

I offer this rapid historical sketch in order to return to the present project with a question: Can the issue of representationality in Diderot's writings be assimilated to the epistemological problem of his entire age in its classical philosophical guise? Or to pose the question in the vocabulary that characterized it in *Les Bijoux indiscrets*, is the sultan's quest a quest for a sight (or an insight) beyond the veil of phenomena, for a literality beyond figuration, or for an epistemological assurance that he at least perceives phenomena correctly and can regulate judgments accordingly?[19] The answer, which is ultimately in the negative, is not simple. Fully within the tradition of philosophy that wants to use metaphor in order to lay claim to a nonmetaphorical, literal truth, Diderot's interest lies—nevertheless—elsewhere.

It is usual to find in Diderot a distillation of all the currents of his time. And indeed, perhaps no one else was so well positioned for that status as the editor of the *Encyclopedia*. But most often one can locate in his reactions to the various intellectual positions and movements a critical awareness of their blind spots—precisely those blind spots most necessary for a system's positivity, as it were, behind the veil.[20] He often seems aware of the discrete philosophical products in his time as truces with the veil, as so many compromise formations passing for solutions. Surely the most impressive example of that stance is his analysis of the *Encyclopedia*'s compromise with its own philosophical ideals.[21] It is for this reason that Diderot was fundamentally a spectator and critic, for all his involvement with the intellectual life of the latter half of the century. In any event, in his own writings we are given to follow the prolongations and the effects of the philosophical metaphors of sun, veil, and mirror with an uncommon degree of complexity and legibility.

He is certainly enmeshed in the century's post-Lockean questions. He makes massive use of the sensationalist vocabulary. And yet, the two most famous early texts on related issues—the *Lettre sur les aveugles* and the *Lettre sur les sourds et muets*, which we shall now examine in the next two chapters, shift the issue away from the "positivist" sensationalism of Locke and Condillac. The representational aspect of sense experience is basic in the writings of Diderot, just as it was in those of Locke and Condillac; but Diderot consistently focuses on the problem of what makes sense representations represent.

From this perspective it can hardly, be overemphasized that his two treatises on sense experience have as their subject the absence of those experiences in the blind and the deaf. It is as if, already at the outset, some manner of blindness and deafness is required in order to produce the metaphors of sight and hearing as nonmetaphorical positivities. His focus on blindness becomes an attention to blindness itself as the "veil of philosophy" that produces the representational positivities that flow endlessly from it as inexhaustible resources.[22]

Consider, for example, the "mirroring" that, consciously or not, links Diderot's descriptions of the human mind, and of the phenomenal world itself. First, from *De l'interprétation de la nature*, is a text on the scientific object that at first seems to exemplify the representational project that Foucault ascribes to the Classical age.

> Once experimental physics is more advanced, it will be recognized that in nature all the phenomena— weight, flexibility, attraction, magnetism, electricity—are only different facets of the same cause [*affection*]. But among the known phenomena that we relate [*rapporte*] to one of these causes, how many intermediary phenomena remain to be found in their identity? That is what cannot be determined. Perhaps there is a central phenomenon that would throw light not only on the phenomena we know, but on all those

we may discover with time, and that unite them all
and form a system. But failing that center of common
correspondence, they will remain isolated. . . . [23]

And here from a later work (the *Réfutation d'Helvetius*) is
one of many texts on the issue of a central, unifying agent
capable of corellating multifaceted data received from the
five senses. The identity and unity that such an agent guarantees to the individual parallels the identity and systemacity that the center of common correspondence would provide for the diverse phenomena of nature. "Without a
correspondent and a common judge of all sensations, without an organ commemorative of everything that happens to
us, the living and sensate organ that is each sense might
have a momentary awareness of its existence, but there
would certainly not be any consciousness of the animal or of
the entire man."[24] The central unifying terms posited in
both instances are homologous, and reflect the same necessity, the same *desideratum*, for a common center.[25] They
both stem from the necessity for a switchboard of common
causality that would be capable of grounding and ultimately
of explaining the "rapports" of the whole person or the
whole world as totalities. Indeed, the mind for Diderot is,
faced with the world, a "sensate mirror, thinking, judging
. . . to whose decision all our sensations are submitted."[26]
But it may well be that what it reflects positively of the
world is doubled by this other reflection of a central "go-
between [*truchement*]" that is required and desired precisely because it is in some way lacking—or at least veiled—
in the self and in the world.[27] If I am correct that the mutual
mirroring of self and world includes this analogous and
shared absence, then it is precisely this negative, this central
and highly productive gap, that Foucault has omitted from
his qualifications of eighteenth-century representation.[28]

At this juncture we can cast a familiar glance back to the
textual network of Diderot's aesthetic writings that we saw
articulated around the same absence: Ariste's lack and need

of a stable basis for true aesthetic and philosophical judgment, the lack and need of an ideal model, the lack of identity ("le propre") in the great actor that causes him naturally to seek different roles, and so forth. Certainly in this generalized feature of Diderot's writings, the later *Neveu de Rameau* is of crucial importance. The nephew's lack of the paternal "fiber" has, paradoxically, defined him by his nondefinition and his concomitant desire to represent himself by means of any identity he can borrow. "We value unity of character in everything," the Nephew lucidly asserts; but he elicits from his interlocutor the equally lucid response that is Rameau's cross: "But this estimable unity of character, you don't yet have it."[29]

We can also adumbrate a reading of "Le Rêve de d'Alembert" in which the problem of a central nerve center or a "common origin which constitutes the unity of the animal" is just as central. But if we search for it in that text we will again find that, as in the actor, as in Rameau's nephew, the sensate network "has at its origin no sense which is proper to it [*aucun sens qui lui soit propre*]." Although the *sensus commune* links together all the divergent elements of the sensorial apparatus, the center itself "does not see, does not hear, does not suffer. It is produced, nourished; it emanates from an inert, insensitive, soft substance [i.e., the brain], that serves as its pillow, and upon which it sits, judges and pronounces."[30] In accordance with the sensationalism of his time, Diderot views the five senses as mirroring a plethora of information from the world they represent; but the agency that makes meaning from that information is, as it were, blind and deaf, insensate. In the plenum of sense representations their essential "truchement" is an empty phantom, a shade in the light, a silence in the noise.[31]

A somewhat different version of the same idea will be suggested in the *Salon de 1767*. "Now you understand what the soft cheese is that fills the volume of your skull and mine. It is the body of a spider whose nerve fibers are its legs or its web. Each sense has its language. The cheese has no idiom proper to it [*Lui, il n'a point d'idiom propre*]; it doesn't see, it doesn't hear, it doesn't even feel; but it is an excellent go-between [*truchement*]."[32]

A "truchement" is an interpreter, a spokesperson, a representative that *causes* understanding or communication to occur between differing or opposing parties. Having no language of its own, the "truchement" causes meaning in one idiom to be comprehended in another idiom—what in Greek was called *metaphorein*, to carry over from the one to the other. To be "rapporté," we might gloss, in an idiom more indigenous to Diderot.

All these issues come together in *Lettre sur les aveugles*, which is Diderot's attempt to resolve William Molyneux's famous question. The latter, as is generally agreed, crystallizes in a single form all the diverse philosophical problems typical of the century.[33] Although Molyneux first formulated the problem in his *Dioptrica Nova* (1692), it was Locke who made it current when he inserted it into a re-edition of his famous *Essay*, from which I am quoting here:

> Suppose a man born blind, and now adult and taught by his touch to distinguish between a cube and sphere of the same metal, and nighly of the same bigness, so as to tell, when he felt one and the other, which is the cube, which the sphere. Suppose then the cube and sphere placed on a table, and the blind man to be made to see; quaere, Whether by sight, before he touched them, he could not distinguish and tell which is the globe, which the cube?[34]

Locke and Molyneux concur that the subject would fail to distinguish the two forms by using only his newly acquired sight. They maintain that only by experience, not through any intrinsic or innate connection, do we associate the different experiences that each sense gives us of the same object. Visually perceived roundness is linked to roundness perceived through touch only by repeated, empirical experience. Although the senses may represent the world, they are not intrinsically connected to each other. Berkeley (in his *New Theory of Vision*, 1709) pursued the issue still further, but in harmony with Locke's original conclusions. In 1728 Cheselden claimed to have verified the proposition through surgical experiment upon a blind boy, but few considered his dubious procedures authoritative.[35] The question becomes current in France through Voltaire's book on Newton (1738), and was taken up by almost all the important French intellects in the middle part of the century.[36] It became the central concern in Diderot's *Lettre sur les aveugles*, his first sustained philosophical work.

Without adding anything remarkably original to the overworked question—at least on the surface of it—Diderot formulates a qualified disagreement with the majority, which thought that the subject would be incapable of discerning the two forms. The specifics of his position—full of caveats about the condition of the patient, his education, preparation, and so forth—are less important here than the central argument of his conclusion. It is an argument that accepts the representational adequacy of sense experience.

Diderot does not doubt that a blind eye that suddenly acquired sight for the first time should eventually "see" objects, "and that it should see them distinctly enough to discern general outlines. To deny it would be to *lose sight* of the purpose of organs, to forget the principal phenomena of vision. It would be to ignore the fact that there is no painter skilled enough to approach the beauty and the exactness of the miniatures that are painted on the backs of our eyes, that there is nothing more precise than the resemblance of the representation to the object represented. . . ."[37]

Diderot's aesthetic writings assume inevitable dissimilarity between representation and object. (No painter can claim to have painted his model's every hair.) Here he describes vision in the characteristic terms of a mimetic representation—in the same passage he goes on to call a retina "the canvas of this painting." But the eye's representations differ from artistic representations at the outset because they are both spontaneous and perfect. In his aesthetic writings, we saw that representation, in its specificity, depends upon difference. Are we now to conclude that for Diderot sensual representation is something approximating undifferentiated repetition of reality in sense impression? Barring one or two characteristically prudent reservations, he seems to be saying just that in his answer to Molyneux.[38]

In the *Lettre sur les aveugles*, then, Diderot's position—which is unusual in the commentary elicited by Molyneux's question—is tantamount to "dissolving the problem."[39] It had been a question asked in order to elicit a negative answer, after all, and thereby to engage battle with the forces of apriorism. By maintaining that the representational function of the eye is ultimately self-sufficient and adequate to the world it must represent, he has robbed the question of its force. At least in this first moment, he has simply granted empiricism its epistemology. The cube *is* square, the sphere *is* round. We see reality accurately. In Jack Undank's characterization of Diderot's attitude toward the visual, "the advantage of true visibility is that it momentarily silences rational consciousness and welcomes trust; the eye is satisfied with its unutterable adequacy, sympathy, antipathy, and intuition. No significance escapes."[40]

But what then, we must wonder, is Diderot's interest in blindness? Indeed—an even more important question—what is blindness in the "economy" of Diderot's writing?[41] In the plenum of sense representation, the blindness to which he devotes an entire treatise inevitably calls up the description from "*Le Rêve*" in which the *sensorum commune* is itself insensate—blind—a copula that is nothing in itself. In the midst of a visual plethora, Diderot's attention is drawn to this gap that makes sense data represent an interconnected, thus meaningful, totality.

He seems to say at one point quite clearly that he is more interested in the philosophical vision of a Tiresias than the physiological vision of a naïve Oedipus: "I would have less confidence in the responses of a [blind] person who sees for the first time than the discoveries of a philosopher who has well meditated upon his subject in the dark—or to speak to you in the language of the poets—who has put out his eyes in order to know [*connaître*] better how vision is achieved" (pp. 54–55).[42] Blindness is then an absence or a gap in the plenum of sense experience that enables one to know what sight is. Blindness in this context is therefore another instance of meaning-producing "truchement," of *metaphora* (transport) or copula. Blindness is this "metaphoricity" itself and can only be signaled through other metaphors— here, through metaphors of dark and light, the poetic language of putting out one's eyes in order to know how vision is achieved. And perhaps most important, Diderot gives evidence of an inchoate recognition—but then, such awareness is perhaps always inchoate—that a philosophical definition of empirical blindness cannot itself eliminate the metaphorical basis of the philosophical enterprise.[43]

And indeed, in the *Lettre sur les aveugles*, Diderot presents himself in the position of a Tiresias, unable to "see" the objects of his discourse. It is addressed in epistolary form to a lady usually assumed to be Mme de Puiseaux. It begins with a reference to a recent event in Paris: Réaumur's removal, before an invited public, of bandages from the eyes of a blind-born girl who had undergone surgery to couch her congenital cataracts. With this case Réaumur had an opportunity literally to perform the experiment projected by Molyneux, and in conditions more controlled than in Cheselden's earlier attempt. To the extent that it promised to provide an empirical answer to Molyneux's hypothetical question, through an operation that could be directly seen, the experiment promised the closest thing possible to absolute sight, to a peek behind the veil of phenomena, a glimpse at the literal nature of vision. It was indeed, as it has recently been called, "the experiment of the century."[44]

But as we are told straight away in the *Lettre*'s first paragraph, Réaumur had denied Diderot admission to the crucial moment when the patient's bandages were first removed. The experiment of the century, in other words, took place in the Philosopher's absence.[45] In his own sensualist terms (coming from Locke), Diderot-Tiresias literally has no "idea" of what he is describing that he could represent literally. (In the article "Invisible," for example, he will write that "if a thing has not been perceptible [*sensible*], one has no representative idea of it.")[46] Not surprisingly, then, from the outset the *Lettre* seems caught up in an ambiguous complex of metaphors relating to sight and blindness, and once again relating knowledge of sight to the experience of blindness.

In the first sentence, for example, Diderot is clearly playing fast and loose with the language of veils, blindness, and ignorance. We learn that the couching of the literal veil (blindness-cataracts) did little to couch the figurative one (blindness-ignorance). "I well suspected, Madam, that the blind-born girl whose cataracts Réaumur has just couched, would not tell you what you wanted to know" (p. 81). There is at the very outset a disjunction of the figure of the veil from its literal grounds; the veil of the cataract and the resulting blindness of the patient has nothing to do with the figurative veil of ignorance, which remains as solidly in place as ever after the cataracts have been couched.

The confusion of trope and nontrope continues apace with a famous insult to Réaumur's mistress. (Unlike Diderot, she had been allowed to witness the experiment.)[47] "Réaumur wanted to let the veil drop only before insignificant eyes [*quelques yeux sans conséquence*]" (pp. 81–82), in which the differing meanings of both "veil" and "eyes" extend the same metaphor as before. Veil-ignorance and veil-bandages fall indeterminately before the eyes-understanding and eyes-eyes of those in attendance. The observers in any case remained no less blind than the patient regarding literal/rhetorical "sight."

It is remarkable, given the tradition outlined above, that Diderot himself should make the connection between these visual tropes and the specifically philosophical aspect of the project in which he is engaged. Rather than positioning his discourse on either side of the veil, as either literally-philosophical or tropological-literary, he stages the conjunction of the two as the nexus from which his text emerges. Referring to his exclusion as an eyewitness, he explains, "I have thus reverted, Madam, to my original plan; and, forced to forego an experiment from which I saw little to be gained . . . I set out to philosophize with my friends about the important question that is its object" (p. 82). Because literally and figuratively he could not see beyond the veil, he philosophizes, as did Socrates, about the questions that the veil produces. Which veil? In one fashion or another, it would seem, that is always the question. Discourse and perception are not ordered as to priority or epistemological reliability.[48]

Let us return to our own question, and ask again: What is interesting to Diderot about this blindness? Can we begin to understand why or how he radically extended this foremost question of that philosophical age while at the same time underscoring rather than suppressing the commerce that philosophy maintains with metaphor?

In his conclusions concerning experiments such as Réaumur's, he catalogues all the reasons for presuming that, at best, "these sorts of experiments will always be very difficult and very uncertain . . ." (p. 65). The subject must be trained in philosophy, for "what precise results can one expect from someone who is not used to thinking [réflechir] and reflecting upon himself [revenir sur lui-même], and who, like Cheselden's patient, is ignorant of the advantages of sight, to the point that he was unaware of his misfortune, and quite unable to imagine that the loss of this sense greatly hinders his pleasures" (p. 65). That surely is absolute blindness: absence of light and absence of awareness simultaneously. And it is not interesting. But philosophy would render the patient self-conscious and, in another essentially visual metaphor, self-reflecting. It would, like a mirror, enable him to "revenir sur lui-même," to go out of himself and come back to himself from another place, "to compare the two conditions through which he has passed, and to inform us of the difference between a blind state and the state of a man who sees" (p. 65). Vision, as a simple positivity, is not interesting. It is not problematic. Nor is blindness when it is understood as a simple negativity.[49] On the other hand, the difference between the two states is both interesting and problematic. Rather, the better conclusion would be that blindness is interesting for Diderot insofar as it is not a state at all but the metaphor for that difference; when it is the veil rather than one of the states—blindness or sight—produced by the veil.

Given this metaphorical function of the veil—which produces such philosophical and empirical effects as blindness and (in)sight—Diderot's analysis of blind people's language rigorously extends these effects quite far. Particularly interesting is the use he makes of Nicholas Saunderson, the blind Cambridge professor of mathematics and, yes, optics. (Diderot's fascination with Saunderson would seem to stem from the latter's virtual incarnation of the link between blindess and knowledge/sight.) With Saunderson, Diderot is already linking sensorial gaps to linguistic metaphor that will become central in the *Lettre sur les sourds et muets.*[50]

But before taking up the links between the veil and language, we need to glance at certain of Diderot's other statements on language that form a point of comparison needed in reading the *Lettre sur les aveugles.* For just as his interest in blindess is set within an overriding conviction that vision represents perfectly, his interest in the lacunae of language needs to be understood against the analogous backdrop of his sometime conviction that language also can represent anything and everything. Six years later the article "Encyclopédie" will express that belief in its most emphatic form. The model for an encyclopedia that aspires to represent and explain all knowledge is, in a first instance, a dictionary of the French language. For a nation's language is "a rather faithful tableau of all the knowledge of that nation." Diderot elaborates:

> Each science has its name, so does each notion in the science: everything that is known in nature is designated, just as everything invented in the arts, as well as phenomena, techniques [*manoeuvres*] and instruments. There are expressions for things outside ourselves, for those inside ourselves . . . abstract and concrete things, particular and general things, forms and states, things in succession—all have been named.[51]

This is only the beginning of a long list that increases in emphatic tone with each successive addition. (It is one of the most elaborate expressions of "Mangogulian" ideology that Diderot ever produced.) Included in the list of what language has the power to name is "the excess beyond all limits, either in nature or in our imagination" (p. 190), not to mention the possible, the impossible, and the infinite. "Language is a symbol for this multiplicity of heterogeneous things" (p. 190). Each of them has its word. There is, or so it seems at this stage, a perfect adequation between the totality of language and the totality of referents, just as there is between things and visual representations on the retina.[52]

With this in mind, let us return to the blind figures described in the *Lettre sur les aveugles.*

In effect, one could virtually hear blindness in Saunderson's speech, which was full of "expressions heureuses."[53] These Diderot defines as expressions "which are proper to one sense, to touch for example, and which are at the same time metaphoric to another sense such as sight, resulting in a double light for the interlocutor: the true and direct light of the expression, and the reflected light of the metaphor" (p. 41). The blindness of Saunderson produces neither the literal nor the figurative meaning of such language. It produces the doubling, both the separation of the meanings and their coalescence in the trope.

The same point can be made about reports of Diderot's earlier conversations with the blind man of Puiseaux whose ability to define a mirror was worthy of a blind Descartes. What is a mirror? " 'A machine,' he responded, 'which puts things in relief far from themselves provided they are appropriately positioned relative to it. It's like my hand [*comme ma main*] that I do not have to place beside an object in order to feel it' " (p. 20). The definition is subtle but wrong. As Diderot explains, the mirror is a flat surface and in fact has no relief. But since it allows sighted people to perceive their own faces, which otherwise can be perceived only through touch, the blind man concluded logically that it duplicates the same tactile relief at a distance. It is therefore "like my hand," only it can feel—that is, represent—surface relief without touching the object.

Such a definition produces the same tropological "double light" as that of Saunderson's figures of speech. If the blind man could see, he would know that the mirror and the hand operate differently, and would not make the tropological error of coupling them (in a simile). For the sighted interlocutor, the mirror and the hand (sight and touch) are palpably different, but are collapsed by the blind man's very persuasive figure. Blindness-veil, copula, "truchement"— produce this "double light," this expression that is "heureuse" precisely because it bears this demarcation within itself. Blindness is the agent of synesthetic conjunction among the senses, the agent of metaphoric meaning production. It is a lack in the plenum that requires the transport of one sense into another, the generalized likeness of figures such as "like my hand."

And moreover, the metaphors of Saunderson's blindness—and genitive here is double—extend to everyone who uses language. "It is obvious that in such instances Saunderson, with all his intelligence, only half understood what he was saying, since he perceived only half the ideas attached to the terms he used." So far, this is sensualist orthodoxy.

The figurality of Saunderson's expressions resulted from the breach, produced by his blindness, between ideas (based upon sense representations) and their linguistic signifiers. Now Diderot goes a major step further: "But who is not in the same situation from time to time?" (p. 41), he asks. Progressively extending the separation, the metaphor-producing blindness, he finally signals its truly general nature. First, idiots and savants alike sometimes say silly things unintentionally, meaning (by analogy to Saunderson) that they use words without realizing the ideas that they designate. But the problem extends beyond the slips made by individuals to become a problem of language itself.

> I have noticed that the paucity [*disette*] of words also produced the same effect on foreigners to whom the language is not yet familiar: they are forced to say everything with a very small quantity of terms, which constrains them to place some of them very felicitously [again, as with Saunderson, the term is "heureusement"]. But *all language in general* being poor in literal words [*mot propres*] for writers who have a lively imagination, they are in the same situation as foreigners who have a lot of wit; the situations they invent, the delicate nuances they perceive in characters, the naiveté of the depictions [*peinture*] they must execute, separate them at every moment from the ordinary way of speaking and *makes them adopt turns* of phrase that are admirable when they are not precious or obscure. . . . (Pp. 41–42; my emphasis)[54]

The breach between the idea and the word is here the same but reversed. For Saunderson (and for all of us who misspeak ourselves occasionally), there is a surplus of words over "ideas" because he uses visual words without being able to perceive their referents. For the foreigner and the writer, on the contrary, there is a surplus of ideas over words. (These ideas are described in the same visual metaphor of "peintures" and perceived "nuances.") But surplus and lack are both versions of the same thing. They both constitute a breach between idea and language—the same needed "truchement"—that produces metaphors. That *is* metaphor.

Language can name everything, as we saw; dictionaries adumbrate encyclopedias. And yet, like blindness in the sensorial gamut, there is "disette [paucity]" in the linguistic gamut of "mots propres" as well. Concomitant to both those lacks, both a possibility and a necessity, there is representation, there is metaphor. In the general usage we have adopted here, both the senses and words can be said to "represent." Diderot has again focused upon the problem of what represents, or what makes representations in the senses and in words. And in the repletion of senses and words, what makes them representative comes to expression in these pages as lack/surplus in the sensorial and linguistic elements. Diderot's interest, then, has again turned to the "ring effect" that makes the representational process so difficult to distinguish from a metaphoric process, philosophy so much like rhetoric.

We seem to have strayed from the terms given in the initial discussion of Molyneux's question. Let us conclude this chapter with a return to the original question in order to seek assurance that, although the particulars are obviously different, the problem for Diderot remains the same.

"It is easy to conceive that the use of one of the senses can be perfected and accelerated by the observations of another; but it is not at all easy to conceive that between their functions there is an essential dependence" (p. 62). Each sense ultimately is self-sufficient; that is his simple response to Molyneux. And yet, at the same time, each sense is undermined by the difference, the very breach of representationality separating it from the object that it "records." The representation that is inaugurated by sight also inaugurates sight as a project, and makes adequation a goal to be accomplished. After affirming the self-sufficiency of each sense, Diderot explains:

It has to be agreed that we must perceive in objects an infinite number of things that the infant or the blindborn [given sight] do not perceive at all, even though such objects be painted upon the back of their eyes the same as ours; that it is not enough for objects to strike us, that we still must be attentive to their impressions; that as a consequence *we see nothing* the first time we use our eyes . . . that experience alone teaches us to *compare* sensations with what occasions them; that since *sensations have nothing* that resembles objects essentially, experience has to instruct us about analogies that seem to be purely conventional: in a word, it cannot be doubted that touch serves a great deal to give the eye precise knowledge of the conformity between an object and the representation of it that the eye receives. (Pp. 61–62; my emphasis)

The representational process of vision proceeds from this possibility of seeing perfectly and yet seeing "nothing"; that between objects and their resemblance on the retina there is again a kind of "nothing"—a "truchement," an agency, a difference—that guarantees accurate representation of objects upon the retina. But such representation is possible and necessary only because of the difference between thing and image. The metaphors that difference produces may be "heurcuses," as in Saunderson's speech, but they also thoroughly contaminate the literality so persistently sought by the descendents of Locke. Diderot makes it plain. We see objects correctly; yet, because we see only representations that are different from what occasions them—"sensations have nothing that resembles objects essentially"—we must ply the space of that difference, back and forth, in the tropological labor of comparison (which is to say, of simile). We have "to compare sensations with what occasions them."

We see accurately, but since "seeing" is "representing," it undergoes all the effects of representationality we have traced heretofore. In Diderot's writing the fictional moment of seeing for the first time communicates with the fictional advent of the magic ring in *Les Bijoux indiscrets*. It begins a figural quest for what Diderot calls "precise knowledge of the conformity between an object and the representation of it. . . ." In the *Lettre sur les aveugles*, blindness is the metaphor for the representational space that both differentiates object and image and poses the very question of their identity or conformity.

To conclude I return to a point made earlier in this chapter, to the mirroring found between Diderot's description of the mind and his qualifications of the phenomenal world. In view of the intervening analysis, the language cited in that segment finds new, more ample resonances. "Once experimental physics is more advanced, it will be recognized that in nature all the phenomena . . . are only different facets of the same cause [*affection*]. But among the phenomena that we relate [*rapporte*] to one of these causes, how many intermediary phenomena remain to be found in order to establish the connections, fill in the gap and show their identity? That is what cannot be determined."[55] These intermediaries, that gap in the identicalness of phenomena, figure in other terms the "truchement"/absence that in the different context of the *Lettre sur les aveugles* is called blindness. Here, and elsewhere, Diderot gives evidence of his deep roots in the philosophical tradition with which be began, when he implies that the veil of phenomena can be progressively parted or pushed back—even if it can never be lifted. The "intermediary phenomena" that would fill in the gap "remain to be found." That attitude and the orientation toward a certain progress that accompanies it has proved to be one of the most lasting legacies of the Enlightenment.

But the veil is also shown to be indispensable to the very representational process whereby the phenomena are understood to have meaning and connection. Their representational "rapport" with other phenomena is first an effect of the very difference that, so far, has made it impossible to "fill in the gap and show their identity." If phenomena can be represented metaphorically as the same—to "show their *identity*"—it is because they are "*different* facets of the same cause." And it is more to the lesson of that difference that Diderot's text persistently returns us. (See the "Postcript to Chapter Seven," linking the analysis of this chapter to Michael Fried's *Absorption and Theatricality*.)

CHAPTER EIGHT

La Lettre sur les sourds et muets

THE HINGING OF SENSORIAL
and linguistic lacks achieved in the *Lettre sur les aveugles* is
the basis for the *Lettre sur les sourds et muets* as well. Just as
blindness was the principle means for knowing sight in the
former, the deaf-mute will serve as a homologous "truchement" in the latter. Again, language, like vision, is a completely adequate mode of representation. And yet, Diderot
is interested in the deaf-mute, whose silence represents the
cusp of articulation between language and ideas. In this
over-abundant plenitude of the *dire*, he is again interested
in "disette [paucity]."[1] He gives clear evidence of his own
sense that this text, explicitly conceived as a sequel to the
commercially successful *Lettre sur les aveugles*, proceeds
from a concept no less strange than the notion of blindness
that emerged there. "It will no doubt seem odd to you to be
referred to one whom nature has deprived of the faculty of
hearing and speech, in order to obtain from him true notions on the formation of language."[2] Strange though it may
seem, that is precisely what Diderot has done, and it is the
basis for a more-than-apparent continuity between the two
works.

Diderot recounts one incident as an explicit prolongation
of the *Lettre sur les aveugles*. Since his deaf-mute has no
direct access to music, Diderot takes him to see Father Castel's "clavecin occulaire [ocular harpsichord]," which dis-
plays ribbons of color corresponding to each note on the
keyboard. This machine (and the experience of music it affords) is, of course, "pleinement métaphorique" (p. 145) for
the deaf-mute, since it shows him something to which

music can be compared, but not what music in itself *is*. And indeed, the man draws some wrong conclusions about the nature of music as a result of the (probably fictional) experience. For example, the "discourse in colors" (p. 146) led him to assume that, like words, each note of music had a meaning. And although he is wrong, Diderot allows as how he had certainly understood the language of music, its overall system, and what we today would call its semiotic nature. Faced with the sensorial veil of deafness, like the blind man trying to define a mirror in the previous *Lettre*, the deaf-mute "philosophizes." He produces meanings and connections that are made both possible and necessary by his infirmity. Diderot says it as clearly as one could ask:

> Is this not, Sir, a faithful image of our thoughts, of our reasoning, of our systems—in a word—of those concepts that have made the reputation of so many philosophers? Every time they have formed judgments about things which seemed to require an organ *which they lacked*, which has often happened to them, they have shown less wisdom . . . than the deaf-mute in question here.
>
> The blind man who was the subject of the *Lettre* [*sur les aveugles*] . . . showed insight . . . his definition of mirrors was surprising. But I find more depth and truth in what my deaf man figured out about Father Castel's ocular harpsichord. . . . If he did not hit exactly upon what it was, he almost hit upon what it ought to be. (P. 147.)

Thus at the outset, through this explicit association with the *Lettre sur les aveugles*, Diderot has imported into the *Lettre sur les sourds et muets* the whole deconstruction of philosophy's traditional exclusion of metaphor.[3] But more than a simple prolongation of the first *Lettre*, this text radicalizes even more thoroughly the traditional protocols of representation.

The *Lettre sur les sourds et muets* was, however, too erudite and too difficult to enjoy the popular success of its predecessor. Its complexity, which can be daunting, stems in part from its situation within a tangle of contemporary works on the central issue that it ostensibly sets out to treat. Just as the first *Lettre* begins as a reflection on Molyneux's question, so the second Lettre is Diderot's most substantive contribution to contemporary theory about language, with particular reference to the problem of direct order as against the inversion of syntax that had been debated for close to a century.

As formulated in the *Grammaire de Port-Royal*, signification already exists before language—ontologically. Language only expresses meaning, it does not create it.[4] The "grammariens-philosophes," adhering to the Cartesianism of Port-Royal, had long shared the corollary assumption that there unquestionably existed a natural order of thought and that it was accurately represented by the grammatical order of discursive language, which in turn was most accurately represented by French.[5] In a word, God created meaning; meaning is syntactic; thought occurs to us according to this natural order of meaning; and French syntax best approximates this natural order of thought. Other languages, Latin and Greek most notably, confidently could be considered to invert the natural order in which thoughts presented themselves prior to being expressed. After Arnauld and Nicole, Lamy, Du Bos, De Cerceau, l'Abbé d'Olivet, Du Marsais, and Beauzée (and the list could be prolonged considerably)—all persisted in perpetuating the basic assumption that discourse as organized by French grammatical norms accurately represented the natural order of thought itself.[6] In his *Avantages de la langue françoise sur la langue latine* (1669), Le Laboureur intended no parody when he advanced a formula that is often repeated nowadays as one of the most outrageous examples of the century's linguistic parochialism: "Cicero and the Romans thought in French before speaking in Latin."[7]

Condillac in his *Essai sur l'origine des connaissances humaines* (1746) first suggested the contrary theory that signs had in fact preceded thought, thereby opposing Descartes and, hypothetically, improving upon Locke by eliminating the need to posit any innate mental faculty capable of ordering sense data. (Recently, Condillac has been described as remaining faithful to the Cartesianism he was trying to escape.)[8]

It is the Abbé Batteux who, against Du Marsais and in support of Condillac, wanted to take the next step and suggest that French could represent the inverted and Latin the direct, or natural, syntactic order. The second volume of his *Cours des belles lettres* ends with a supplement entitled *Lettres sur la prose française comparée avec la phrase latine*, addressed to the Abbé d'Olivet. The first of these letters declares that thought itself can be inverted relative to "the order in which things are found."[9] Varying subjective interests must be taken into account, for they influence the order in which we are prompted to generate our thoughts. Thought itself can be reversed in the same way that expression can be reversed relative to thought. But this revolutionary position was fundamentally compromised when Batteux maintained that, although the order of our thoughts depends on subjective more than objective determinants, we are all made alike. In effect then, there is after all a natural order of thought, and thus of expression, which Batteux decided was best represented by Latin.[10]

It is within such a network of texts that Diderot's *Lettre sur les sourds et muets*—in the most modern sense of the term "intertextually"—introduces a series of subtle shifts, displacements, and outright contradictions that radicalize the problem and that make this one of his very significant works.[11] Its difficulty also stems from the lack of narrative linearity in the organization of its arguments, a feature that itself becomes a central theme in the later discussion of linear expression as a perversion of simultaneous thought. (In a real sense, the entire *Lettre* could make ideal sense only if it could be read in a single instant. But more on that issue later.)

The *Lettre* is addressed to Batteux. In it, Diderot agrees

with Condillac that temporary subjective interests can determine word order, at least sometimes (as in the examples
of "serpentem fuge" and the "Pro Marcello" [pp. 155 ff.].)
but he also agrees that perceived qualities (color, size, shape,
and so on) are logically prior to any abstract "substances"
they may be thought to qualify. There is then a "natural
order" of discourse comparable to that defined by Condillac,
based on sensualist assumptions regarding the order in
which things are ordinarily perceived. (From this perspective we see that an object is tall, green and stationary before
we deduce that it is an exemplar of "treeness.") Seen in this
light, the French order would seem to be unnatural, an "ordre d'institution," since, for example, the adjective most
often comes after the noun.[12]

Diderot also allows for an "ordre scientifique" or an "ordre didactique," which is an analytical order based on logical
relations according to "the mind's views when language was
wholly formed" (p. 137). From this perspective the substantive is normally prior to the adjective because (since Aristotle, to whom Diderot refers on this point) there logically has
to be a "substance" that supports accidents such as color,
size, and so forth.[13] So, although genetically speaking adjectives precede nouns, logically speaking nouns should precede adjectives. (Of course, such "logic" is the product of
language already formed according different principles altogether.[14] But Diderot is tracking other game and moves
on without stopping at this problem.)

There is yet a third factor that is thrown into the discussion. From a quite different perspective, empirically, French
does not invert, in the sense that French order is almost
always the same. In practice Latin and Greek do invert because one can say with equal correctness (as in Condillac's
example), "Alexander vicit Darium," or "Darium vicit
Alexander," since the subject and the direct object are
clearly marked by case endings. French is devoid of such case
markers and thus relies primarily upon a standardized order
to distinguish subject and predicate. This is, of course, a

merely empirical aspect of the question, unrelated to the ontological question underlying the preceding arguments.

Thus the very proliferation of differing meanings of the terms "order" and "inversion"—sometimes with an empirical and historical, sometimes with an ontological reference —already goes far toward robbing the problem of the stable coordinates that could promise a simple a priori solution. Without warning, Diderot can and does leap from one of these definitions of the issue to another (e.g., pp. 139, 153). It is difficult to believe that he was in control of the logic of his argument at all points. He can, in the same paragraph, say: "I would not want to suggest generally and without distinction that the Latins do not invert, and we do invert"; and, "In French we say things as the mind is forced to consider them in whatever language one writes" (p. 164).

In part the confusion results from the complexity of the problem. As Diderot himself insists, "I exhort you, sir, to weigh these things if you want really to know [*sentir*] how complicated is the question of inversions" (p. 162). At the same time, he confesses that (an implicit comparison to Socrates) he is "more occupied with creating clouds than dissipating them, with suspending judgments than making them" (p. 162). I think that the difficulties also result from Diderot's propensity for dialogical writing. That is to say, virtually every sentence of this text is inscribed within an implicit dialogue with competing formulations by other writers. The frame of reference and the direction of the argument shifts as the implicit intertext changes. The dialogical tendency that is often a great strength in Diderot's writing is here a challenge to understanding.

Rather than retracing the meandering course of the argument (which has been carried out amply by Hobson, elegantly by Genette, and with admirable thoroughness and clarity in the scholarly apparatus that Jacques Chouillet has provided in the *D.P.V.* edition of the text), my intention is to focus again on the representational space that makes so many shifting dichotomies possible. For it is my contention that it is this "truchement" which is the elusive object of the *Lettre* and which can best account for its organization and aims. But where does one look to find it? By now one is not too surprised if it seems a good idea to begin with Diderot's assertions concerning the mind's ideal unity, generally acknowledged by the most forceful part of the *Lettre* and most specific to Diderot.

> The state of the mind [*âme*] in an indivisible instant was represented by a multitude of terms which linguistic precision required, and which distributed a total impression into parts: and because these terms were pronounced in succession, and were comprehended only as they were pronounced, one was led to believe that the state [*affections*] of the mind which they represented existed in the same succession; but this is in no way true. The state of our mind is one thing; quite another thing is the account we give of it either to ourselves, or to others: the total, instantaneous sensation of that state is one thing; another thing is the successive and detailed attention that we are forced to pay in order to analyze it, to manifest it and make ourselves understood. Our soul is a moving picture, a model according to which we are constantly painting [un tableau mouvant d'après lequel nous peignons sans cesse]: we employ a great deal of time rendering it faithfully; but it exists in entirety and all at once: the mind does not proceed by measured steps as does expression. (P. 161)

In the previous *Lettre sur les aveugles*, the rift between discourse and thought was expressed in terms of a superabundance of perception over the paucity of language, and/or the paucity of perceptions underlying the language of a blind man. Now here, there is no less of a generalized breach, but it is presented as that between the simultaneous unity of complex thought and the protracted linearity of discourse, between temporal axes one could think of as horizontal and vertical. Complex ideas and states of mind exist in a synchronic instant. They are all of a piece, like a single picture. Language comes along to paint a picture of that unitary picture—to represent this ideal image. But since language is syntactic, it is always too late, always a deferral of ideal expression, its mental object having moved on even before language can lay it out in syntax.

Thus ordinary language is again a figurative modification of the idea, metaleptic because periphrastic: using too many words to express a state of mind as if it were present although it is in fact past, left behind by the mental "tableau mouvant" that it labors to catch up with and to represent. "The creation of languages required breaking up [of thought into its components]; but seeing an object, judging it beautiful, feeling an agreeable sensation, desiring possession is a single instant of the mental state. . . . Ah! Sir, how our understanding is modified by signs; and what a cold copy is even the most lively discourse on mental events" (p. 162).

In this first instance, then, ordinary language trails after the moving tableau of the soul that it is commissioned to represent. But as in all its other guises, the differential space around which this text is organized disallows any ontological priority of *représenté* over *représentant*, of mental state over linguistic expression.

> Sensation does not have in the mind [*âme*] this successive development characteristic of discourse; and if it could command twenty mouths, with each mouth saying its piece, all the preceding ideas would be expressed at the same time. . . . But *in the absence* of [*au défaut de*] several mouths, here is what was done: several ideas were attached to a single expression. If these energetic expressions were more frequent, instead of language having constantly to trail after the mind, the number of ideas expressed all at once could be such that, with language now the faster, the mind would be forced to chase after it. (P. 158)

Moreover, this reversal of thought and language is not just hypothetical. (Real instances of such a reversal were also discussed in the *Lettres sur les aveugles*.) Latin and Greek are full of such expressions to which several ideas have been attached. Instead of "What a nice fruit! I'm hungry. I'd gladly eat it," the Roman in Diderot's example said it all with the simple word, in a single instant: "Esurio" (p. 150).

Diderot concludes with what is tantamount to a final dismissal of the whole question of inversion versus natural order. If one really understood the significance of complex words such as "esurio," infrequent in French but abundant in other languages, "what would then become of inversion, which supposes decomposition of the mind's simultaneous movements and multitude of expressions?" (p. 158). What indeed? The entire argument depended upon the priority of thought (as signified) over language (as signifier). But if, as Diderot claims, that priority could be reversed and language can and does precede thought, the very grounds for the debate dissolve. There is a thought of language and a language of thought.

The clear consequence for the whole question of inversions of discourse relative to thought, or of thought relative to "the order in which things are found" (Batteux), is a dissolution of the problem. Thought itself has no essential order, and so any sequential concatenation of its elements— in other words, all sequential discourse—is a misrepresentation of non-sequential mental states. ("A consequence of the preceding is that there is not and perhaps even there cannot be inversion in the mind . . . " [p. 163].) And secondly, because the entire issue of direct and inverted order is a problem of proper representation of thought by language in traditional, mimetic terms, the issue is again dissolved because neither language nor thought is always the prior model for the miming of the other. One can imagine a language whose words (like "esurio") contain so many representational elements that its use would precede thought. Thought would thus re-present the ideas contained in just-spoken words. This is then yet another sort of reversibility, quite different from that of syntax relative to thought. For if there is a reversibility of *représenté* and *représentant*, the entire mimetic system within which the debate had been situated is denied its natural authority.

The *Lettre sur les sourds et muets* has thus far concentrated upon the failure of language to represent adequately the mind's state, upon the "défaut" of twenty mouths, upon the inevitable metaphoricity of signs that alter rather than reproduce understanding, and upon the reversibility in the priority of language and thought. To use the essay on "Expression" as a point of comparison, we have reached a stage parallel to the stage at which the artist has first used paint or marble to fashion the divine image. But the magic has yet to occur that conjoins representation and model to make them both effectively divine. The mind's ideal unity has been posited and anticipated as a model. But it has undergone change and vicissitude in verbal expression, such that verbal expression has up to now been marked by disjunction and failure to coincide. The comfortable (if fruitless) debate over direct or reverse syntactic order has been left light years behind.[15]

Appropriately, therefore, here ceases all mention of syntactic inversions. Here ceases all reference to experiments involving deaf-mutes—real or conventional—to discover which order occurs spontaneously or naturally once one accedes to language for the first time. Critics have seen this juncture as an unexpected discontinuity in the text, not prepared by what precedes it.[16] I disagree. Diderot has dissolved the problem of inversions, which is an argument of ontological priority. The argument now focuses on the "sortir du temple" (to continue the parallel with "Expression"), on the moment when grounding in traditional mimetic protocols dissolves, and when ideality is effectively expressed/created. Not at all a break in the text's trajectory, it is this last third of the *Lettre* for which, almost like an entelechy, the foregoing has been longing.

At the threshold between the last section and the foregoing, there is a one-sentence summary of the basic argument up to now: "It is necessary to distinguish thought from expression in all discourse in general . . . " (p. 169). It appears odd, however, to present as a prescription what earlier was presented as an inevitability. Yet the rest of the sentence makes it clear that the basic disjunction of thought and language has been argued, and is recalled here, as a necessary prelude to this moment of ideal fulfillment that becomes all the more pointed for being unexpected and even unnatural.

Here is the whole passage:

> It is necessary to distinguish thought from expression in all discourse in general: if thought is rendered with clarity, purity and precision, that is enough for familiar conversation: join to these qualities word choice, along with measure and harmony of the rounded sentence, and you have the style appropriate for the lectern; but you will still be far from poetry. . . . In poetry, there passes into the discourse of the poet a spirit which moves and vivifies all the syllables. What is this spirit? I've sometimes felt its presence; but all I know of it is that it alone causes things to be *said and represented* all at once; that at the same time that the understanding grasps them, the soul is moved by them, the imagination sees them, the ear hears them and that discourse is no longer a mere concatenation of energetic terms which expose thought with force and nobility, but more still a tissue of hieroglyphs heaped one upon the other which paint it. In this sense I could say that all poetry is emblematic. (P. 169)[17]

The insurmountable breach between unitary thought and concatenated discourse—which Diderot begins the paragraph by reiterating prescriptively—seems now to be necessary *in order* to be transgressed, and thus experienced in the epiphany of an ideal *dire/représenter*. The disjunction, the difference, has become agency, "truchement."

In the "hieroglyphic" discourse of poetry, words signify according to the usual rules of syntax and semantics that betray the unity of thought; but they also signify in a fashion that, although dependent on ordinary language, supplements the deferred with an immediate signification. Here is one of Diderot's examples from Voltaire's *Henriade*: "Et des fleuves français les eaux ensanglantées / Ne portaient que des morts aux mers épouvantées" (p. 169).[18] In his analysis of the verb "portaient," for example, Diderot maintains that the first syllable gives one to "see the waters swollen with cadavers, and the course of the rivers as if suspended by this dike"; and in the second syllable, one can "see" the dike bursting, allowing the jam of corpses to spill forth and flow to the sea (p. 169). He is not claiming that the verb "portaient" signifies such a grisly event all by itself. Obviously, the semantic context provided by the rest of the line—protracted and distorted though it may necessarily be—is essential. This becomes explicit in his next example. "The seas' dread [*effroi*] is indicated to any reader in 'épouvantées'; but the emphatic pronunciation of the third syllable reveals to me their vast expanse" (p. 169). The "revelation" and "perception" of the signified—with obvious privilege accorded as usual to visual perception—remains within the order of the unified and simultaneous intellect. The single syllable "por-" gives us to see in a single instant a complex of ideas that requires several sentences to elaborate in normal prose. But like all the other modes of ideality we have seen—like the sacred in the profane, the profane in the sacred—the hieroglyphic element by itself is not intrinsically ideal. It is ideal only in its differential relation with the prosaic and periphrastic context that is its other, but with which it is thoroughly coupled and embedded.

A recent critic has attempted to derive an entire stylistics from various modes of referentiality through which Diderot supposedly insists upon the thing, the "object sensible" to the exclusion of abstractions and tropes.[19] The present theory of poetic hieroglyphs itself is perhaps the most powerful antidote to Mangogul-critic.

Both the entire syntactic unit and the hieroglyphic overlay "refer" less to real things than to each other. Their artic-

ulation hinges upon the difference that they represent between literal simultaneity and periphrastic prolongation. It
is their difference that produces the ideality of poetic representation, and not their traditional referential function.[20]
(To what, after all, do elements such as "por-," "taient," or
"-vant-" refer?) The prosaic opens to signification through
elements that have no intrinsic signification; but those elements also open to the prosaic signification that is not only
unpoetic but a basic perversion of the ideal, unitary mind.
The ideality of poetic expression flows from the interface of
the two in the moment of their wholly tropological, differential representation of each other. Diderot's theory could
not be further from a unidirectional translation, or positive
reconstitution in the mind of things previously perceived by
the senses.

Diderot insists that poetic hieroglyphs cannot be translated into another language (p. 171), which is another indication that they do not refer, simply, to an external world of
things. They can only be repeated in other artistic media,
and he even provides an example of the "same" hieroglyph
in Virgil and Lucretius, in an engraving by Frans Van Mie-
ris, and in a musical phrase by an unidentified composer
(pp. 183 ff.).

What emerges then is a Diderotian poetics that is appli-
cable to all the arts, and that is explicitly opposed to the
naiveté of Batteux's notions of mimesis (p. 182). Each art
that "imitates nature in a single object" (p. 182) is not imitating "nature" as a given and self-evident phenomenon to
the mimed in classical terms. The object of imitation is
again, in terms of the article "Beau" (written in the same
year), the differential "rapports" that make beauty more
than the "things" in which those "rapports" are marked.

The choice of the term "hieroglyph" to designate the
ideal representation of a "rapport" as against a mimetic
copy of an object is surely significant in this regard.[21] It has
rarely been mentioned, however, that despite the attempts
of Warburton (*The Divine Légation of Moses Demon-*

strated [1737–41]) and others, nobody in the eighteenth century could in fact read hieroglyphics. Before Champollion realized that it was in part a phonetic writing, it had seemed obvious that it must be ideogrammatic, based on mimetic representations of objects and actions.[22] It seems safe to assume that Diderot's use of the term stems in part from such a view, that hieroglyphics mediated both the abstract idea and the immediate image of the "thing itself" at the same time, each representing the other as well as the referent. And yet, in conjuring up the metaphor of "hieroglyphics" in poetic representation, Diderot is invoking a representation whose link to its referent was in fact, for his time, blocked. The hieroglyph's illegibility is then an emblem of the rift, the differential space that makes ideality and that we have been tracing all along.[23] And because the illegibility of the hieroglyph represents that breach, it is but another avatar of blindness, deafness, and muteness. The hieroglyph comes in its appropriate time and place as the concluding development of the *Lettre sur les sourds et muets*. At this point, I rejoin Marion Hobson's suggestion that the concept of imitation itself is "frittered away" by the multiple crosscurrents of Diderot's text.[24] But I am also inclined to accept a hypothesis that she tends to discard, that the hieroglyph is a "bastard representation of representation" (p. 321). However, what is represented, just as in the case of the "ideal model," is representation-as-difference, the double presence/absence that comes with the word "re-presentation."

And what of the deaf-mute, who is indeed the subject of this treatise? He has disappeared from the scene, but the issue articulated on the basis of his infirmity, like blindness in the previous *Lettre*, like the philosopher's vicissitude in *De la poésie dramatique*, never leaves center stage.[25] The deaf-mute disappears from the treatise only to return, in the very lack of signs capable of truly representing our real mental state, and in all analogical, metaphorical supplements that such lack produces throughout the text.[26] He disappears and returns in the *Lettre* much in the same way that, in Jacques Chouillet's astute observation, the theory and the very term "hieroglyph" disappears from Diderot's writings after the *Lettre* only to reemerge as the "ideal model" after 1758.[27] And if we were to seek out other avatars by surveying even broader terrain governed by this extraordinarily fertile copula—in a proleptic glance forward toward work remaining to be done—Roger Lewinter could point the way with his discussion of the term "molécule" in Diderot's scientific writing. I conclude then with this coincidence of critical insights, and with the amplitude of resonances that it leaves humming in the ear:

> The concept of "molecule" is itself double: [first] the "original" molecule is the suprasensitive which precedes all sensate matter: [and second, it is] the "living" molecule. If the original molecule was not unitary—unaltered by the alterations it undergoes—there would be several different kinds of basic matter in the universe, which would then become heterogeneous. At the same time however, if the living molecule were not always other—changed by life in a process of "différance"—the universe would be nothing more than an amorphous mass. It is this which defines all reality as "representation" (deformed presence) of the "ideal model" (a primary absence), the non-existence from which results all existence.[28]

The blind man and the deaf-mute of 1749 and 1751 have, it would seem, an extensive career ahead of them.

CHAPTER NINE

"Chasing after Advances"

Je suis un hors d'oeuvre.
—Diderot, Letter to Sophie Volland

THE *ENCYCLOPEDIA* OF DIDE-rot and d'Alembert is a vast pedagogical project whose aim is to represent everything. To do so it lays out the state of contemporary knowledge globally and systematically. "The goal of an encyclopedia is to assemble the knowledge scattered far and wide on the surface of the earth, to expose its general system to our fellow men with whom we live and to transmit it to those who will follow us, so that . . . our sons, by becoming more educated, might become at the same time more virtuous and happy. . . . "[1] A traditional commentary on this passage reads: "Here in a few lines is the whole program of what was to be called the 'Age of Enlightenment.' Here is the philosopher's confidence in the beneficent effect of expanding knowledge. Here is a hopeful belief in progress through education."[2] This would certainly seem to be an accurate appraisal.

As we saw before, Michel Foucault has suggested some of the most basic reasons why a philosopher such as Diderot would have been able to feel "confidence" that an encyclopedic representation would fulfill such goals in the Classical age: "The continuum of representation and being, an ontology defined negatively as an absence of nothingness, a general representability of being, and being manifested by the presence of representation—all this is a part of the overall configuration of the Classical episteme."[3] As we saw in chapter 1, the *Encyclopedia* occupies the privileged space opened by language, and through that space, language has a "relation to the universal" (p. 86) and to being. If one accepts Foucault's analysis, language itself promises success to a work attempting to represent the totality of the known.[4]

Coming from a consideration of the *Lettre sur les sourds et muets* as we are, this optimistic and positive thinking about the possibility of passing seamlessly from knowledge to linguistic expression may well astonish. And yet it is indeed true that Diderot shared the philosophical confidence of his age in many respects. As he himself claims, "the *Encyclopedia* could only be the endeavor of a philosophical century" (p. 232).

If that is so, the place to look for an elaboration of the link between optimistic philosophy and this particular work would be at its meta-encyclopedic heart, that is, in its self-definitional article in volume 5 that is itself entitled "Encyclopedia" (1755). And yet, in this peculiar text, rather than luxuriating in the positivity one associates with such a confident epistemology, we find Diderot nail-biting over the difficult conditions of its possibility. The least we can say about this latter problem is that logically it ought to be anterior to any philosophical confidence. Confidence would presume the problem resolved. But it is not the case here: Diderot is both "confident" and at the same time clearly imbued with a sense of the intrinsic impossibility of a true encyclopedia, and of all the hopes for which it is the vehicle.

The very existence of the article bears witness to this point. Even if we accepted the epistemological protocols described by Foucault, we would still have to wonder to what necessity Diderot was responding when he wrote "Encyclopedia." If the *Encyclopedia* could represent all knowledge and expose its system through the medium of the word, to what imperative was he responding when he added a meta-discursive article whose purpose was to represent the system of the system at another remove—to represent the representation? "Encyclopedia" didactically elaborates the pedagogy of the entire work. It self-consciously teaches how the great Book teaches. On the one hand, it is in the alphabet—in volume 5, under E, between the entries "Encroué" and "Endécagone"—and like all other terms it can derive its full meaning only by being in its place within that system. But it is also necessarily different from the system, objectifying and defining it as if from the outside.[5] (In this sense it is fully as preliminary as either the "Prospectus" or d'Alembert's "Discours préliminaire.") It is a liminal demarcation of inside and outside, of *représenté* and *représentant,* of spectator and spectacle embedded deeply within the encyclopedic body. And it is in this threshold article that the borderline of despair and optimism is most clearly to be traced. By reading it we can get some sense of how those attitudes are related, and of how they emerge from the differential space that has produced Diderot's other lasting works.

"Encyclopédie" brings with it a vocabulary and a range of concerns that by now are familiar. In describing a work that aims to expose the system of knowledge for all time, it necessarily comes upon the basic epistemological issue of how to know that we know. Diderot formulates the problem explicitly. "In everything there is an unvarying and common measure, *failing* which we know nothing [*on ne connaît rien*], we can appraise nothing, nor can we define anything . . . " (p. 206; my emphasis). In fact, "measure," and its synonym "model" are two of the text's master terms. They are avatars of the ideal model and the poetic hieroglyph. They are the focus of a central desideratum

> *If* we could define [words] according to unchanging nature, and not according to human conventions and prejudices which change continually, such definitions would become seeds for discoveries. Let us observe here again the *continual need* we have of an unvarying and constant model to which our definitions and

descriptions might refer, such as the nature of man, of animals or of other beings always extant. All the rest is nothing. . . . (P. 257; my emphasis)[6]

Diderot raises this issue of a stable measure relative to all levels of encyclopedic strategy and always in the same way. The first section of the article, for example, deals at length with the question of how to assure the legibility of the work for future generations. Our descendants will be unable to read it at all if the references, the literal meanings of metaphors, the linguistic codes necessary for its understanding are no longer known. Without an assured reference point, the *Encyclopedia* will be quickly superannuated. What is required therefore—but once again, not necessarily granted—is "a permanent model" (p. 193), or a "poetics of the genre according to real and thoughtful understanding of the human heart, of the nature of things and of right reason, which are the same in all times" (p. 185).[7]

In terms of vocabulary, where measure equals "definition," the encyclopedist must take care to define all root words in Latin or Greek, dead and thus unchanging models. In another instance the use of synonyms, beyond a certain measure that remains to be determined, is deleterious to clarity of meaning. Here the measure must again be determined by the needs of posterity: "Above all, it is posterity that must be kept in mind. There is yet another measure. It is useless to add shades of meaning to words that are not likely to be misunderstood once the language is dead" (p. 208). Or in yet another instance, the encyclopedist needs a stable measure in order to determine the proper length of articles relative to the exact importance or place that their subject matter occupies in the scheme of things. Some articles are too long, some too short, in the current work, "but *failing a common and constant measure*, there is no compromise; everything that a science comprehends must at first be included . . . " (P. 214; my emphasis).

Diderot often reiterates that this is at best a "first attempt" (p. 214), necessarily flawed: "If our descendants work on the *Encyclopedia* without interruption, they will be able to bring the organization of its material to some degree of perfection" (p. 214). He anticipates "a great number of editions perfected successively" (p. 215). In yet another formulation, he writes, "I am forced to confess that hardly two thirds of an *Encyclopedia* such as ours would be included in a true encyclopedia" (p. 236).

The basic difficulty is clear then: in order for the *Encyclopedia* to fulfill its pedagogical mission for future generations, a stable epistemological measure must be found, but the present generation of encyclopedists does not yet possess the means to derive such a model.[8] Because it is indeed "failing," it remains a desideratum and a projection. For not existing, however, its effects are nonetheless real. But that remains to be seen.

In *The Philosophy of the Enlightenment*,[9] Lucien Goldmann characterizes the problem as typical of the situation faced by the essayist—which is his view of Diderot the encyclopedist.

> What matters to the essayist is not the actual process of examining the theoretical basis of particular truths or values. Instead he is concerned with showing that such an examination is both possible and necessary, and, at the same time, that it is both important and impossible to give answers. He is looking for theoretical answers to a series of questions fundamental to human existence which can have no prospect of ever being answered from his point of view. (Pp. 45–46)

In Goldmann's view the essay is a philosophical form insofar as it raises basic issues that are conceptual and abstract, and therefore aiming at general truths. It is a literary form to the degree that, in the first place, it has no means to answer such abstract and conceptual questions: and in the second place, it raises them relative to concrete and particular occasions or events. (One thinks of Montaigne reflecting on a text read or an important experience.) "The true essay thus necessarily inhabits two worlds, and is necessarily ironic: it seems to be talking about particular people and situations, but these are mere 'occasions' for the essayist to raise crucial abstract questions." The *Encyclopedia* is related to the essay form, but is different precisely in that the genre pretends fully to answer the questions it raises. The irony is similar however, because "the encyclopedists realized that this knowledge constituted only a small part of what generations to come would add to the amount hitherto amassed. The progress of knowledge knows no limits" (p. 45).

The ironic point of view is, as always, powerful and persuasive—if for no other reason than that no one wants to miss an irony. It goes far in defining certain givens of the article "Encyclopedia": Diderot writes an "essay," raising basic and abstract epistemological issues that he and his collaborators cannot resolve, but that must be resolved for the *Encyclopedia* to fulfill the mission it has assigned itself. Yet the figure of irony that Goldmann privileges through his reading of Diderot's importance to the Enlightenment, though in keeping with the German idealism from which Goldmann inherited, does not account for the major operation in "Encyclopedia," which is, as we shall see, governed by a different figure.

The fundamental epistemological principle that consistently emerges in "Encyclopedia"—the "unvarying and common measure, failing which we know nothing"—is indistinguishable from anticipation of its future availability, or reference back to its past availability in old models such as Greek or Latin. Both operations define such a principle as a prolepsis.[10] Encyclopedic knowledge, therefore, because it is not-still or not-yet available, is itself less ironic than it is proleptic. The answer to the fundamental question of a constant epistemological model is not impossible, as Goldmann suggests. Rather it is in referral or deferral, radically forwarded or sent back—all of which is signified in the term "renvoyé."

The complex and laborious set of strategies for deferral must be linked to the work's pedagogical aspirations. But how? The willing learner who is beguiled by the ringing call for a constant point of epistemological reference is repeatedly disappointed to discover upon closer examination that all specific reference points are only virtual. (Diderot even equivocates about the infallibility of Greek—which sometimes must be supplemented by Latin, which is sometimes from unreliable manuscripts, and so forth.) What kind of instruction is this? What real and empirical knowledge is in fact being represented in "Encyclopedia"?

Even though we may be comfortably ensconced in our skeptical modernity, it is not so easy simply to dismiss the problem of an unchanging epistemological measure by pointing out that it is absent or necessarily ironic. What is more, such measures are not totally in default within the *Encyclopedia*. Or rather, it is their "défaut"—indistinguishable from their "renvoi"—that in a real sense *is* the *Encyclopedia*, its "instruction" and its ideal.

Already at its inception, the article "Encyclopedia" is in part conceived as a prosthetic operation, required because of a "défaut" in the *Encyclopedia* that is significant enough to undermine the great hopes of the entire project.

> Familiarity [*connaissance*] with the language is the basis of all these great hopes. They will not be secure unless language is stabilized and transmitted in all its perfection [read: ideality] to posterity, which means that, properly speaking, language was the most important of those objects that encyclopedists should have treated in depth. We realized it too late and from that oversight, *imperfection has sprung up* throughout the work. The treatment of language has remained *insufficient* [*faible*] . . . and for that reason it ought to be the principle subject in an article in which one is examining one's work impartially, seeking ways of correcting its defects [*défauts*]. I am there-

fore going to treat the question of language, specially
and as I should. (P. 188; my emphasis)

Here we are on fully familiar terrain. There is faith in the
representational adequacy of language (as Foucault suggests), but just as in the two *Lettres* there is also "disette"
and "défaut." Here at the meta-discursive heart of the *Encyclopedia* is a quick remedial fix of the essential language
element in which for the Classical "episteme," being and
representation are conjoined. Prosthesis is thus an integral
part of what is being represented as an encyclopedia. Recognizing a lack and proffering a supplement is therefore,
literally, a part of the *Encyclopedia*'s definition of itself.
That is what the *Encyclopedia* "is."

What is more, the remedial theory of language that
ensues is only a complex of speculations about the future
and about how diachronic language will have to be rendered
stable some day through linkage to unchanging referential
constants such as nature, the structure of the bocal cavity,
dead languages, euphonics, and ultimately to "general and
rational grammar" (p. 206). Diderot seems to confirm the
reader's response to this linguistic dog chasing its cratylistic
tail when he writes: "One can see just how long, difficult and
thorny this labor really is" (p. 205). He is implicitly granting a presumed objection by the reader—another form of
prolepsis frequent in the article—that the stable linguistic
model actually exists in no other guise than anticipation of
the final, perfect model. In this instance the radically prospective nature of the model can be detected in the very
proliferation of different models, each more unlikely than
the other.

Just as the *Encyclopedia* is a permanent anticipation of its
epistemological model, the text is itself an anticipation of
the object—knowledge—that it is supposed to represent.
Diderot explains that only a group can write a successful
Encyclopedia because only a group could accomplish the
task in a reasonably brief period of time. The currency of any

knowledge quickly fades. An encyclopedia must fix the totality of knowledge in one moment, like an image of the national mind that will itself become a stable measure by which future progress can be gauged. Quick completion guarantees the integrity of such a moment, the presence to itself of a mind/measure frozen in time. Yet Diderot himself then proceeds to shatter the very presence and integrity he sought to assure the encyclopedic moment.

> In any work intended for the general instruction of mankind, it is therefore necessary to start by conceiving one's object in the widest possible context, by becoming familiar with the mind of one's nation, by knowing in advance the direction it is going to take, by overtaking it quickly so that instead of leaving your work behind, your work might be in advance of the national mind, which will then come upon it ahead of itself. (p. 186)

As in the *Lettre sur les sourds et muets*, représenté and représentant are in fact reversible; the *Encyclopedia* (like a language full of "mots-discours") can come before the knowledge that it represents. The national mind, then, would chase after, would re-present the *Encyclopedia*.

The figure of prolepsis, then, emerges in such disparate moments of the text as to suggest that its effects are general in "Encyclopédie." The system of "renvois" (references) from article to article is the most ample of these effects. Understanding of a term in its present context is presupposed while, at the same time, being recognized as future by virtue of the fact that the term "wants" some further elaboration. The system can produce complex relations. In the article "Encyclopedia," for example—an article that is setting out *to define* its object as would any other article—there is a "renvoi" to the article entitled "Definition." (Here Foucault looms large for the modern reader.) "A good wordbook will never be created without the cooperation of a large number of talents, because definitions of names are

not different than definitions of things (See the art. Definition) . . . " (p. 177). It is supposed that the reader knows
what a "definition" is. Yet at the same time, the "renvoi"
makes it obvious that the term is not yet fully understood,
that it will be understood only after a future reading of the
article "Definition." Once again the supposedly transparent
linguistic medium of representation brings with it this proleptic relation of "défaut/renvoi."

In Diderot's estimation the "renvois" are the "most important part of the encyclopedic order" (p. 221). Knowledge
exists as a whole. All its parts are of a piece, existing simultaneously in one arborescent system (p. 227). The problem
of representing such a monolithic whole in discrete articles
arranged alphabetically was similar to the problem analyzed
in the *Lettre sur les sourds et muets*: how can a simultaneous
but complex perception or action be expressed in discourse
that is necessarily protracted, incremental, and syntactic?
With the system of "renvois," however, something like a
hieroglyphic effect is achieved. Both the partial and local
integrity of each article of the syntagmatic chain is assured,
and the simultaneous integrity of Knowledge as a whole is
signified in the same process. An organic, integral system is
superimposed upon an arbitrary, alphabetical system.[11] A
familiar rhetorical logic transpires, however, in Diderot's
language. Temporal becomes spatial prolepsis:

> All the sciences encroach on each other: they are con-
> tinuous limbs branching from the same trunk. When
> someone writes a work, he does not enter his subject
> abruptly, close himself off rigorously within it, leave it
> brusquely: he is *compelled to anticipate* upon terrain
> neighboring on one side, his conclusions often lead
> him into another contiguous area on the opposite
> side, and through how many other *necessary excur-
> sions* within the body of a work. There is no end
> [*Quelle est la fin*] to the forewords, the introductions,
> the prefaces, the exordia, the episodes and conclu-
> sions. If everything that is off the subject [*hors du
> sujet*] being treated were rigorously culled out, virtu-

ally any work would shrink to a fourth of its original volume. What is accomplished by encyclopedia-style concatenation, that rigorous circumscription? It demarcates the limits of a subject so strictly, that only what is essential remains within an article. (P. 227; my emphasis)

The deprecation of "forewords, introductions and prefaces" is a topos, often occurring in a preface (in the preface of Hegel's *Logik*, for example), that betrays an undecidable relation between what is "essential"—book, inside, work—and what is "hors du sujet"—preface, exteriority, writing.[12] Sooner or later, however, because of the system of "renvois" every element of this Book at some point should be enclosed in quotation marks, the way *Encyclopedia* is here called "Encyclopedia"—exterior and anticipatory, not yet the thing itself. "Preface" and its synonyms (for example, "discours préliminaire") are only different names for the same prolepsis.

But is the *Encyclopedia* not an exception? Precisely, the concatenation of terms quaranteed by the system of "renvois" is supposed to eliminate such superfluity. Yet it is Diderot himself who, a few pages later, will write the lines quoted above: "I am forced to confess that hardly two-thirds of an *encyclopedia* such as ours would be included in a true *encyclopedia*" (p. 236). The present version is, again, only an introductory offer, a foretaste of the real thing, which exists but which exists elsewhere, on the next page, in the next volume, in another article, in the next century. If there is in this text (returning to our standard commentary) a "whole program of what was to be called the 'Age of Enlightenment' . . . a hopeful belief in progress through education," that program and that belief are not to be located in any empirical time. The "essentiality" of the *Encyclopedia*—its status as concept, interiority, Book—is indistinguishable from the effect of its proleptic reference to the text to come. The text was what is was (and is what it is) through what it was to be; but the *u-topos* of the book to be was (in) the book that it was, not in the real future.[13] Diderot recognizes more than he misprizes that, when someone writes, "he is compelled to anticipate." And, as more often than we usually acknowledge, his text contemplates its own effects in the duplicity of the phrase "Quelle est la *fin* des avant-propos?" Indeed, what "purpose" and what "duration" can we ascribe to the task of anticipating on the definitive representation or the ideal model to come?

For to what does a "renvoi" refer but to another "renvoi," to the very deferral in function of which the "encyclopedic concatenation" seems to have been imagined? Diderot is categorical on this point: "The *renvois* in an article are like those toothing stones ["pierres d'attentes," literally: "stones in waiting"] that can be seen at the ends of a long wall . . . and whose crenellation anticipates similar crenellation and similar toothing stones waiting elsewhere" (p. 230).

Moreover, what limits a "renvoi" to a single reference or destination, to the confines of a single volume or series of volumes? Like the earlier form of "renvoi" with which Diderot defined the beautiful (in the article "Beau"), once there is presumption and anticipation of *rapport*, things can be represented by an ever-expanding field of other things— ad infinitum. So what assures a reader of Diderot's "Encyclopedia," for example, that he or she will not wind up off the track or on one of those "many other necessary excursions?" To be "renvoyé," after all, also means to be shown the door, to be kicked out, perhaps into what Diderot calls the "dehors du sujet." Perhaps even into Jacques Derrida's essay under the parallel designation of "Hors livre," which deals precisely with the status of what Diderot above called "Forewords, introductions, prefaces, exordia, episodes and conclusions."

Implicitly, then, this is what we find in "Encyclopedia": See "Hors Livre." Diderot refers us to Derrida, anticipates Derrida. We certainly can follow this "renvoi" to Derrida's essay and find passages such as this one, which is itself centered around a verb in the "futur antérieur": "And if we wanted . . . to know this system in the form of this-equals-that, we lose just about everything in the waiting: neither pre-face or pre-dicate. Toothing stone [*pierre d'attente*], corner stone, stumbling block—beginning at the threshold of dissemination, but also earlier—will all have provided the deadfall hindering examination by the petrified reader. So many stones!" And we find ourselves, perhaps unwittingly, involved in what Derrida goes on to call a "reconstruction of the textual field beginning with intertextual manoeuvres, or with the endless *renvoi* from traces to traces. . . . "[14]

But, you may be asking (proleptically, that is), whether there is not at the heart of this lapidary system, lurking, a hidden touchstone, a truly common measure that is more than an anachronistic anticipation, a premature birth? After all, Diderot does write, "I have wanted even the most unimportant objects [in the *Encyclopedia*] secretly to refer to man . . . "(p. 255). Diderot the humanist? Enlightenment theology? Perhaps. This text has been put to such uses, as we saw earlier. (Humanism and theology meld, in the traditional view, as the human center of the work figures, in displaced form, the divine center of the universe.)[15] If indeed man is that point of reference to which the most indifferent objects "refer"—"sont rapportés"—we are still left once again to examine the nature and the function of that "rapport."

Diderot seems to conceive of it visually, spatially, as a relation between man and a kind of mirror.[16] (But as we shall see, it both includes and surpasses the role of the mirror that Richard Rorty placed at the center of modern epistemology.)[17] Referring to man Diderot asks: "Is there in infinite nature some point from which we might extend, to greater advantage, the immense lines that we propose to send out to all other points? What intense and pleasant reactions will ensue, between nature and man, from man to nature?" (p. 212). The Encyclopedia must be made to correspond to the organization of the human intellect, to the flawed features of the human mind rather than to "the absolute perfection of a universal plan" (p. 212). Otherwise we would be faced with the same infinite complexity in reading the texts that we already face when we attempt to understand the universe itself. If the Book really represented the universe in its ideal totality, "all the different parts of our knowledge would become just as isolated as they already are; we would lose our grasp of the inductive chain, we would lose sight of the links that precede and those that follow, and soon we would be faced with the same gaps and the same doubts that we face now" (pp. 211–12). That is not the stuff of "intense and pleasant reactions" between man and world.

The world is immensely complex, well beyond our powers of perception, and yet perfectly logical and coherent in itself. Faced with the world we are like the blind ("we lose sight"), we lack cognitive access to its perfect system. Only a mirror-like correspondence between the encyclopedic system and the lacunary capacities of its human center would provide that center with an image of itself cured of confusion and weakness. Again, this vast compendium of things and knowledge is designed to give humanity a corrected image of itself.

Ariste faced the same difficulty in *De la poésie dramatique* as he sets out to form an ideal model of the philosopher. In both cases one projects a model of perfection that reflects one's own imperfections, but reversed and thus remedied, mirror-like. Here the *Encyclopedia* is that mirror, linking people and things "by immense lines," but in such a way that the human center no longer experiences its usual inadequacies when faced with the world. The severance between human and world, like blindness, both makes possible and requires figurative, orthopedic representation in the mirror.

Given the subject-mirror nature of this "rapport" with our surroundings, what then is its pedagogical function? It is here that we are most irresistibly "renvoyés" and the "renvoi" is once again "en dehors du sujet": see "Mirror Stage." For I believe that Lacan's elaboration of an infant's experience before the mirror in which the "I" is constituted as a prolepsis, permanently chasing after an anticipation of itself, provides the best understanding of the human figuration in the *Encyclopedia*.

The infant before the mirror in Lacan's analysis has not formed ego and is "still sunk in his motor incapacity and nursing dependence."[18] She or he cannot stand alone and has no mastery over body movements. Like the human figure of "Encyclopedia," the infant is characterized by "insufficiency" (p. 4). But then the child sees, and recognizes as self, an image in the mirror. "This act . . . immediately rebounds in the case of the child in a series of gestures in which he experiences in play the relation between the movements *assumed* in the image and the reflected environment, and between this *virtual* complex and the reality it reduplicates—the child's own body, and the persons and things around him" (p. 1; my emphasis).

The mirror reflects the child in his or her surroundings at a moment "of an organic insufficiency" (p. 4)—the infant has no motor control. But what the fledgling subject gets back from the mirror is an image of the body as a whole, as moving together and as relating as a whole entity to its surroundings. (Lacan invokes the notion of a Gestalt.) That image is only a "virtual complex," however, because it is the image of a reality that the infant does not yet experience empirically. (The child still knows only fragments of experience that would correspond, no doubt, to Diderot's fantasy of the five senses without unifying *sensorum commune*.) Having captured this image of self as a whole, the infant undergoes a "drama whose internal thrust is precipitated from insufficiency to anticipation—and which manufactures for the subject, caught up in the lure of spatial identification, the succession of phantasies that extends from a fragmented body-image to a form of its totality that I shall call orthopedic . . . " (p. 4).[19]

Through this mirror image, the child passes from "insuf-ficiency," not to sufficiency, but to an anticipation of a sufficiency—motor ability and subjective definition—that he does not yet enjoy. For Lacan identification with a pro-leptic image at the mirror stage is the core of all future iden-tifications, of all future identity. In this way identity is alien-ating because it is eternally in anticipation of itself.

Like the infant, the human experience in the encyclopedic mirror stems from the insufficiency that it both remedies and perpetuates at the same time. The orthopedic, ideal im-age reflected back to us inscribes our epistemological ground, like our "ideal-I," in a permanent relation to our "coming-into-being [*le devenir*]" (p. 2). Therein lies its pedagogical effect. The *Encyclopedia* gives us the confi-dence we can know everything by teaching us to know our desire in the present and to desire the knowledge that is ours already in the future. It is an enormous, Rabelaisian compendium that tries and fails to include knowledge of all things. The object of its lesson is less in the contents of its articles than in this example of its desire.

But what of the "intense and pleasant reactions [that] will ensue between nature and man, from man to nature?"

In the mirror stage, the little human overcomes "motor incapacity" (p. 2) in an experience that Lacan at first calls "a flutter of jubilant activity" (p. 1), and later calls a "jubilant assumption of his specular image" (p. 2). The infant should jubilate while she or he can because the mirror stage termi-nates in the "identification with the image of the counter-part [*semblable*] and the drama of primordial jealousy" (p. 5). The little apprentice in humanity is still unaware that "desire of the other" is concomitant with a "competition or cooperation of others" that inevitably entails alienation and aggression.

One suspects that the reason for Lacan's repeated refer-ence to the infant's jubilation, otherwise unexplained, is to underscore the naïveté of the victim that will then be "pierced" by the ironic blade of one in a position to know.

For the ecstatic child is only the first incarnation of the blind idealist, who will return a few pages later: "We place no trust in altruistic feeling, *we who pierce through to reveal* [*nous qui perçons à jour*] the aggressivity that underlies the activity of the philanthropist, the idealist, the *pedagogue*, and even the reformer" (p. 7; my emphasis). From the idealistic, pedagogical perspective of "Encyclopedia," such a statement invites a certain number of impertinent questions: Who is this "we"? What is its position? What is its interest in piercing the illusions of the naïve? Since Lacan is clearly not himself indulging in veiled (altruistic) aggressivity—his aggression is piercingly obvious—how should we characterize his own posture in an article that presumably is also attempting to do something like represent and teach?

To the extent that Lacan's "we" is enunciated from the analyst's position of dominion over the difference between what is said and what is meant, it is the "we" of a master ironist. (But only to that extent.) It is even a royal "we" insofar as, through irony, he may be seeking to remain in a position of overseer, dominating from above the oversights of the naïve and the suspicious intentions of the idealist. More than once Diderot experienced piercing interruptions of his encyclopedic project, as in 1759 when the king's council revoked for the second time the royal privilege to print it. With a little violence to historical verisimilitude, one could spin a fantasy in which Lacan would be a metaphor for Louis XV, suspecting pedagogical altruism as a mask for aggression against the crown or, more precisely, against the condition of possibility for what I am calling royal irony. And indeed, in that suspicion Louis and Lacan would have been correct.

Consider Diderot's subtle but explicit critique of at least one aspect of the monarchical order: "Works commanded by sovereigns are never conceived on the basis of their usefulness, but always on the basis of [the king's] personal dignity, which is to say, they embrace the widest possible scope . . . " (p. 182). Diderot reveals a view of kings that is strangely similar to Lacan's view of altruistic pedagogues: kings are not really interested in benefiting others (altruism), but only in the widest possible expansion of their egos (aggression). Any interruption in the royally commissioned project is therefore "deadly" (p. 182) for its successful completion. In its specificity the royal ego, the ego as king, does not want to accommodate negativity.

That is one of the reasons for which Diderot insists on the intimate link between his conception of the *Encyclopedia* and its composition by a group of individuals motivated—precisely—by a proleptic ideality. In the event that such an individual is interrupted in his project, "he at least gathers together the fragments of his enterprise: he carefully stores materials that can be useful when times are better; he chases after his advances [*il court après ses avances*]. The monarchical spirit disdains such prudence" (p. 183). The sovereign ego disdains relations to its own being as project; the encyclopedist's being is in "chasing after advances," running both ahead of and behind himself because his "advances" represent work already done and work to be done, an image in the mirror. The *Encyclopedia* arises from this interruption of the proleptic future as a differentiating a royal project is "deadly."

As part of his anxiety in "Encyclopedia," Diderot tirelessly catalogues the obstacles and inadequacies that would render his enterprise "ironic" in Goldmann's sense of the term. He spells out the reality principle according to which the "we" represented in the *Encyclopedia* remains an interminable project, an interminable failure in the face of its *imago*. In the midst of such negativity, the more pertinent query, finally, is why Diderot was able to persevere at all. In answering just this question, he shows signs of a certain passion, a certain jubilation that is perhaps not unlike that of the infant before the mirror.

> We felt rekindled by that thought so sweet and consoling, that men would speak of us, men for whose edu-

cation and happiness we were sacrificing ourselves, men whom we esteemed and loved even though they had yet to be born, but whose voices we were given to hear through that too voluptuous murmur on the lips of certain of our contemporaries. . . . In effect, man is seen by his contemporaries and sees himself just as he is, a bizarre composite of sublime qualities and shameful deficiencies. . . . [But when he dies,] there remain only those qualities eternalized in the monuments he has raised to himself or that he owes to public veneration and recognition, honors that his own self-esteem allows him already to enjoy in an anticipated ecstasy [*jouissance*], ecstasy that is just as pure just as strong, just as real as any other ecstasy, and in which there can be nothing imaginary except the credentials on which his aspirations are based. Our credentials are forwarded in the present work; posterity will judge them. (Pp. 232–33)

The idealist, the pedagogue, the reformer speaks altruistically about his work in which he sacrifices himself now to something to come only later. In terms of present reality, to his contemporaries, he is like the *Encyclopedia* itself, a "bizarre composite of sublime qualities and shameful deficiencies," in which there are many echoes—of the "deficiency of understanding" that the work sets out to remedy; of the early reference to the "treatment of language that has remained insufficient," thus requiring remedial treatment in the article; of Ariste's vicissitudes; of Saunderson's blindness; of the lack of "mots-discours" in modern languages. But also, he is already what he will be, as reflected in what the ironist could only see as an orthopedic mirror.

The movement is indeed one of precipitation from insufficiency to identification with an ideal image. But just as Lacan's analysis of the mirror stage neglects the repeated detail of the infant's jubilation at the moment of anticipatory projection (in reality the beginning of his lifelong alienation), an "ironic" reading would neglect to account for the encyclopedist-pedagogue's analogous "jouissance".[20] In this moment of ideal fulfillment, does the infant jubilate because she or he is naïve, or because she or he knows; in spite of or because of that knowledge? Our reading would anticipate that it is both, that both are necessary precisely in their difference from each other.

Diderot's text opens onto what may be another scene, in which the jealousy and aggressivity of *je* always denied its ideal has for a moment become affirmation and confidence, not of any real future enjoyment of that idea (which for Diderot is as irreducibly prospective as it is for Lacan), but of *real working* done in its image. In the working, paradoxically, "there can be nothing imaginary." The work is—good or bad, useful or useless, read or forgotten. The "affairement jubilatoire" in Diderot has prolonged itself in the affair of writing an encyclopedia. In the glassy, representational space between himself and his book, between himself and his measure, there is this future possibility and this past history of a "jouissance" that no measure can know.

CHAPTER TEN

Renvoi

Je suis dans ce monde et j'y reste.
—Rameau's Nephew

*T*HE SPECULAR LINK BETWEEN
mind and world that organizes the *Encyclopedia* brings
with it the effects we have found accompanying representation in other moments of Diderot's writing. The volumi-
nous monumentality of the *Encyclopedia* becomes expectation, desire, passion, affirmation.

It is no doubt significant that two of the better recent
books on Diderot have each found its metaphor for some
extraordinary power to create and affirm. For Jack Undank
it is the metaphor of intersubjective "space," across which
desire orchestrates its ever-new negotiations; for Elizabeth
de Fontenay it is the collapse of the matter-mind dichotomy
into a "jonglerie" that supplants their traditional representational link.[1] These authors' tone and preoccupations, their
continuous shuttling between Diderot's writing and modern theoretical texts, suggests that they consider Diderot as
a virtual contemporary whose texts are actively engaged in
dialogue with modern thought. And it is with just this question of Diderot's "modernity"—which is our antiquity—
that the present study will conclude.[2]

Diderot's writings allow us to ask the ever-new, ever-old
question of representation, and to focus (blindly perhaps)
on the liminal space, the stage that makes and marks its
texts. This entire study has been a polymorphous "mira!
mira!" which is all too easily confused with the narcissistic

"mirror, mirror." We, like Foucault, have pointed to something radically other that is at the same time a reflection of ourselves, of our own episteme. We have been trying to "see" the place of representation that Derrida must have had in mind when he wrote referring not to Diderot but to Artaud: "The West—and such is no doubt the energy of its essence—has probably never labored at anything but the effacement of the stage."[3] Diderot's writings have "shown" us this stage that demarcates the beginning of the visible, the intelligible, the legible—this threshold that has forever been overlooked in favor of the oppositions it produces. Their interest in *allowing* stage effects is what links such heterogeneous figures as Artaud and Diderot—or Brecht and Diderot (but that would require another chapter).[4]

For both the stage is a "space produced from inside itself and no longer ordered according to an absent locus . . . [or] an invisible utopia" such as an "author god," or according to some fiction of temporality expressed in "phonetic linearity."[5] For Diderot the representation of divinity in a statue was less the product of an artist than the effect of a threshold; in his analysis of poetic hieroglyphs, prescisely, phonetic linearity was interrupted by a quite other temporality in which things were "said and represented at the same time." "Archi-manifestation de la force ou de la vie," writes Derrida of Artaud's stage (p. 349), but the qualification suggests something of the productivity and fertility of Diderot's copulas and thresholds as well. As "*archi-* manifestation" the stage antecedes all the appearances or performances that it allows. As "archi-*manifestation*" the stage is all the same a revelation of something prior whose existence can be deduced retrospectively. However one seeks to arrest the spiraling regression, the result is that theater and a certain theatricality, a certain literarity of experience, does not allow itself to be slavishly derived from a certain "life," or "history."[6] It is in terms of this experience that the author of "drames bourgeois" and the author of "théâtre de la cruauté" communicate across the historical differences from which we construct their specificity. For the experience that each makes legible can open within any historically discrete moment.

And yet, it is not a question of ignoring history. "Diderot" is not "Artaud." The subject "Artaud" constituted itself in and through a dialectical negation of a tradition (a tradition that of course includes Diderot's teary bourgeois dramas). Writing must always be situated within the particularity of its time. The Enlightenment must necessarily be conjured up if one is to appreciate Diderot's adherence, his negation, his deflections and deconstructions of its ideology. But as we have seen, once there is representation, everything is representational, and can enter into the endless virtuality of "rapports." Diderot can be linked to Artaud, as he has been tied to figures such as Descartes, Montaigne, Gide, and Sterne.[7] But more important, he is a writer who has frequently taken this "sens copulatif de l'être [copulative meaning of being]," as Vincent Descombes has recently called it, as the object of his discourse in all its varied genres.[8] To see Diderot "in" Artaud, or to see ourselves in Mangogul (as did Foucault), for Diderot to see himself in Seneca, is to participate in and to restage the differential conjunction of identity and representation that we have seen preoccupying his writing

The materialist vocabulary that Diderot inherited was certainly an obstacle to any systematization of such inchoate understandings. But they are there. Diderot "understood" the intercourse of being and identity with difference, which was to play such a part in thought after Hegel. (The latter's extensive use of *Le Neveu* in the *Phenomenology of Mind* suggests that at least Hegel thought as much.) And most remarkably of all, the "copulative meaning of being" did not constitute a loss or a source of nostalgic regret for Diderot. No doubt as a consequence, he shows little inclination to insert it into a teleology or to save us from its effects by promising the advent of a real term to its *rapports*. In Diderot there is no Absolute comparable to Hegel's absolute spirit—itself an elaborate representational notion, as Descombes's analysis suggests.[9]

Diderot may have been one of the rare philosophers to have written his way into the complex commerce of identity and difference while remaining so sanguine, even affirmative, about the consequences. His texts manifest no single-minded desire to exclude them or to leave behind our traditional need for such mimetic or referential underpinnings, for a connection to the "real" or to an absolute capable of underwriting representation's double function. Texts from all periods of his career attest an acceptance of the imperative for ontological grounding that underlies traditional philosophy, even as, in effect, they deconstruct such a possibility.

Consider the passage in the *Entretien d'un philosophe avec la Maréchale de* *** (1774), which affirms the Maréchale's need to believe in God, in spite of the atheism that characterized the latter part of Diderot's own life. "For you it is consoling to imagine beside you, overhead, a great and powerful being who sees you walking upon the earth; and that notion emboldens your step. Continue, Madam, to derive the benefits [*jouir*] of this august guarantor of your thoughts, this spectator, this sublime model of your actions."[10] This is not just an eighteenth-century version of tolerance. After all, in 1758 (in *De la poésie dramatique*) and in 1767 (in the *Salon* of that year), Diderot had conjured up a similar relation between the philosopher or artist and their own "ideal models," with results that we have examined already. Moreover, one notices how much of the key vocabulary from those works finds its way into this passage, the very terms that earlier served as conduits for differential effects: a "spectator" who "sees" the Maréchale as a spectacle, and which is simultaneously a "sublime model." Diderot's tolerance for the Maréchale's dependence on a divine guarantor is not concocted or condescending. Her relation to "God," at bottom, is no different from Plato's to the ideal, from the actor's to his role, Rosalie's to Dorval,

Jacques and his master's to the great scroll, from Diderot's to posterity in "Encyclopedia" or the *Lettres à Falconet*.[11] From the child's before the mirror. Through such "rapports" this divine underwriting, this ultimate referent of our earthly performance that Diderot allows the Maréchale, undergoes the deconstructive effects we have seen in all such relations to models. One can surmise, then, that the model—God—finds its model in the Maréchale's sense of her own deficiencies, that it is an instance of her very difference from herself, of the ubiquitous proscenium that marks both representation and object in the representational moment.[12] This is what Diderot's whole writing career could lead him to affirm in the Maréchale's relation to "God."

But surely the most extravagant instance of Diderot's proto-Nietzchean affirmation, springing from the unfettered, non-logocentric effects of representation, is *Le neveu de Rameau*. A number of years ago, Leo Spitzer recognized that Rameau was severed from the Logos.[13] That precisely is the Nephew's situation. In addition, all the attendant resonances that such a statement causes to sound in the contemporary ear are also valid. If severed from the Logos, then we would expect him to be severed from his identity as presence, from personal and social ideals, from his father as origin and underpinning for filial re-presence, and so forth. And we would be right. As I have argued elsewhere, the Nephew's relation to his famous uncle is one of quite undecidable similarity-difference, in constant oscillation.[14] The "paternal molecule" linking the uncle-model and the nephew-representation, would seem to assure the double function of similarity and difference we have discovered in other texts fueled by this issue. One would do well here to recall that Lysimond's paternal prayer in *Le Fils Naturel* was, "May heaven which blesses children through their fathers and fathers through their children, grant you offspring that resemble you. . . ."[15] But that patriarchal wish is exploded forever, since, borrowing a recent formulation by Elizabeth de Fontenay concerning the Nephew, "if difference speaks in its own name, nothing can continue to remain the same [*pareil*]."[16] And with Jean-François Rameau, that is surely what occurs (except, perhaps, that difference has no "propre nom"). According to one of the dialogue's most-quoted phrases, "Rien ne dissemble plus de lui que lui-même [Nothing resembles him less than himself]."[17] In the Nephew the fundamental principle of non-contradiction is suspended; identity and difference are confused; the clear-cut relation of identity and its re-representation is impossible.

Hegel's unsurpassed analysis in the *Phenomenology* focuses on this absolute "sundering [*Zerrissenheit*]" that is the Nephew, "a consciousness of absolute inversion of reality and thought."[18] The dialogue's Latin epigraph is a line from Horace invoking Vertumnus, the god who presides over changes in weather and season and who is, in de Fontenay's exegesis, "the god who can imitate everything" (pp. 245–46).[19]

The absolute sundering and absolute reversibility of thought and reality, language and thing, representation and object—such "is" Rameau's nephew. He "is" what we have been calling representationality itself, representation-as-difference. He figures again the liminal space around which such terms as master and slave, original and copy, nature and art, author and work, parent and child, actor and audience, model and imitator come to be organized. And as precarious products of a liminal space, we can see that they are always ready to reverse.[20] *Lui* figures something like a stage that itself is not referential or representational, but which provides the framing necessary for any representation to work. He is an abstract agency (a "nothing" in itself) that causes things to appear—as in a stage appearance— what they "are." Although a pure hypocrite, he is the "speck of yeast that leavens the whole and restores to each of us a portion of his natural individuality. He stirs people and gives them a shaking; he causes approbation or blame; he makes the truth emerge . . ." (p. 35).[21] He is the procurer, pimping between being and appearance in the "grand branle du monde" (p. 105).

He is also the "homme-clavecin" that is figured in the *Rêve de d'Alembert*, in which de Fontenay has found a basis for reading much of Diderot. In this metaphor ideas are compared to vibrations of a chord that can be struck by the harpsichord itself or by an external agent. One idea or resonance causes sympathetic vibrations of other chords, either those in contiguity or those at considerable harmonic intervals. For de Fontenay, Diderot thus finesses the question of adequation to the real that idealisms guarantee through God, the soul, absolute spirit (p. 222). The musical metaphor that marks so much of Diderot's writing renders inoperative the basic incompatibility of materialism and idealism. It is fundamentally a nonexclusive trope.[22] The concatenation of multiple ideas that result when a chord is plucked points to notions of pleasure more than the labor of adequation, "allowing us to glimpse just how far the abandonment of classical notions of truth has gone" (p. 225). De Fontenay also suggests that, homonymically, the Cartesian "raisonner" (to reason) has been supplanted by a much less domitable order of "résonner" (to resonate).

More precisely, however, Rameau is himself less comparable to the homme-clavecin as an entity—metaphoric though such a creature might be—than to the harmonic principle that makes resonance possible. For in order for one chord to vibrate sympathetically, it must be both in "rapport," and yet different from, the other objects or chords. It is to this intermediary function that Rameau can best be compared. In his own view "one must learn how to prepare, place and resolve dissonances in the social harmony. Noting more dull than a sequence of perfect chords. There must be something that prods and breaks up the beam of light and scatters the rays" (p. 111). Uncle Rameau's theory of the "basse fondamentale" is replaced by the nephew's disseminating theory of dissonance, breaking

the monolithic and the monological into ever new and surprising representational links, produced by ever new disso-
nance/difference. "Individualité naturelle" is forever rene-
gotiated, recreated anew. De Fontenay's conclusion is apt:

> The consolation of resolution [of a dissonance] lasts
> only an instant, even if it can by rights repeat itself
> infinitely. Musical construction cannot be credited
> with a referent, and produces no meaning. There is
> only patriation and rapatriation—but to what *patrie*?
> To the major mode? The dominant? This manner of
> denying the strictly historical character of the compo-
> sition procedures that order our musical sensibilities
> is only a theological mirage! Expatriation and repatri-
> ation, due to the nostalgia without object which they
> induce in us, know no transcendence of the future, and
> know eternity only as beginning anew. (p. 242)

And finally, summing up these remarks, she writes, "Far
from making music think, Diderot makes philosophy sing"
(p. 243).

Although we entered Diderot's writing through the *Bijoux indiscrets*, we might well have begun with *Le Neveu de
Rameau*. For the nephew's status as universal copula—an
agency of "rapport," of separating and joining—certainly
finds sympathetic resonances in Cucufa's magic ring of language. Initially Mangogul labored to domesticate the differential effects that proliferated through use of the ring. He
was like *Le Neveu de Rameau*'s philosophical interlocutor,
"Moi," who always insists on the monological and eternal
verities. In that mode Mangogul sought to subjugate the
heterogeneous connections to one meaning, ideal and ontological. He sought the one answer to his question: What is
Mirzoza? And to that extent, he was a bad theorist, a bad
critic. When finally he addresses this one object of his desire
as radically differentiated, he passes from a domain of restricted representation to general representationality; he
accedes to another register in which difference is the

springboard for affirmation. One could think of it as forgoing "raissoner" for "résonner."

Thus *Bijoux indiscrets* was a fiction about theory, a theory about fiction. It insinuated us into the space conjoining and dividing fictitious, imaginary criticism and the critical fictions theorists construct in order to represent and name their objects in the most literal way they can.[23] *Le Neveu de Rameau* indulges that space and elaborates it in one of the most disruptive texts ever written. But its principal figure, *Lui*, nevertheless claims for himself an absolutely mundane reality as well: "Je suis de ce monde et j'y reste [I am in this world and here I stay]" (p. 120).

He is abstract representationality, but he explicitly disclaims the very classificatory activity that Foucault saw at the heart of the contemporary episteme based on representation: "Go and perch on the epicycle of Mercury, if it appeals to you, like Réaumur while he classifies flies into tailors, surveyors and harvesters, you can divide men into cabinet-makers, carpenters, runners, dancers, singers. It is your business, and I am not interested" (p. 120). In that, Rameau is perhaps an important model: both absolute other, and inextricably a part of his world. (It is indicative in this regard that any modern reader has to rely heavily on footnotes to grope through the profusion of highly specific and concrete references to contemporary events, people and places on which the dialogue relies. *Lui* is indeed embedded within the concrete materiality of his world.)

Difference, limen, gap that naturally creates scenes—*Lui* is all these things—and he is materiality, subject, body, reality. He is the strange that makes the familiar, that always inhabits the familiar and can always reorder, renew, or "alienate" it (in Hegel's and Brecht's sense of "entfremden"). He is a certain "virtuality" that theory wants to articulate and that reality can always release. He is the possibility that allows alteration in the representations by which we live and through which we know. Just as Foucault found an "emblem" of ourselves in Diderot's sultan, I would propose the Nephew as an emblem of that which preoccupies our thinking today, drawing it like a magnet.

In the most general terms, our modernity has proceeded from a radical mistrust of representation that has appeared a lie to be disparaged in increasingly nonrepresentational literature and art. Viewed from the vantage point we now occupy, here at the end of this foray into the eighteenth century, the renunciation of representation and "aboutness" in so much modern cultural activity can be seen as something of a failure. It is first a failure to affirm or even to allow the differential effects figured—for example—by *Rameau's Nephew*. And too, it has been a failure in that the loss of representational illusions has not been without naïveté in another guise. In fact, "nonrepresentational" art and fiction do seek to represent. What they would represent is simple aesthetic activity itself, fully differentiated from mimetic tradition. And aim to represent *only* aesthetic activity itself, as disembodied semiosis.

Paradoxically, this is an art predicated on the conviction of its own self-identity.[24] It dreams of supplanting difference *within* representation and world by a far more manageable difference *between* the real and the purely aesthetic production. The hypostatization of a frontier between *représentant* and *représenté* condemns much contemporary art to the fruitless pursuit of tautology and denies it a transgressive intercourse of diacritical differences within and between itelf and the world. It strives for self-absorption and eschews the "copulative sense of being." Contemporary art is at an impasse.[25]

To make this claim here, after the foregoing reading of Diderot, is not to suggest that any programmatic solution is to be found in his writings. If there were anything pertinent that could be offered at this juncture, it surely would point away from any attempt to *spare* us the illusions of representation. Whatever positive model there may be here would be derived first and foremost from the unflinching affirmation of the entangled "rapports" of naïveté and awareness that are disseminated in his writing.

Such affirmation, which the *Le Neveu de Rameau* exemplifies yet again, has nothing to do with what Paul de Man has recently stigmatized as "the 'overcompensation of a programmatically euphoric utopianism" in some modern theoretical discourse.[26] (Diderot is not Habermas). Rather, my point is, first, that the same limitations on our certainty about language's links to the world affected Diderot and can be traced in his writing. (De Man would seem likely to concur since he also thinks that the difficulties that are thought to characterize modernist discourse are, "to some extent, a-historical in the temporal sense of the term.")[27] And second, I have maintained that what we find in Diderot is nonetheless an affirmation of representation that is exactly concomitant with an inchoate awareness of the part that its radical unreliability plays in its effectiveness.

Again, the unreliability of representations—linguistic or other—derives from their difference from what they represent, but that difference is precisely what must be marked—both in the real and in its image—in order for the representation to be efficacious. In a word, representations depend for their effect on the difference that makes them unreliable. What Diderot's writing gives us to glimpse are the possibilities—for experience, for thought—that are thereby opened up to us once representation is severed from an incestuous attachment to the real—which is not the same as being severed from the real altogether.

We are left with no privileged meta-representational space in any way free of the unreliability—the blind spot—in all representation.[28] But representation there is. If it has enslaved us, it also frees us. For like Rameau's Nephew—and everything is in the "like"—one can choose to linger as much as possible at that threshold from which one is given to see the similarity of two texts in their difference, hear the sound of different chords in their sympathetic resonance, recognize ourselves in a past that is irretrievably lost to us.

Writing a book on the question of representation in Diderot opens onto a limitless range of "rapports," none of which is in fact privileged or prior to any other. One is trapped in textual linearity, however, which only resonance and "renvoi" can relieve. The reader has at best been given to hear certain specific harmonies. And yet, by them, nothing is defined. No meaning is enshrined. One can hope only that they have melded into a chorus of other voices.

This is, alas, not a fairy tale. But once again, "like" Mangogul, we can throw away the ring of power—in some ways, at some moments—if sometimes we can embrace the unruly proliferation of its symbolic effects.

Virtue and Identification:
Diderot and Sade

The suggestion that virtue for Diderot has more to do with aesthetic impact than ethical content may seem strange for anyone familiar with the tradition of Diderot scholarship. It is not commonly held that the force of the dramatic effect or aesthetic experience that Diderot generally prescribes is promulgated as an end in itself.[1] The end that he advocates is not usually thought to be the mere shattering of the spectator invaded by forceful effects of representation and difference. Rather, theater is more commonly understood as an ethico-aesthetic experience that leads us to choose a role for ourselves, and to choose in favor of virtue. In his *Eloge de Richardson* (1762), for example, Diderot writes, "Oh Richardson! whatever our resistances we take a role in your words, we get involved in the conversation, we approve, we blame, we admire, we become irritated, we become indignant."[2]

But if we examine such descriptions of the aesthetic experience more closely, we discover that here too it is our sympathetic vibration with the diacritical oppositions within the text that mark the reader, that are imprinted upon us.

These same imprints are subsequently metaphorized as seeds: "Richardson sows seeds of virtue in our hearts which remain there . . . until an occasion comes along which stirs them up and makes them blossom" (p. 214). When reading Richardson, our soul is "open to the truth" (p. 214). Diderot does not mean open to the formulaic truth of the maxim that "by itself imprints no sensate image upon our mind" (p. 214), but rather open to the differential truths of theatricality that prompt us "to take a role," to see others in roles, to experience a certain representationality when, as it happened to the faithful leaving the Greek temple, something comes along that makes a representational-differential connection to the characters a writer has imprinted within us.

About the virtue that Diderot seems to want to posit as the surefire effect of such sympathetic identification, we can say, with Leo Bersani, that "the very operation of sympathy partially un-

dermines the moral solidarity that we like to think of as its primary effect."[3] Bersani's cogent assessment of the links between
sexual excitement or violence and mimetic representations, partially derived from Laplanche, includes as a necessary moment the
speculation that desire "perhaps always includes, within itself, the
disruptive effect on the other's equilibrium, which is now an effect
on an internalized order" (p. 148). Desire would then be constitu-
tively sadomasochistic. In other words, Bersani concurs with the
suggestion he finds in Freud that "the spectacle of pain stimulates
a mimetic representation that, so to speak, shatters the subject
into sexual excitement" (p. 149). The image of violence done to
the other represents violence to ourselves. "Who would want to
be Lovelace with all his advantages?" asks Diderot rhetorically.
"Who would not want to be Clarissa, in spite of all her misfortunes?" (p. 215). He makes the point more directly still in a subsequent passage: "In [Richardson's] work, as in the world, men
are divided into two classes; those who enjoy [*jouissent*] and those
who suffer. He always gives me the latter for associates [*c'est
toujours à ceux-ci qu'il m'associe*]" (p. 216). If virtue is for Diderot
"always a sacrifice of oneself" (p. 214), the representation of that
sacrifice in Clarissa's pain issues unmistakably in the reader's
pleasure: "[Richardson] left me with a melancholy which pleases
me and which lasts" (p. 216).[4]

There is surely reason, therefore, for one's thoughts at this
point to turn to Sade, who clearly could teach us something about
both Diderot and Rousseau. Again, in Bersani's words:

> What Sade rejects is not the mechanism of sympathetic pro-
> jection assumed by theories of benevolence, but rather the
> pious view that we are stirred by virtuous identification
> with others. Virtue is irrelevant to the agitations induced by
> the suffering of others. It is the identification itself—that is,
> a fantasmatic introjection of the other—which appears to
> be intrinsically sexual. Such introjections make us "vibrate."
> (P. 150)

Such vibrations characterize the "virtuous" self-sacrifice prescribed in *De la poésie dramatique* and in the *Eloge de Richardson*, when, through the mechanisms of identification or pity, we
are invaded by the differential spectacle of vice and virtue. As
Bersani notes, both Laplanche and Sade use the word "ébranle-
ment" to describe such psychic shattering.[5] And for Diderot
drama must unleash an effect so violent that "spectators, like
people during the quaking of a part of the globe, see the walls of

their houses vacillate, and feel the earth disappear beneath their feet" (pp. 197–98). The seat of one's identity, like one's house, is sundered by the spectacle of vice/virtue.

Although we shall not pursue these connections explicitly, I do not think that we shall ever stray very far from their ramifications as we go on now to ask to what extent Diderot was able to sustain this differential, vibratory movement at the heart of his most cherished investments. Important among them is the notion of an ideal model. On the face of it, one could hardly imagine an ending more incompatible with what we have found in the preceding treatise, since any appeal to an "ideal model" brings with it connotations of an original, immutable reference point wholly apart from the quicksands of psychic fluidity. But Diderot's interest for us moderns is precisely his capacity to articulate the incompatibility of both these spheres while ultimately privileging neither.

Idealism and Reversal:
On a Note by Jacques Derrida

Again, if the argument closely approximates the terms of Platonic idealism, that similarity again serves primarily to deconstruct classical "ideology." (See *Republic*, bk. 10, and "Phaedo".)[1]

In its relation to particular, real creations of the artist, Diderot's ideal, like Plato's, is also that to which works refer and toward which they "strive." But the referentiality, the tropism of a "likeness," is the same as that which opens within its model. In Diderot the "shortfall" that Plato limits to "likenesses" is generalized absolutely; the thing itself, the model, "falls short" of absolute presence to itself at the same time and in the same way as its likeness. Representation thus becomes, yes, the "equality" of those two lacks, their communications, their "striving"—but their striving toward and in function of each other. It is "shortfall," and "striving" therefore, that produce (an effect of) ideality, rather than a preexisting Ideal that defines "shortfall" absolutely and a priori.

Clearly, Diderot's "solicitations of the mimetological machine" (as Derrida called them) have issued in more than a simple reversal of Platonic idealism. Derrida amplifies his point about reversals in Diderot by referring to a highly pertinent passage from the *Pensées détachées sur la peinture*, in which Diderot approves the sentiment of a contemporary who had maintained, "If possible, we should make the figures of our painting the living models of antique statues, rather than allowing those statues to become the originals of the figures we paint."[2] Certainly this phrase seems to imply a reversal of model and copy. But, imported and reinscribed into Diderot's writing, something happens to its direct simplicity. The "modèles vivants" in the quotation resonate strongly with the "original vivant" of the goddess, which, in the essay "Expression," is neither more nor less original than her representation in the temple. And if we return to the next development of the *Salon de 1767*, we find that, symptomatically, Diderot turned precisely to the problem of antiquity as model, without in any way proposing a simple reversal of the Platonic order of original and copy.

"And if there were no antiquity," asks Diderot, "how would you proceed? . . . I am going to try to give you an explanation of how the ancients, who had no ancients, attacked the problem" (p. 12). The speculation that follows is clearly guided by his preceding theory of model-as-difference. Its first object is the anthropomorphic model whose ideal would be imaginable as a perfectly beautiful man or woman, perfectly apt for all human functions, but who would reach adulthood without ever having performed any of them. Such a body would bear no mark of its difference from what it either was or should be. From where does such an intuition of ideality emerge? "Perhaps because of a project, natural to idolatrists, to elevate man above his condition and to imprint a divine character upon him . . . [the Greeks] began by perceiving [*par sentir*] *the great alterations*, the most obvious *deformities*, the great sufferings" (pp. 12–13; my emphasis). By a very long process—"through long and painful groping, through an unspoken and secret notion of analogy" (p. 13)—the real human model was reformed into something approximating its nonexistent "original" state that its deformity gave the Greeks to imagine. But once again that ideality (the imprint of "divine character") has no other being than the perceived and felt difference in/between both the natural model and idealized representation. These are each brought into being first as diacritical representations of each other—like a "bizarre mixture of sacred and profane"—in which each is what the other is not.

Greek art notwithstanding, therefore, no representation is in itself an ideal for Diderot. His earlier reasoning about "portraits" applies here as well: when the artist represents an idealized model of the human form, "there is [yet again] a thing which is not the thing you have painted" but whose "presence" is felt. The ideal model is an imagined, pristine form unaltered by experience and use; but its ideality is produced through difference with the natural reality of which it is, precisely, an alteration.

Therefore, we cannot take the Greek ideal as simple acquisition to be copied in order to elevate our creations above the level of mimetic portraits, to the loftier spheres of ideality. If what the Greeks "revealed" was less a product than a relationship, then the only possible imitation of the Greek model would be—not just a reversal—but a repetition of the process through which that relationship is marked. That is what Diderot states with all the earmarks of simplicity in a passage that, in fact, contains hardly a word that can be read according to Platonic norms.

The fact is that, due to the models the Greeks left us, we have never been able, as they did, to attain the beauty of those models incrementally and slowly. The fact is, we have made ourselves into more or less servile imitators, portraitists. We have had the ideal model, the true line, only artificially, indistinctly, dimly. The fact is, if these models had been destroyed there is every reason to presume that, forced as they were to trail after a deformed, imperfect and vitiated nature, we would have reached an original, primary model just as they did. . . . (P. 16)

One cannot "possess" the ideal as a borrowed object. One must accept, as it were, to live proleptically in the differentiating space "within" the real, referring and deferring, always "trailing after."

Blindness and Absorption:
On Michael Fried's
Absorption and Theatricality

Blindness in the *Lettre sur les aveugles* is also the analogue of the proscenium in Diderot's writings on theater and theatrical aesthetics, of the liminal demarcations in all forms of artistic representation, and of the fundamental lack that produces the metaphoric models of ideality in their various guises. More than being simply analogous, these vocabularies are ordered by "object" because one can attribute to it a certain continuity from one set of concerns to another (from aesthetics to philosophy, for example); "impossible" because it is finally only a nothing, a space that marks things as both different and representative of each other at the same time.

The reason for a postscript to the complex of effects attendant upon blindness in the *Lettre* is to bring to bear the recent work of Michael Fried in his *Absorption and Theatricality: Painting and the Beholder in the Age of Diderot*.[1] Different in focus—it is a work of art history—it provides counterpoint to the preceding chapters and amplification of their basic metaphors into another sphere. Fried's title already suggests connections to the present analysis, including as it does notions of enthrallment and theatricality relative to artistic representation.

His claim is that in the 1750s French painting underwent a significant shift away from the classical doctrine (Aristotle to Du Bos) according to which "the art of painting at its highest consisted in the representation of significant human action" (p. 73). Great art could not represent subject matter that was trivial in itself. A rigid hierarchy of genres predicated on that principle placed history painting in a position of superiority over other genres because its subjects were considered to be intrinsically most significant. At mid-century (e.g., Chardin), there occurred an important move away from that doctrine, a move in which Diderot was deeply implicated. (In Fried's study, at least, Diderot plays a more essential role than any single painter [p. 3].) As a result of the shift around 1750, the question of subject loses its central importance and history painting loses its preeminent position. But the changes that occurred then were not the result of any explicit theoretical reorientation regarding subject matter per se—history painting as against genre scenes, for example. Rather, changes in that sphere "were largely determined by other, ontologically prior concerns and imperatives" (p. 75).

Fried lists three such concerns: (1) for a dramatic conception of painting; (2) for pictorial unity, with causal relations of all elements immediately obvious to the viewer; (3) for a new link between the painting and the beholder of the painting (pp. 75–76). The third of these concerns depends on the first two and is, in effect, the major focus of the author's analysis.

The new and essential link between painting and beholder is not only theatrical, as between a spectator and a play, but is one in which the beholder views the painting in a suspended state of complete enthrallment. That effect is achieved not by representing subjects that are in themselves captivating (as in Du Bos and the classical tradition) but rather by representing scenes in which the viewer is figured as absent, closed out of the scene that is taking place unmindful of the viewer's intruding eye.[2] This is what Fried calls the "supreme fiction" toward which the paintings he analyzes were striving.[3] One immediately thinks of Diderot's recommendations in *De la poésie dramatique* and elsewhere that actors should above all avoid playing to the audience, and should perform as if the spectator did not exist at all. (Not to mention the complex issue of audience in the *Fils naturel* and its appended *Entretien*; see chapter 6 above.) Fried himself makes reference to most of these texts.

I shall do less injustice to the multifaceted and richly documented argument of his study by resorting right away to the specific example of blind Belisarius receiving alms, which was the subject of several significant engravings and paintings of the time. It is not just any example, however, but is the culmination of all the mid-century changes that Fried is exposing.

The legend results from embellishments of Procopius' sixth-century account of a Roman general, Belisarius, who after winning many victories for Justinian fell under unwarranted suspicion. As a result, he lost his position and eventually died in poverty and disrepute. Legend adds that he was blinded and reduced to beggging for his subsistence (p. 146). Marmontel's *Béli-*

saire (1767) disseminates the legend in the late eighteenth century (p. 147). French artists after 1770 become very interested in it due to the popularity of an engraving of the subject incorrectly thought to be by Van Dyck. (Fried reproduces it on page 146).

According to Fried, "Diderot saw in Van Dyck's composition a double paradigm, or paradigm of paradigms: for pictorial composition generally and for the painting-beholder relationship on the establishment of which the success indeed the validity of the pictorial enterprise seemed to him to depend" (pp. 150–51). The engraving shows the blind Belisarius seated on the far right, his hand extended to receive alms from a group of three women, busily involved in extracting and handing over coins. On the outer edge of their semicircle, one hundred and eighty degrees from Belisarius, is a soldier who is standing with his hands clasped and hanging, observing the scene of the alms-giving with utter dreamy enthrallment. He is no doubt contemplating the irony of his former commander fallen to such a lowly state. (In any case that is the assumption made by Diderot.)

Diderot had an argument over this engraving with his friends Suard and Mme d'Houdetot that he reports in a letter to Sophie Volland dated 18 July 1762.

> It is certain that it is the figure of the soldier that holds our interest, and that it seems to make us forget all the others. Suard and the countess said that this was a flaw. As for me, I claimed that it was precisely that which made the painting moral, and that the soldier was playing my role. Van Dyck has rendered the thing itself and is reproached for having done so. Many delicate and subtle things were said on both sides. If when one makes a painting, one supposes beholders, everything is lost. The painter leaves his canvas, just as the actor who speaks to the audience steps down from the stage. In supposing that there is no one else in the world except the personages of the painting, Van Dyck's painting is sublime. Now this is a supposition that must always be made. If one were alongside the soldier, one would have his facial expression, and one would not notice it in him. Does not the figure of Belisarius achieve the effect that he must achieve? What does it matter if one loses sight of him?[4]

Suard and the countess may be thought to represent the Classical, subject-oriented theory of Du Bos, for example. (See his *Réflexions critiques sur la poésie et sur la peinture*, 1719.) In that view Van Dyck's engraving is flawed because its principal subject, Belisarius, is upstaged by a secondary figure. Indeed, it would be difficult to imagine a clearer example of adherence to a notion of representation antithetical to that expounded by Diderot. His opponents' position could be fleshed out as follows: Belisarius' experience of fate's injustice is the principal referent to Van Dyck's representation. It can and should be expressed directly. The central experience should receive central attention, without competition from another subject or action such as the soldier's musings.

Diderot's opinion is that, on the contrary, "Van Dyck has rendered the thing itself." What then is the "thing itself" in this painting for Diderot? It is not Belisarius, nor is it the observing soldier. It is the relation between the two, and the relation between the viewer and the entire painting that is figured by the former relation. If the viewer were to become one of the figures in the scene represented, one would *have* the soldier's expression instead of *noticing* it. Thus Fried concludes, the soldier is a "natural synecdoche, [mediating] between the actual beholder and the painting as a whole" (p. 150).

Fried continues in a development of highest interest in the present context:

> On the one hand, the actual beholder, in this instance Diderot, was led as it were to see himself in the figure of the soldier and thus was granted an especially intimate mode of access to the world of the painting . . . On the other hand, that mode of access by its very nature involved a blindness, or at least a degree of indirection or inadvertence, which effectively removed the actual beholder from the front of the principal figure—Belisarius—whose exemplary obliviousness to being beheld was in that way made all the more secure. In fact by virtue of the same synecdoche, one might say that removing or displacing the beholder from in front of the principal figure went along way towards neutralizing the fact of his presence before the painting as a whole. (P. 150)

It is that "neutralization" that is the "supreme fiction" in Fried's analysis, and that in fact precipitates the actual viewer's absorption in the scene that excludes him. It is again perfectly parallel to what Diderot proposes for dramatic representation in the theater.

But the "blindness" or "indirection" represented by the soldier's synecdochal representation of the viewer has further consequences of significance here.

It is implicit in Diderot's observation that it is precisely the dominance of the figure of the soldier that makes the painting moral, by which I take him to mean that it is the viewer's conviction of the soldier's utterly concentrated and intense response to the sight of Belisarius [the sight of blindness, I would add] that establishes the hero's full identity and thus secures the moral meaning of the composition as a whole. The notion of absorption is also implicit in Diderot's statement that Belisarius' effect—which can only mean on the soldier—is exactly what it ought to be. . . .

I suggest that, in Diderot's view, that effect was achieved in and through the persuasive representation of absorption, above all the absorption of the figure of the soldier, who thus was felt to determine not just the expressive tenor and moral significance but also, more important, the ontological status of the painting as a whole. And of course Belisarius' blindness, which rendered him unaware of being beheld, at once set the stage for the soldier's absorption and could be perceived as an exemplary mode of obliviousness in its own right. (Pp. 148-49)

The "moral" quality of the painting is not in the subject of a good man's misfortune that it depicts. Rather, as always for Diderot, it results from a differential, representational space. The primacy of the soldier over Belisarius "made the painting moral" in Diderot's argument. But it is precisely his absorption that makes the soldier more interesting than Belisarius. And it is precipitated by Belisarius' own absorption in the form of blindness or obliviousness to those around him, cutting him off in the manner of a proscenium, placing him in a differentiated space, as if other, as if a spectacle. Indeed, as in Fried's felicitous phrase, Belisarius' blindness "sets the stage for the soldier's absorption." The soldier's own blind absorption, provoked by that of Belisarius, in turn precipitates the absorption of those who behold the engraving. (And Fried has found the theme of absorption to be a major one in the period and a frequent focus of Diderot's commentaries.)

Here Fried for an instant falls somewhat short of the implications of his own, very persuasive argument. For Diderot is expressing his thought quite straightforwardly when he asks, "Does not the figure of Belisarius achieve the effect that he must achieve? What does it matter if one loses sight of him?" Clearly one sees him the way one is supposed to see him *because* one "loses sight of him," *because* Belisarius' blindness is less a subject or content of Van Dyck's representation, less a depicted state than the representational, differential mark that alone makes painting affecting for Diderot. We lose sight of him as a simple mimetic presence on the canvas as he enters into a representational "rapport" with the soldier, who in turn enters into a similar relationship to the beholder, who is himself now marked by the same blindness-obliviousness that so often offers one up to spectacle in Diderot's writing.

Compare the following text from the *Entretien sur le fils naturel*, in which Dorval's obliviousness to, or unawareness of, his interlocutor has a similarly contagious effect.

> Dorval had been the first to arrive. I approached without his hearing me. He had given himself over to the spectacle of nature. His chest was expanded. He was breathing heavily. His attentive eyes focused every object. I followed on his face the diverse impressions he was experiencing, and I was beginning to share his rapture when I cried out, almost without wanting to, "He is under the spell."[5]

Whatever it is that makes nature into a representation, a "spectacle," communicates itself to Dorval, who becomes a spectacle himself for the narrator, and continues its contagious expansion to the narrator and perhaps even to the reader-viewer as well. Like Belisarius, the expansion of Dorval's theatrical "effect" is a witness to the contagion of the "obliviousness," "indirection," or "blindness" that makes representation.

NOTES

The following abbreviations will be used:

A.-T.: *Oeuvres complètes*, eds. Assézat and Tourneux, (Paris: Garnier, 1875).

CCE.: *Correspondance de Denis Diderot*, eds. Varloot and Proust (Paris: Minuit, 1955–).

D.P.V.: *Oeuvres complètes*, eds. Dieckmann, Varloot, and Proust (Paris: Hermann, 1975).

O.E.: *Oeuvres oesthétiques*, ed. Paul Vernière (Paris: Garnier, 1959).

O.Ph.: *Oeuvres philosophiques*, ed. Paul Vernière (Paris: Garnier, 1961).

O.R.: *Oeuvres romanesques*, ed. Henri Bénac (Paris: 1962).

All translations, unless otherwise indicated, are my own.

CHAPTER ONE

1. Henri Lefebvre, *La Présence et l'absence: contribution à la théorie des représentations* (Brussels: Castermann, 1980). All further page references will be given in the text.

2. *Les Mots est les choses* in English is entitled *The Order of Things*, translator not indicated (New York: Random House, 1970).

3. D'Alembert, *Oeuvres complètes* (hereafter *O.C.*) (Geneva: Slatkine Reprints, 1969), 1:44–46. All further page references will be given in the text.

4. *An Essay Concerning Human Understanding*, ed. Alexander C. Fraser (New York: Dover Publications, 1959), 1:171–72.

5. Ibid., pp. 172–73.

6. Jerry A. Fodor, *Representations: Philosophical Essays on the Foundations of Cognitive Science* (Cambridge, Mass.: M.I.T. Press, 1981), p. 203.

7. "The Phaedo," transl. B. Jowett, in *The Dialogues of Plato* (Oxford: Oxford University Press, 1926), 2:214–15.

8. Ibid., p. 215.

9. Ibid., p. 216. See Gilles Deleuze, *Logique du sens* (Paris: Minuit, 1969), pp. 341–61, for a superb summary of "mimesis" and "simulacrum" in Plato. Suffice it to say here that, in sum, I am trying to show that in

Plato there is a margin of simulacrum in all mimesis, that the mimetic that Plato approves is dependent upon the simulacrum that he wants to limit and control.

10. For a general treatment of the problem, see Richard Rorty, *Philosophy and the Mirror of Nature* (Princeton, N.J.: Princeton University Press, 1979). In this limited sense, the question of representation that I am trying to introduce here bears comparison to the unconscious and to ideology: the unconscious, which Freud said was eternal, despite the empirical historical specificity of its contents; to ideology, which Marx in *German Ideology* characterized as having no history. Cf. Louis Althusser, *Positions* (Paris: Editions Sociales, 1976), pp. 98–101.

CHAPTER TWO

1. Diderot, *Les Bijoux indiscrets, O.R.* All further page references will be given in the text.

2. Clearly then, there is already imperfection in the Edenic scene with which the novel opens, and the pure presence located at its origin is compromised even before the events that I shall analyze below. But it is nevertheless the case that the myth of that plenitude is invoked by Diderot, and for that purpose the "orientalist" setting—even if it is the "Congo"—is not without significance, even for the eighteenth century. Edward Said writes: "The Prophet is he who has completed a world-view; thus the word heresy in Arabic is synonymous with the verb 'to innovate' or 'to begin.' Islam views the world as a plenum, capable of neither diminishment nor amplification. Consequently, stories like those of *The Arabian Nights* are ornamental, variations on the world, not completions of it . . ." (*Beginnings* [New York: Basic Books, 1975], p. 81). (Arthur Wilson agrees that the Congo is here only a geographically confused rendition of the literary "Orient"; see his *Diderot* [New York: Oxford University Press, 1972], p. 735 n. 6.)

3. On the "imaginaire" see Lacan's "Mirror Stage" in *Ecrits* (New York: Norton Press, 1977), trans. Alan Sheridan, pp. 1–7; and "Aggression in Psychoanalysis," ibid., pp. 8–29. See also Laplanche and Pontalis, *Dictionnaire de la psychanalyse* (Paris: P.U.F., 1967), pp. 195–96.

4. Mirzoza's situation thus reveals itself to be surprisingly resonant with the worker's situation as now classically defined under capitalism. Work, once an experience lived in the immediate, is now measured and categorized, placed in alienating equivalences to things other: time, products, gold, and even the philosophical "concept" of work. As Henri Lefebvre has recently written, "The worker does not quite understand what is happening. He understands poorly and conceives only vaguely something like the *substitution*: the measure substituted for his activity. He believes he is receiving for his work the *equivalent* in money. . . . He is

inserted into an ensemble of *equivalences*, whose injustice is apparent to him, but whose logic he accepts" (*La Présence et l'absence: contribution à la théorie des représentations* [Brussels: Castermann, 1980], p. 30).

5. Jack Undank accurately captures what I would call the "sultanesque" thread in Diderot's writing when he comments, "In the beginning . . . was not metaphor, but those feelings of immediacy and relationship that metaphoric signs and representations sprang up to communicate—redemptively already looking behind, but with salvation necessarily in what they promised on ahead." (*Diderot: Inside, Outside, and In-Between* [Madison, Wisc.: Coda Press, 1979], p. 94) I think, however, that, as we shall see, *Les Bijoux indiscrets* is typical of Diderot's writing in that it presents such "immediacy" only as a necessary foil for something other.

6. See Michikazu Tamai, "Autour des *Bijoux indiscrets*: réflexions sur le rapport de Diderot avec ses oeuvres romanesques," *Etudes de langue et littérature françaises* 22 (1973): 61–72.

7. See David Adams, "Experiment and Experience in *Les Bijoux indiscrets*," *S.V.E.C.* 182:223–29. More to the point here, however, is Richard H. Brown's parallel understanding of the persistent ideal of so-called scientific language: "To report the facts objectively, the voice of science ideally must correspond to its objects in this one to one fashion. . . . The part of communication that cannot be reduced to pointer readings or mathematics is declared to be subjective and hence epistemologically invalid—a kind of symbol cloak beneath which reality remains hidden" (*Poetics for Sociology*, quoted by Elizabeth W. Bruss, *Beautiful Theories* [Baltimore: Johns Hopkins University Press, 1982], p. 35).

8. In a recent publication whose argument serves to extend this analysis, Elisabeth de Fontaney has written that for Diderot, "[woman] constitutes the ungraspable principle of difference" (*Diderot ou le matérialisme enchanté* [Paris: Grasset, 1981], p. 152).

9. See Bruss, *Beautiful Theories*, p. 131. In more philosophical language, one could also say that the sultan has understood the relation that Alexander Kojève describes between the gold of a ring and the hole/nothingness that gives it its identity (see the *Introduction à la lecture de Hegel* [Paris: Gallimard, 1947], p. 487n). Death is here the difference between being and nothingness that, according to Kojève's reading of Hegel, exists just as much as being itself, since "without it, if there were no difference between Being and Nothingness Being itself would not be" (p. 491).

10. *D.P.V.* 7:189–90.

11. As we saw in the preceding chapter, this is a major thesis in *The Order of Things* (New York: Pantheon Books, 1970). (All further page references will be given in the text.) See pages 46–47 for an example of the position in summary form.

12. See *The Order of Things*, pp. 86 ff., on the place of an *Encyclopedia* in the Classical episteme.

13. For an assessment of the place of taxonomy in contemporary discourse, see Bruss, *Beautiful Theories*, pp. 101–2: "The low esteem of

taxonomy in scientific circles," she summarizes, "is a reflection of the fact that it can organize information without otherwise illuminating or explaining it" (p. 101).

14. *The Order of Things*, pp. 217-387.

15. See the special issue of *Littérature* on "Métalangage" (No. 27, October 1977). Consider this elegantly simple explanation by Elizabeth Bruss, both defining the attraction of meta-language in general and aptly characterizing the procedures my reading of *Les Bijoux* sought to exemplify: "Recently, meta-languages have become models in a second sense as well, appropriated from their original domains to apply to new objects—narratives and myths, clothing and architecture, economic and psychological behavior—that are not, literally, languages or systems of logic. The transfer to a new domain results in a reinterpretation, turning the object under study into a kind of language at the same moment that its 'syntax' is being catalogued and explained. The popularity of these models twice-removed is due partly to the aptness of the categories and explanatory framework they offer, and partly to the very considerations that they exclude—the traditional literary concern for representational fidelity, moral assessment, relative aesthetic merit" (p. 96).

16. "We would prove to have been mistaken if we establish a theater [in Geneva], we will be wrong to let it continue, we will be wrong to curtail it: after the first mistake, we will have only bad choices left to make" (*Lettre à d'Alembert* [Paris: Garnier-Flammarion, 1967], p. 232). Although the *Deuxième discours* deals ostensibly with different issues, one can easily surmise that the broad problem of representation in all senses is common to both these texts. For, argues Rousseau, once there are "signes représentatifs des richesses," the unconscious wealth and beauty possessed as a gift of nature becomes an object of competition and semiotic pursuit, and thus, cause for strife. Once there was representation "it was necessary for one's advantage, to show oneself as other than what one in fact was. Being and seeming became two, quite different things" (*Oeuvres complètes* (Paris: Pléiade, 1964) ed. Gagnebin and Raymond, 3:174-75. In this *Discours*, Rousseau's famous analysis of mankind's "perfectibility" is entirely predicated on the regrettable effects of representation.

17. Culler's relation to the problem is quite different, of course, and yet he too lays claim to his own style of meta-representational space: "Since [works] participate in a variety of systems . . . critics can move through texts towards an understanding of the systems and semiotic processes that make them possible" (*The Pursuit of Signs* [Ithaca, N.Y.: Cornell University Press, 1981), p. 17.

18. Stanley Fish, *Is There a Text in This Class?: The Authority of Interpretive Communities* (Cambridge, Mass.: Harvard University Press, 1980).

19. This, in short, is the argument of Gerald Graff in *Literature against Itself* (Chicago: University of Chicago Press, 1979), for example, p. 170. Wayne Booth's *Rhetoric of Irony* (Chicago: University of Chicago Press, 1974) is another example of a similar project, namely, that of ac-

crediting a non-ironic critical grounds for measuring and controlling all irony.

20. Michel Foucault, *Will to Knowledge*, Vol. 1 of *History of Sexuality*, trans. Robert Hurley (New York: Vintage Books, 1979), p. 77. All further page references will be given in the text.

21. The question of the various words for *representation* ultimately would lead to the complex of issues consecrated by later German philosophy from Kant to Hegel to Heidegger (*Vorstellung, Darstellung,* etc.), which would lead us too far astray. See Henri Lefebvre's analysis, *La Présence,* pp. 32ff.

22. Of the many references to Derrida implied here, perhaps the most cogent is his seminal article "La Différance," in *Marges* (Paris: Minuit, 1972), pp. 1–29. For example, page 13: " 'Différance' is that which makes the movement of signification impossible unless each so-called 'present' element, appearing on the scene of presence, relates to something other than itself, keeping within itself the mark of the past element and allowing itself thus to be hollowed out by the mark of its link to the future element . . . constituting what we call the present by this very relation to what is not present: absolutely not present. . . . An interval must separate it from what is not present in order that the present be itself present. . . ."

23. Norman Bryson has discussed this notion of history in *Word and Image: French Painting of the Ancien Régime* (Cambridge: Cambridge University Press, 1981), pp. 35, 39, 40. See also Pierre Trotignon, "Réflexions métaphysiques sur le concept de représentation," *Revue des Sciences Humaines,* No. 154 (Spring 1974), pp. 195–201.

24. The tension I am here locating within Foucault's writing could be found between different contemporary theorists as well (for example, between Gadamer and Jameson): "It will become clear in the course of my subsequent discussion that a Marxian conception of our relationship to the past requires a sense of our radical difference from earlier cultures which is not adequately allowed for in Gadamer's influential notion of *Horizontverschmelzung* (fusion of horizons)" *The Political Unconscious* [Ithaca, N.Y.: Cornell University Press, 1981), p. 75 n. 56.

25. Since I shall be following a different path altogether, I should say a brief word here about René Girard's use of "representation" in his hypothesis of an original scapegoat that comes dialectically to represent the social unity that his expulsion and murder render possible. Neither for the Girard of *La Violence et le sacré* (Paris: Grasset, 1972) nor for his disciples (such as Eric Gans) does the efficacy of representation depend on its failure, as it paradoxically does for Mangogul-Diderot. For both Girard and Gans, the advent of representation coincides with transcendence of difference and the advent of a transcendental signifier that, as will become clear below, is incompatible with Diderot's experience of it. See Gan's *The Origin of Language: A Formal Theory of Representation* (Berkeley: University of California Press, 1981).

26. See my "Diderot and the Pleasure of the Other: Friends, Readers, and Posterity," *Eighteenth-Century Studies* 2 (Summer 1978): 439–56.

CHAPTER THREE

1. *O.E.*, pp. 391–456. All further page references will be given in the text. A necessary complement to the analysis that follows is Jacques Chouillet's discussion of Diderot's borrowings (and alterations) from Père André's *Essai sur le beau* (1741), in *La Formation des idées esthétiques de Diderot* (Paris: Armand Colin, 1973), pp. 265–73.

2. See Diderot's *Encyclopedia* article entitled "Pyrrhonienne," *D.P.V.*, vol. 7, and his *Pensées philosophiques* (nos. 30, 31, 24) in *O. Ph.*, pp. 27–29. See also Ernst Cassirer, *The Philosophy of the Enlightenment*, trans. F. C. A. Koelln and J. P. Pettegrave (Boston: Beacon Press, 1955), p. 117 ff.

3. In his *Oeuvres esthétiques* edition, Paul Vernière documents sources of the opposing theories that Diderot discards in the first section of his essay, most notably Plato (of whom more later), Père André, Wolff, Crousaz, Hutcheson and Shaftesbury.

4. See Cassirer, *The Philosophy of the Enlightenment* pp. 275–360, for a general discussion of Enlightenment aesthetics. See also Paul de Man, "The Resistance to Theory," *Yale French Studies*, No. 63 (1982), p. 8. Also helpful is Chouillet's *Esthétiques des lumières* (Paris: P.U.F., 1975).

5. Michel Foucault, *The Order of Things* (New York: Pantheon Books, 1970), p. 311. All further page references will be given in the text.

6. Diderot's use of "différence spécifique" is partly a reference to the old scholastic distinction between *differentia specifica*, that which defines an entity as a kind in itself, as against *genus proximum*, or "next genus above." For a discussion, see Cassirer, *The Philosophy of the Enlightenment*, p. 253 ff.

7. Diderot will later refer to the "differential" character of the beautiful in general as "rapports" (p. 428).

8. For a different view of the whole question of unity in multiplicity, see Cassirer, *The Philosophy of the Enlightenment*, p. 213 ff., and Chouillet, *Formation*, chap. 4, pp. 193–257.

9. Or, according to Foucault, "there can no longer be any signs except in the analysis of representations according to identities and differences. That is, all designation must be accomplished by means of a certain relation to all other possible designations. To know what properly appertains to one individual is to have before one the classification—or the possibility of classifying—all others. Identity and what marks it are defined by the differences that remain. An animal or a plant is not what is indicated—or betrayed—by the stigma that is to be found imprinted upon it; it is what the others are not; it exists in itself only insofar as it is bounded by what is distinguishable from it" (*The Order of Things*, pp. 144–45).

10. Diderot elaborates: "All these ideas [of "rapports"] come from the senses and are factitious; and we have progressed from the notion of a multitude of artificial and natural beings, arranged, proportioned, com-

bined, balanced, to the positive and *abstract notion* of order arrangement, proportion, combination relation, symmetry, and to the abstract and negative notion of disproportion, disorder and chaos" (p. 416; my emphasis). Cf. also in "Beau," p. 432, for an explicit definition of the intellectual operation called "abstraction."

11. Diderot recognizes this objectivity explicitly: "My mind [*entendement*] puts nothing into things and takes nothing out. Whether or not I am thinking of the Louvre's facade, all its component parts nevertheless have such and such a form and are arranged in such and such a fashion among themselves. Whether there be men or not, it is no less beautiful, but only for beings really possible and constituted like us in body and mind; because, for other creatures, it could well be neither beautiful nor ugly, or even ugly altogether. From which it follows that, although there is no absolute beauty, there are two kinds of beauty relative to us, a real and perceived beauty" (pp. 418–19).

12. Most succinctly in a letter to Sophie Volland: "A whole is beautiful only when it is one" (*CCE*, 2:208).

13. For sources, see, for example, Plato's "Sophist," 218d; *The Republic*, 383a; and numerous passages of Aristotle's *Poetics*.

14. As does the Abbé Batteux in his famous *Beaux-Arts réduits à un même principe* (Paris: Durand, 1746).

CHAPTER FOUR

1. For reasons that should become clear as this analysis develops, I am not respecting the traditional Aristotelean distinction of representation and imitation. As a justification in the immediate, I would refer to the new translation of the *Poetics* by R. Dupont-Roc and Jean Lallot (Paris: Seuil, 1980), in which "mimesis" is translated as "representation," and is thereby denied any particular link to theater. Thus understood, the epic poem and the dance represent as fully as do plays. On this point see Francois Rigault, "Nouvelle lecture de la poétique," in *L'Ane* 1 (April-May 1981): 5, 58.

2. *Essais sur la peinture*, ed. Roland Desné (Paris: Editions Sociales, 1955), p. 63. Further page references will be given in the text. Translation of "l'image d'un *sentiment*" necessarily truncates the complex resonances in French, essential to the word's eighteenth-century connotations especially: sentiment, feeling, perception, awareness. Materialism as a philosophical movement is predicated on a notion of generalized "sentience," as in the famous formulation from the *Rêve de d'Alembert*, "Il faut que la pierre sente."

3. "There is no felt pleasure that is unreal [*chimérique*]; the imaginary invalid is really invalid. The man who believes he is happy is happy" (*Lettres à Falconet, A.-T.*, 18:88). This invites reference to the Platonic canon

with which, in such moments, Diderot breaks quite abruptly. Cf. the "Philebus," especially 34c–55d.

4. Compare to simpler forms of the same logic that emerge in other texts, for example, in the *Entretiens sur le fils naturel, A.-T.* 7:154–55.

5. For many resonances in another, but related, analysis, see Paul de Man's *Allegories of Reading* (New Haven, Conn.: Yale University Press, 1979), on Rousseau's *Pygmalion,* pp. 160–87: "Valère . . . could just as well be in love with difference as resemblance; resemblance is 'loved' because it can be interpreted as identity as well as difference and is therefore unseizable, forever in flight" (p. 168).

6. A similar logic is to be found in the *Eloge de Richardson,* in which Diderot describes the experience "inside" Richardson's *Clarissa* in terms not unlike experience inside the temple in the present essay. He addresses the English novelist in these resonant terms: "Coming away from reading you [*Au sortir de ta lecture*], I was the same as a man at the end of a day spent doing good. . . . I had become a spectator of a multitude of incidents, I felt that I had acquired experience" (*O.E.,* p. 30).

7. For a clear idea of the extent to which Diderot's analysis can be seen to differ widely from Rousseau's attitudes concerning these and similar issues, see Jacques Derrida, *De la grammatologie* (Paris: Minuit, 1967), pp. 290, 296, 303.

8. As Diderot writes in the later *Salon de 1769* about the faces painted by Raphael, "although they may not exist anywhere in reality, it seems all the same that one has always seen them . . ." (*A.-T.,* 11:413).

9. Compare to Lévi-Strauss's logic in his "Introduction à l'oeuvre de Marcel Mauss": "Following a transformation that it is not the task of the social sciences but of biology and psychology to study, a passage took place between a stage at which nothing had meaning, to another at which everything had meaning." And later: "The universe signified well before we began to know what it signified; doubtless, that goes without saying. But from the preceding analysis, we can also conclude that it signified, from the outset, the totality of what humanity can expect to know of it" (in Marcel Mauss, *Sociologie et anthropologie* [Paris: Presses Universitaires de France, 1950], pp. xlvii–xlviii; my emphasis).

10. See below, chap. 9, p. 000.

11. "Philebus," 39b–39c, in *Plato* (Cambridge, Mass.: Harvard University Press, 1592), trans. W. R. M. Lamb and H. N. Fowler, 3:301. In Derrida's *La Dissémination* Paris: Seuil, 1971), p. 215, one finds the following characterization of this Platonic ideology: "The painter who works after [*d'après*] the writer, copying him [*d'après lui*], the worker who comes along behind him, can, precisely by an exercise of analysis, of separation and reduction, purify the pictoral, imitative and imaginal essence of thought. The painter is thereby able to restore the bare image of the thing, just as it lends itself to intuition, to sight, in the intelligibility of its *eidos* or the palpability of its *oration.* It strips it of everything added on by language, of the envelope around the kernel, the epidermal tissue."

12. As Elizabeth Bruss writes, "Thus the paradox—and the threat to those who would prefer their implements of thought less slippery and

less often double-edged—of figures is that they can die into a perfectly literal afterlife" (*Beautiful Theories* [Baltimore: John Hopkins University Press, 1982], p. 56).

CHAPTER FIVE

1. Jacques Chouillet, *La Formation des idées esthétiques de Diderot* (Paris: Armand Colin, 1973); and more recently see his *Diderot* (Paris: S.E.D.E.S., 1977); Lester Crocker, *Diderot's Chaotic Order* (Princeton, N.J.: Princeton University Press, 1974.

2. *Republic*, bks. 3 and 10; *Sophist*, to mention only two.

3. For a full discussion of sources and antecedents, see Chouillet's *Formation*, pp. 481–89; and more generally his *L'Esthétique des lumières* (Paris: P.U.F., 1975).

4. *O.E.*, p. 277.

5. Chouillet, *Formation*, p. 479. All further page references will be given in the text.

6. See *La Dissémination* (Paris: Seuil, 1972), p. 216 n. 2.

7. Note the difference of Diderot's notion of theatrical impact and Aristotle's emphasis on catharsis through identification in the *Poetics*.

8. This notion was amplified earlier in the *Lettre sur les aveugles* (*A.T.* 7:329; *O.E.*, p. 213): "If nature never combined events in an extraordinary manner, everything the poet imagines beyond simple, cold uniformity of common things would be unbelievable. But that is not the way it is. So what does the poet do? He seizes upon these extraordinary combinations or he imagines similar ones."

9. Cf. Aristotle's very different position in the *Poetics*, 1460a26.

10. In *Rêve de d'Alembert* (1769), he will write: "Imagination is the memory of form and colors. The spectacle of a scene, of an object, necessarily winds up [*monte*] the sensate instrument in a certain manner; it then rewinds itself by itself, or is rewound by some external cause. Then it quivers inside or resonates outside; it records for itself in silence the impressions that it has received, or it causes them to burst forth by conventional sounds [i.e., language]" (*O. Ph.*, p. 367).

11. The diacritical "rapport" of justice and injustice brings with it the baggage of differential relations at the heart of the essay on "Expression" and the article "Beau." (See also the *Apologie de l'Abbé de Prades*, *D.P.V.*, 4:352–54.)

12. The contrast between styles of contrast is an important one for Diderot. In the *Essais sur le peinture*, seven years later, he will repeat the same argument relative to painting: "Contrast poorly understood is one of the most deadly causes of mannerism. There is no true contrast except that which springs from the essence of action, or from the diversity either of bodily parts or of interest. Look at Raphael, Le Sueur; they sometimes

place three, four, five figures standing next to each other, and the effect is sublime" (p. 40; *A.-T.*, 10:466; my emphasis).

13. I shall merely signal the multiple connections between the problem of the "empreinte" so basic to any reading of these texts, and Derrida's readings of "writing" and the "trace" in Rousseau and others in *De la grammatologie* (Paris: Minuit, 1967), pp. 135–59.

14. As Paul de Man shows in his reading of the related *Second Discourse* in *Allegories of Reading* (New Haven, Conn.: Yale University Press, 1979).

15. *Discours sur l'origine et les fondements de l'inégalité parmi les hommes*, in J.-J. Rousseau, *Oeuvres complètes*, ed. Bernard Gagnebin and Marcel Raymond (Paris: Gallimard, Bibliothèque de la Pléiade, 1964), 3:155. All further page references will be given in the text. All further references to the works of Rousseau are to this edition.

16. In the *Contrat social*, for example: "All institutions that put man in contradiction with himself are worth nothing" (3:464), and that is exactly what happens to wicked men at the theater when they identify with the misfortunes represented on the stage.

17. See de Man for a discussion of other pertinent terms, such as "judgment" (*Allegories of Reading*, p. 242).

18. Quoted and translated by de Man, ibid., p. 222.

19. Diderot thereby situates Ariste in the grand philosophical tradition, both explicitly and through the Platonic scene that is replayed when Ariste finds that his interlocutors are absent. Explicitly through the following remark: "The cloak of a former philosopher was virtually the only thing he lacked for his status as philosopher to be complete" (p. 282). Here is the Platonic scene that Ariste is implicitly repeating: In the "Philebus," Socrates describes a man who is trying to identify an object that he can perceive only dimly and at a distance.

SOCRATES: And if someone is with him, he might repeat aloud to his companion what he had said to himself, and thus that which we called opinion [*doxa*] now becomes a statement [*logos*]? PROTARCHUS: Certainly. SOCRATES: But if he is alone when he has this thought, he sometimes carries it about in his mind for a long time. PROTARCHUS: Undoubtedly. . . . SOCRATES: I think the soul at such a time is like a book. PROTARCHUS: How is that? SOCRATES: Memory unites with the senses, and they and the feelings which are connected with them seem to me almost to write in words in our souls; and when the feeling in question writes the truth, true opinions and true statements are produced in us; but when the writer within us writes falsehoods, the resulting opinions and statements are the opposite of true." (38e–39a in *Plato*, 3:299–301.)

Even in thinking in complete solitude, like Ariste severed from his interlocutors and thus from the *Logos*, Plato maintains that thoughts can be, and are, measured in relation to standards of absolute Ideality. (See Derrida's analysis in "La Double Séance," in *La Dissémination*, p. 211.) As we shall see, the same cannot be said of Diderot-Ariste.

20. "We can be assured that the simple ideas that a single object excites in different people are as different as the likes and dislikes they are found to have. It is even a truth about perception [*sentiment*]. It is no more unusual for several people to differ among themselves in the same moment relative to the same simple ideas, than for the same man to differ from himself in different moments. Our senses are in continual vicissitude" ("Beau," *O.E.*, p. 433).

21. Elizabeth Bruss has recently formulated an analogous insight in her study of contemporary theoretical practices: "The new respect for theory comes from recognizing that one cannot extract a framework directly from the data, but must already have some framework to establish which data are relevant and which are not" (*Beautiful Theories* [Baltimore: Johns Hopkins University Press, 1982], p. 35). "Lack" then provides the negative, the critical grounds, the framework, for the ideal model. Just as human "défaut" provides the theoretical model for God in Descartes's *Discours de la méthode*, pt. 4. (See below, chap. 10 n. 12.)

22. Louis Marin, "Disneyland: A Degenerate Utopia," *Glyph I*, 1977, p. 53.

23. Bruss, *Beautiful Theories*, p. 90.

24. *Salon de 1767, A.-T.*, vol. 11. All further page references will be given in the text.

25. Yet the reference to Plato is unmistakable: see "Phaedo," 74d; 75a-b, for example. The "bed argument" in the *Republic* (bk. 10, 597-bff.) is clearly repeated here, at least in form. Diderot again invokes classical models only to alter them.

26. See W. J. Verdenius, *Mimesis* (Leiden: Brill, 1962), pp. 14–16, 40–41; and Norman Bryson, *Word and Image: French Painting in the Ancien Régime* (Cambridge: Cambridge University Press, 1981).

27. In his analysis of Rousseau's *Pygmalion*, Paul de Man writes: "The general model is not a combination of miscellaneous traits (as if Galathea were an amalgamation of the various invidual women that animated Rousseau's erotic reveries), but the attraction of the individual stems from its resemblance to a prior general model that is, in fact, an emanation of the beautiful and desirable. Aesthetic generality is the precondition for resemblance which also means that it is constitutive of metaphor" (*Allegories of Reading*, p. 183). On this and most other points, the present reading is in opposition to the analyses of Yvon Bélaval in his *Esthétique sans paradoxe de Diderot* (Paris: Gallimard, 1950), who at times (especially pp. 93ff.) seems to repeat the fundamental misunderstanding perpetrated by Grimm (and reproduced by Belaval [p. 101]) in the *Cooréspondance littéraire* of 1 August 1760: "*Monsieur Diderot has treated the same subject at the end of his treatise De la poésie dramatique.* He creates for himself an ideal model from beauty found scattered throughout nature, whose parts he gathers in order to form an ensemble to which he later refers his judgments of art works."

CHAPTER SIX

1. "We should at least recognize that . . . the *Entretiens sur le fils naturel* had more consequences than the *Préface de Cromwell*" (Paul Vernière, *O.E.*, p. 3). Vernière also cites (p. 149 n. 1) apparently direct borrowings in Beaumarchais's 1767 *Essai sur le genre dramatique sérieux.*

2. Jacques Chouillet, *La Formation des idées esthétiques de Diderot* Paris: Armand Colin, 1973), p. 457.

3. *Le Fils naturel*, in *D.P.V.*, 10:55. All further page references will be given in the text.

4. Anne-Marie Chouillet addresses the issue in her introduction to *Le Fils naturel.* After quoting Diderot's call for a theater that brings terror to the hearts of the audience, she comments: "These words are strong. If a doubt were permitted, it would bear less on the choice of means proposed by Diderot, than on the imbalance of a program in which we see so much force, enthusiasm and extremism on one side, and, dare I say, so much timidity on the other" (*D.P.V.*, 10:xvi).

5. "You might still say to me that the orator, the preacher lose themselves [*paie de leur personne*] just as the actor does. The difference is very great. When the orator presents himself, it is in order to speak, and not to offer himself as a spectacle; he is representing only himself, he plays only his own role, speaks only in his own name, and is saying, or should be saying only what he really thinks; since the man and the role are the same being, he is in his place [*à sa place*] . . ." (*Lettre à d'Alembert*, ed. Michel Launay [Paris: Garnier Flammarion, 1967], pp. 164–65).

6. Diderot, *O.E.*, pp. 285–86.

7. As Diderot writes in *De la poésie dramatique*: "The more one expands one's knowledge, the greater and more rigorous the ideal model will become"; and again, once the ideal model has been conceived, its destiny is to be constantly changed or "re-modeled": "But once I have it . . . what use shall I make of this deal model? . . . I shall modify it according to circumstances. That is the second project to which I shall have to dedicate myself" (*O.E.*, p. 286).

8. To be precise, Dorval is only Rosalie's half-brother, Lysimond's bastard son (thus the play's title). Their desire for each other is nevertheless incestuous. This is also Jack Undank's view of the meaning of incest in this play: "It is not only the case, as Palissot noticed, that the author (Dorval) is also the subject and protagonist of his own play, but also that this self-propagation—repetitious overlappings of the same—is echoed and figured in the incestuous or narcissistic relationship of the characters" (*Diderot: Inside, Outside, and In-Between* [Madison, Wisc.: Coda Press, 1979], p. 99). Undank's chapters are the best texts I know on *Le Fils naturel* and its *Entretiens* (see his pp. 95–109). Our analyses of the play run a parallel course until it comes time to account for the relation between the play and the *Entretiens*. Undank's conclusion takes rather

more literally the natural and undifferentiated "inside" represented in the play by Dorval's incestuous, familial enclosure (see his p. 106).

9. J. Chouillet makes this same point (*Formation des idées esthetiques*, p. 461).

10. "In the mimetic art of antiquity, the instability of fortune almost always appears as a fate which strikes from without and affects only a limited area, not as a fate which results from inner processes of the real, historical world" (Eric Auerbach, *Mimesis*, trans. W. R. Trask [Princeton, N.J.: Princeton University Press, 1953], p. 29).

11. Sophocles, *Oedipus Rex*, trans. D. Fitts and R. Fitzgerald (New York: Harcourt, Brace, 1939), p. 49.

12. In an analysis that nicely complements my own, Roger Lewinter rightly pegs Constance's relation to virtue as purely narcissistic: "Constance is drunk on virtue, her sole sensuality [*volupté*]. And in the final analysis, the adoration of virtue brings her back to herself, since it is she who practices virtue. To adore virtue to such an extent is tantamount to adoring herself, to adoring the image of the virtuous ego who practices virtue more than virtue itself . . ." (L'Exaltation de la vertue dans le théâtre de Diderot," *Diderot Studies* 8 [1966]: 14).

13. A psychoanalytic reading, which this play demands and which I shall only adumbrate at the conclusion of this chapter, would have to account for the absence of a concrete representation of the mother and her concomitant omnipresence. Here, virtue is a maternal presence, "giving birth" to a nontransgressive love.

14. "On Narcissism: An Introduction," *The Complete Works of Sigmund Freud*, ed. J. Strachey (London: Hogarth, 1953; rpt. 1978).

15. Jeffrey Mehlman has written, "The message that is transmitted in Dorval's annual ritual is thus the prohibition of incest." And later, "*Le Fils naturel* increasingly begins to take on the appearance of a mawkish version of *Totem and Taboo*" (*Cataract: A Study in Diderot* [Middletown, Conn.: Wesleyan University Press, 1979], p. 35).

16. It will be recalled that in the *Salon de 1767*, Diderot distinguishes repeatedly between the "primary image" and "a portrait or a copy of a copy . . . the phantom and not the thing." (*A.-T.*, 10:9.)

17. Philippe Lacoue-Labarthe writes, in "Diderot, le paradoxe et la mimésis" (*Poétique* 43:277): "At whatever level you take it—in the copy or the reproduction in the actor's art, in mimicry, disguise, dialogical writing—the rule is always the same: the more it resembles, the more it differs. The same, in its sameness, is the self-same other, which in turn cannot be called 'same,' and so on *ad infinitum*."

18. Cf. Aristotle's *Poetics*, 1448b: "Imitation is natural to man from childhood . . . he is the most imitative creature in the world, and learns at first by imitation" (*The Basic Works of Aristotle*, trans. Ingram Bywater [New York: Random House, 1945]). Diderot passes on this Aristotelean commonplace, but as usual, alters its classical import by privileging virtue over other mimetic objects, and by the context in which Constance's message is enunciated. The nature of that context, as it will

be clarified below, suggests that Diderot's relation to Aristotelean mimesis is not that of the simple disciple.

19. Something of the underlying significance of these tensions, with their appearance and (for the moment) their odd disappearance in Diderot's writings, are broadly suggested in a resonant text by Paul de Man. The passage from the classical to the romantic "is generally understood as the passage from mimetic to a genetic concept of art and literature, from a Platonic to a Hegelian model of the universe. Instead of being mere copies of a transcendental order, *Nature or God*, 'all things below' are said to be part of a chain of being underway to its teleological end. The hierarchical world of Ideas and Images of ideas becomes a world of means moving towards an end and ordered in the prospective temporality of a genetic movement" (*Allegories of Reading* [New Haven, Conn.: Yale University Press, 1979], pp. 79–80).

20. Some examples from *De la poésie dramatique*: "There is nothing sacred for the poet, not even virtue upon which he will heap ridicule if the character and the situation demand it" (*O.E.*, p. 252). Or again: "One must present virtue on the stage "without hindering the violent and rapid course of dramatic action" (p. 197).

21. These are the words of Anne-Marie Chouillet. (See n. 4, above.)

CHAPTER SEVEN

1. *Traité de l'âme* (1745), quoted by E. Cassirer, *The Philosophy of the Enlightenment*, trans. F. C. A. Keolln and J. Pettegrove (Boston: Beacon Press, 1955), p. 67.

2. In the *Paradoxe* Diderot has "Le Second" raise precisely this argument against the notion of the ideal model. "But since it is ideal, it doesn't exist: and as we know, there is nothing in the understanding that wasn't first in the sensations" (*O.E.*, p. 339). For another instance of Diderot's ratification of this fundamental principle, see the *Suite de l'Apologie de l'Abbé de Prades*, *D.P.V.*, 4:352.

3. See Richard Rorty, *Philosophy and the Mirror of Nature* (Princeton, N.J.: Princeton University Press, 1979), pp. 131–64, for a discussion.

4. This is fundamental to virtually all definitions of "Enlightenment" *per se*, and especially of intellectual-historical definitions. See, for example, Cassirer, *The Philosophy of the Enlightenment*, or Hegel's *Phenomenology of Mind*, trans. J. B. Baillie (New York: Harper Torchbooks, 1966), pp. 559–98.

5. "White Mythology," in *New Literary History*, vol. 6, no. 1 (1974), p. 29. All further page references will be given in the text.

6. *Republic*, bk. 7, 516-a: "When he approaches the light [of the sun] his eyes will be dazzled, and he will not be able to see anything at all of what we now called reality." Note the continuation of the same metaphor in Descartes's third Meditation: "It seems to me right to . . . contem-

plate God himself . . . the beauty of this light so resplendent, at least as far as the strength of my mind, which is in some measure dazzled by the sight, will allow me to do so" (quoted by Derrida, *White Mythology*, p. 70).

7. Commentators as diverse as Franco Venturi and Paul de Man give further evidence of the persistence of the same metaphor. The nineteenth century (specifically, Croce) erroneously saw the eighteenth century as having "groped in the dark or else undergone the blinding of a false light" (Venturi, *Jeunesse de Diderot* [Paris: Skira, 1939], p. 239). De Man talks of a reader who "has to undo the explicit results of a vision that is able to move toward the light only because, being already blind, it does not have to fear the power of this light. But the vision is unable to report correctly what it has perceived in the course of its journey" (*Blindness and Insight* [New York: Oxford University Press, 1971], p. 106).

8. Quoted by Cassirer, *The Philosophy of the Enlightenment*, p. 67.

9. One need only recall the set of issues so organized in Starobinski's classic *Jean-Jacques Rousseau, la transparence et l'obstacle* (Paris: Gallimard, 1971).

10. *La Promenade du sceptique*. D.P.V. 2:78. I cite this example rather than other, frequently mentioned works in which Diderot specifically invokes Plato's cave allegory. For being implicit, the reference here is no less precise. In the *Republic* (bk. 7, 515-e), we read, "And if he is compelled to look straight at the light, will he not have a pain in his eyes which will make him turn away to take refuge in the objects of vision which he can see, and which he will conceive to be in reality clearer than the things which are not being shown to him?"

11. Rorty, *Philosophy and the Mirror of Nature*, p. 45.

12. Quoted by Cassirer, *The Philosophy of the Enlightenment*, p. 56.

13. *D.P.V.*, 7:210.

14. See Rorty, *Philosophy and the Mirror of Nature*, pp. 132 ff.

15. Cassirer, *The Philosophy of the Enlightenment*, p. 98. In this regard see also his chapter 3, "Psychology and Epistemology."

16. Rorty, *Philosophy and the Mirror of Nature*, p. 140.

17. Ibid., p. 136.

18. For Foucault the representational model is simply given in the epistemic break with the Renaissance, and can be recognized as the organizing principle of knowledge in the seventeenth and eighteenth centuries. Rorty is interested in a more conventional historical account of the particular philosophical articulation which gave rise to (which "caused" in some sense) the problem of representation that, as a result, epistemology rose to resolve.

19. An interesting digression that I forgo in the interest of economy would be the relation of this philosophical issue to the so called "rehearsal plays" that flourished particularly in England during the first two thirds of the century. It seems to me that much of this sub-genre could be understood as symptomatic of a desire to achieve precisely what is designated in the title of one of Garrick's better-known plays of this type, *A Peek Behind the Curtain.*

20. One has only to think of Diderot's pointing out Batteux's blind spot in reducing all art to simple imitation of "la belle nature" without ever feeling called upon to define a "Beautiful" as opposed to any other variety of "nature" (In *Les Beaux Arts réduits à un seul principe*, 1746).

21. In the *Encyclopedia* article entitled "Encyclopédie" (*D.P.V.*, 7:174–262). See chap. 10, below.

22. Jacques Chouillet makes an astute remark that bears on this propensity in Diderot: "At every moment, Diderot behaves as someone who does not want to lose his attachments to the philosophy of 'enllghtenment [*des lumières*],' but for whom the exploration of the 'shadows of the cave' constitutes the essential tack of the critic" (*La Formation des idées esthétiques*, p. 190).

23. *De l'interprétation de la nature* (1753), *O. Ph*, p. 220.

24. *Réfutation d'Helvetius* (1773–75) *O. Ph.*, p. 585. See also p. 606 of the same work, and in the *Rêve de d'Alembert*, *O. Ph.*, pp. 306, 330, passim.

25. It will become increasingly obvious in this chapter that once again I part ways with those authors who have understood the theme of unity ("l'unité de l'esprit" especially) to be the keystone of Diderot's vision of human kind in its actual state. "Unity" functions in his writing as an ideal desideratum that is much more often portrayed as suspended or abstracted than it is celebrated as an achievement. As the most massive recent example of the opposing view, see Chouillet's *Formation des idées esthétiques*, especially pp. 193–257.

26. *Réfutation d'Helvetius, O. Ph.*, p. 612.

27. The term "truchement" recurs on several occasions, e.g., in the *Réfutation d'Helvetius* (p. 583), or in the *Salon de 1767, A.-T.*, 11:146). Before the passage from the *Réfutation d'Helvetius* quoted above, Diderot is presenting this thought in dialogue form, with one voice claiming that the head is like a book which we cannot judge by its cover: "I would open heads in vain, I couldn't read anything inside them," he maintains. The response is telling: "And why would you read in them? The alphabet of this living book is not yet known to you, and perhaps will never be known to you; and yet, that's where the depositions of the five witnesses [i.e., the senses] are consigned, combined, compared and confronted" (p. 584). Again, the central agency exists, but is not perceptible or knowable as an epistemological positivity. This is a constant feature of Diderot's treatment of epistemological issues. (See chap. 10, below.)

28. In Foucault's analysis, there were only positivities that were to be represented on the absolute table or grid of representational correspondences, according to their categorical similarities and differences.

29. *Rameau's Nephew*, trans. L. W. Tancock (Middlesex, England: Penguin Books, 1966), p. 93. See my "Never de Rameau: The 'Diary' of a Reading,' *MLN* 95 (1980): 995–1004. Hegel's analysis of *Le Neveu* is unsurpassed in this regard. See *The Phenomenology of Mind*, trans. J. B. Baillie (New York: Harper Torchbooks, 1967), p. 543–45, or indeed the entire section entitled "The World of Spirit in Self-Estrangement," pp. 509–58.

30. *Rêve de d'Alembert, O. Ph.*, pp. 330–31. Again, one is reminded of the pure, abstract agency of Rameau's nephew who, although "nothing" in himself, agitates and prods others in society: "He causes approbation or blame; he makes the truth to emerge [*il fait approuver ou blamer; il fait sortir la vérité*]" (*Le Neveu de Rameau,* p. 35).

31. Contrast the metaphorics of such texts by Diderot with a representative text from the *Logique de Port-Royal*: "Just as there is no need of marks to distinguish light from darkness, except for light itself which makes itself felt, so also there is no need of other marks to recognize truth except for clarity itself which surrounds truth and which . . . persuades the mind in spite of itself [*malgré qu'il en ait*]" (ed. P. Clair and F. Girbal [Paris: P. U. F., 1965], p. 20).

32. *A.T.,* 11:146.

33. In Cassirer's terms, "The investigation of the individual problems in all their abundance and apparent dispersion comes back again and again" to this question (*The Philosophy of the Enlightenment,* p. 108).

34. *An Essay Concerning Human Understanding,* ed. A. C. Frazer (New York: Dover, 1959), part one, pp. 186–87.

35. For example, see Condillac's *Essai sur l'origine des connaissances humaines* (Paris: Galilée, 1973), pp. 188–90, which also includes a quote from Voltaire and an analysis by Condillac of the experiment's inconclusiveness.

36. Chouillet (*Formation des idées esthetique,* pp. 139–46) lists some twenty-five references to other works that take up the question. See also Robert Niklaus's annotations in his edition of the *Lettre* for *D.P.V.,* 4:87 n. 78; and still others by Paul Vernière in *O. Ph.,* pp. 75–76. Also helpful is Andrea Barnabei, "Il cieco di Molyneux: Un problema di percezione visiva nella Francia illuminista (1731–1754)," *Rivista Critica della Storia di Filosofia,* 30 (1976); pp. 132–66. Franco Venturi has provided a useful caveat concerning work in this field. He considers Molyneaux's question to have been too frequently only "an abstraction that different significations fill in one after the other," depending upon the particular interests of each author (*Jeunesse de Diderot,* p. 277).

37. *Lettre sur les aveugles, D.P.V.,* 4:63. All further references will be given by page number in the text.

38. For example: "But from the fact that our sense are not in contradiction with each other concerning forms, does it follow that forms are better known to us? Who has told us that we aren't dealing with false witnesses?" (p. 72) But even given a perfect and reliable sensorial apparatus, many questions remain, and Diderot is well aware of them all. Just how does the accurate but different information from five different sources combine to produce unified mental operations? (See also pp. 159–60.) More basically still, how are the senses as a whole represented in rationality and then in language? See Chouillet (*Formation des idées esthetiques,* p. 476) on the intermediary role of imagination, for a different line of inquiry.

39. Jeffrey Mehlman, *Cataract: A Study in Diderot* (Middletown, Conn.: Wesleyan University Press, 1979) p. 13.

40. Diderot, *Inside, Outside, and In-Between*, p. 69.

41. See Elizabeth Bruss's discussion of the "Economic" metaphor in contemporary critical discourse in *Beautiful Theories* (Baltimore: Johns Hopkins University Press, 1982), pp. 124–28. Particularly pertinent here is her contention that "the economy of theoretical discourse is, then, a system for the production and distribution of attention; it establishes what we usually think of as the 'themes' of the text, which are made up of the interplay of its own various levels and what passes from this text to others" (p. 124). The transmissive function of Diderot's interest in a certain "blindness" will become increasingly manifest as our analysis continues.

42. And on page 48 we read, "For what was this Tiresias who had read the secrets of the gods . . . if not a blind philosopher . . . ?"

43. See Paul de Man, "The Epistemology of Metaphor," in *New Literary History* 5 (Autumn, 1978): 13–30.

44. The phrase is Chouillet's, *Formation des idées esthetique*, p. 132. See also Arthur Wilson's *Diderot* (New York: Oxford University Press, 1972), pp. 97–100, for a nice account of the various intrigues at play in the episode and their probable relation to Diderot's imprisonment at Vincennes.

45. In her sometimes unreliable memoirs, Angélique Diderot suggests that her father was in fact present at the crucial experiment, but that it was obvious that the patient had been coached in advance (*A.-T.*, 1:xliii). If this is true, the fact serves the present argument quite well. For, in that case, why is Diderot prompted to discuss the issue underlying an experiment he saw performed as if he had been absent? The rhetorical-philosophical necessity for "blindness" would become all the more evident for being contrary to his actual experience.

46. *D.P.V.*, 7:547. See "White Mythology," p. 51, in which Derrida quotes Aristotle's Topics: "Every object of sensation, when it passes outside the range of sensation, becomes obscure; for it is not clear whether it still exists, because it is comprehended only by sensation."

47. See Wilson, *Diderot*, p. 97.

48. In *Beautiful Theories*, Elizabeth Bruss offers a generalization that is pertinent here: "When only seeing is believing and perceptual knowledge is esteemed more certain than inferential knowledge, theoretical discourse (indeed discourse of all kind) is devalued, reduced to an ancillary device for summarizing past observations and calculating the likely outcome of future observations" (p. 35). Against this backdrop Diderot's procedures in the *Lettre sur les aveugles* show up clearly as, on the contrary, a mode of insisting on the necessary conjunction of perceptual immediacy and its other. Discourse springs up at that conjunction and is in no way secondary to perception.

49. As a counter example of philosophical "blindness" as a simple negative, consider Buffon: "Far from being discouraged, the philosopher should applaud nature at the very moment she appears miserly and mysterious towards him, and be happy that to the degree he lifts a part of her veil she allows him to glimpse an immense quantity of other objects that

are all worthy of his research" (quoted by J. Roger, *Les Sciences de la vie dans la pensée française au XVIIIe siècle* [Paris: A. Colin, 1963], p. 565). The veil itself is interesting to Buffon only insofar as it can be lifted. It is clear that for him nature's hidden riches are in no way produced by the veil.

50. Although hardly necessary, I must underscore my complete divergence from the grounding assumptions of J.-P. Séguin's recent *Diderot, le discours et les choses* (Paris: Klincksieck, 1978). Séguin's main point is that Diderot's discourse is not based on figures.

51. *D.P.V.*, 7:189.

52. Franco Venturi is correct, as he so often is, when he notes that in this article, "The artistic and poetic side of language is left aside" (*Jeunesse de Diderot*, p. 260). He is also short of the mark, however, because in the article "Encyclopédie," just as in the two *Letters*, representational adequacy is only the backdrop for the transforming power of all representation. (See the following chapter.) In *Les Mots et les choses* (p. 102), Foucault quotes this passage as an indication of language's ability to contain all knowledge in the representational mode of the Classical "episteme." In this he has taken only half of what Diderot has to say about language and left aside language's inherent inadequacy.

53. For a concise account of such eighteenth-century versions of the "synesthesia" to come with Baudelaire and Nodier (as well as numerous other concerns pertinent to the present study), see Gérard Genette, "Peinture et dérivation," in *Mimologiques, voyage en Cratylie* (Paris: Sueil, 1976), pp. 85–118, especially pp. 99–100.

54. In the *Salon de 1767* (*A.-T.*, 11:130–39), Diderot will further expand the notion of a severance between ideas and words in a lengthy section of dialogue from which I quote only the conclusion: "It is the variety of accents that makes up for the dearth of words [*supplée à la disette des mots*], and which abolishes the identities that are so frequent among [linguistic] effects produced by the same cause" (p. 135).

55. Source cited above, n. 23.

CHAPTER EIGHT

1. *The Dictionnaire étymologique de la langue française*, 5th ed. (Paris: P.U.F., 1968), says of the word "disette," in part: "Perhaps derived from the verb *dire* in the sense it has in expressions such as *trouver à dire*, 'to regret the absence of something. . . .' "

2. *Lettre sur les sourds et muets*, *D.P.V.*, 2:142. All further page references will be given in the text. In this text there are other analogies and resonances with putting out one's eye "in order to know better how vision is achieved" from the *Lettre sur les aveugles*. For example, Diderot's stopping up his ears in order better to gauge the efficacity of acting on the stage (p. 148), the "muet de convention" who refuses to speak so as to know how one orders signs naturally (p. 138), and so forth.

3. It may be possible here to lay to rest a question wrongly understood by commentators concerning one of the most quoted lines of this text: "But I leave this figurative language . . . and return to the tone of Philosophy *à qui il faut des raisons et non des comparaisons.*" This last phrase, italicized by Diderot, is usually understood to mean that philosophy "needs reasons and not similes," literal language and not rhetoric. And, of course, as I have maintained all along, Diderot was situated squarely within the traditions of philosophy that could prompt him to adopt just such an attitude. But the text also deconstructs the philosophical certitudes that it proffers. Philosophy is also shown to proceed as did the deaf-mute when faced with Father Castel's harpsichord, and as did the blind man when required to define the mirror: that is, by metaphor and analogy. When this passage is read within that network, one suspects that the reason the key phrase is italicized by Diderot is to alert us to its problematic nature. For the word that Diderot consistently uses to describe mental operations carried out upon the data derived from different senses is "comparaison." There is no difference between this basic philosophical operation native to the human intellect and the rhetorical operation that seems to be excluded in statements like this. One must use a simile to say/know what sight is like.

4. For a pertinent discussion, see Marion Hobson, "*La Lettre sur les sourds et muets* de Diderot: labyrinthe et langage," *Semiotica* 16 (?) p. 303.

5. This relates in pertinent fashion to a lengthy tradition extending well before the seventeenth- and eighteenth-century grammarians, at least to Aristotle's "categories." For a modern prolongation of a very similar set of issues, see Emile Benveniste, *Problèmes de linguistique générale*, vol. 1 (Paris: Gallimard, 1966); and Derrida's response and analysis of Benveniste in "The Supplement of the Copula: Philosophy before Linguistics," trans. J. Creech and J. Harari, *Georgia Review* 30 (Fall 1976): 527–64.

6. If one can afford to be schematic here, it is because this basic problem for the eighteenth century has recently received the admirable scholarly attention it deserves. Most helpful to me, in addition to Marion Hobson's article (see note 3, above) have been G. Genette's invaluable *Mimologiques, voyage en Cratylie* (Paris: Seuil, 1976), particularly the chapters entitled "Peinture et dérivation" (pp. 85–118), and "Blanc bonnet versus bonnet blanc" (pp. 183–226); J. Chouillet's *La Formation des idées esthétiques de Diderot* (Paris: A. Colin, 1973), particularly pp. 151–257.

7. Quoted, for example, by Genette, *Mimologiques*, p. 188, and indirectly by Diderot himself in the present *Lettre*, p. 164. See Chouillet's editorial note, p. 164 n. 85, in the *D.P.V.* edition.

8. See Chouillet, *Formation des idées esthétiques*, pp. 160, 172. See too Franco Venturi, *La Jeunesse de Diderot* (Paris: Skira, 1939), pp. 247ff., for another interesting viewpoint. Appearing too late to be included in the discussion here, but of real significance, is Hans Aarlsleff's *From*

Locke to Saussure (Minneapolis: University of Minnesota Press, 1982), especially his pages on Condillac (pp. 224–46).

9. Quoted by Chouillet, *Formation des idèes esthetiques*, p. 173.

10. See ibid., pp. 173, 175.

11. Genette (*Mimologiques*, p. 206) suggests something of the work's importance: "Diderot inaugurates, but with more genius, the often naïve practices of so-called modern stylistics for which the supreme beauty of style seems always to be to double signification with imitation; but also he anticipates by more than a century an idea of 'poetic language' in which we will find one of the great refuges of cratylian desire."

12. In this way Diderot both recognizes Aristotle's importance, while at the same time echoing Locke's criticism of "substances" in the *Essay* (bk. 3, chap. 1, para. 5).

13. See pages 137–38, where Diderot maintains that "peripatetic" philosophy—Aristotelean, Greek, Ancient—is paradoxically responsible for the absence of Greek-style inversions in French.

14. Some three years later, a similar problem will be raised by Rousseau in his *Second Discourse*, concerning whether there was society before their was language, or language before society (Pléiade ed., 3:147–51). Rousseau uses several sets of analogous terms; for example, did man have to be a philosopher before becoming a man?

15. In his introduction to the *D.P.V.* edition of the *Lettre*, Jacques Chouillet correctly maintains that "the absolute originality of [Diderot's] position makes him pretty much unclassifiable" (p. 117). And again (p. 118), "All the alternatives of traditional aesthetics here lose a little of their reality."

16. E.g., Genette, *Mimologiques*, pp. 204–5.

17. "Emblème" connotes the visual effects of the pictoral epigraphs that introduced much sixteenth-century poetry. See J. Doolittle, "Hieroglyph and Emblem in Diderot's *Lettre sur les sourds et muets*," *Diderot Studies* 2 (1952): 148–67.

18. Daunted by the irony of translating poetry that Diderot calls untranslatable, I offer a rendition of the line in prose: "And the bloodied waters of France's rivers bore only the dead to the horrified seas.

19. Jean-Pierre Séguin, *Diderot, le discours et les choses*, (Paris: Klincksieck, 1978), p. 17. Here is, it seems to me, Séguin's basic point of departure: written language "reconstitutes in the imaginary the world of objects perceptible to the senses: such is the referential basis of Diderot's philosophical writing" (p. 34). From that point, Séguin goes on to suggest, in the logic of his analysis, that Diderot's texts do not really rely upon metaphor (p. 133), nor simile (p. 145). My point is that the necessary metaphoricity of language is indeed exemplified by Diderot's writing, and nowhere more obviously than in his analysis of "poetic hieroglyphs."

20. Compare to Chouillet's quite cogent analysis, *Formation des idèes esthétiques*, p. 222, according to which the poetic, is assimilated less to a differential experience than to a capacity "to go beyond the now illusory antithesis of thought and expression." Poetic intelligence consists in the

awareness of the new totality, "not in disjoining but in reuniting elements of the text. . . ." My point is that the greater weight is placed by Diderot on the disjunction so that the simultaneous whole of the poetic expression would be experienced as an ideality, marked as are all idealities by the difference of the terms conjoined in the representational moment.

21. See Chouillet's treatment of the question, *Formation des idées esthétiques*, p. 223.

22. See Lieselotte Dieckmann, *Hieroglyphics* (Saint Louis, Mo.: Washington University Press, 1970).

23. Something of this understanding of hieroglyphs, although not linked to Diderot, finds its way into John T. Irwin's *American Hieroglyphics* (New Haven, Conn.: Yale University Press, 1980). The question of access to language in the American nineteenth century leads to familiar formulations of the problem: "[As Humboldt seems to have understood], origination cannot be understood in terms of temporal priority precisely to time. 'Man and language (thought) come into existence simultaneously through a continuous network of mutually constitutive, differential opposition; yet the ground of this network by which man and language exist in time is itself, insofar as it is simultaneous, above the flow of time. Whether we call it the synchronic aspect of language as opposed to the temporal, it involves, as the origin and ground of human consciousness, the simultaneous, mutual constitution of sameness and difference. In the originating act, the knowing subject and the known object are simultaneously held apart as different and held together as same" (p. 51). In Irwin's analysis, the hieroglyph became the focus for this problem in the American Renaissance where he finds a myth of "the simultaneous origin of man and language," of "the origin of art—of symbolization or representation— . . . depicted as a form of hieroglyphic doubling" (p. 64).

24. Hobson, "La Lettre sur les sourds et muets," pp. 321–322.

25. Doolittle, "Hieroglyph and Emblem," p. 161, writes: "The poet who grasps and would speak of things in nature beyond the jurisdiction of reason and logic, has a problem of expression, and his critical problem of apprehension, which are analogous to those of the deaf-mute in the ordinary world just as the deaf mute uses and understands gesture to signify things for which he has no words, so the poet and the critic rely on hieroglyphic representation to communicate and comprehend things for which no conventional verbal expression is adequate."

26. Just such supplementarity is what underlies Diderot's often-discussed description of Père Castel's "ocular harpsichord" (pp. 145–46), and provides a rich subject of comparison with the analogous object in the *Lettre sur les aveugles*, namely, the mirror.

27. Chouillet, *Formation des idées esthétiques*, p. 255: "The hieroglyph conceived of as 'painting,' as 'moving tableau, a model according to which we are constantly painting,' is nothing more than the first, distant avatar of the 'ideal model.' "

28. *Diderot, ou les mots de l'absence* (Paris: Editions Champs Libre, 1976), p. 151.

CHAPTER NINE

1. "Encyclopédie," *D.P.V.*, 7:174. All further references will be given in the text.

2. George Havens, *The Age of Ideas* (New York: Henry Holt, 1955), p. 295. Or alternatively, see a similar appreciation in Franco Venturi, *Jeunesse de Diderot* (Paris: Skira, 1939), pp. 260–61. The same passage was recently the object of a quite different evaluation: "In fact, this mission of the *Encyclopedia* does not coincide with its historical role . . . since man's self-concept and action also result from a whole process of denegation that allows the system to function" (Groupe d'Intervention Lettres Nantes, "Lire 'L'Encyclopédie,' " in *Littérature* 42 [May 1981]: 30). The point of this article, I think, is that the *Encyclopedia* creates its audience as much as it instructs readers, and that the encyclopedic "narratee" turns out upon examination to correspond to a less idealistic model.

3. *The Order of Things* (New York: Random House, 1970), p. 206. All further page references are given in the text.

4. Foucault writes, "Though the being of language had been entirely reduced to its function within representation, representation, on the other hand, had no relation [*rapport*] to the universal except through the intermediary of language" (ibid., p. 86).

5. It would seem then that "Encyclopédie" owes its existence to a phenomenological imperative whose earliest exponent is often thought to be Hegel. As Vincent Descombes has recently noted, "Geist" is precisely what is "capable of becoming the concept of itself, i.e., is capable of conceiving its own identity. . . . In other words, the system contains one part . . . in which it is explained how the system is possible, or how this discourse was capable of being enunciated" (*Modern French Philosophy*, trans. L. Scott-Fox and J. M. Harding [Cambridge: Cambridge University Press, 1980], pp. 40–41).

6. Compare with the passage we saw before from *De la poésie dramatique* (*O.E.*, p. 284): "It is certain that there will be no term to our disputes if each person takes himself as a model and judge. There will be as many measures as judges. . . . That suffices, it seems to me, to feel the necessity of seeking a measure, a model [*modulc*] outside myself. . . . But where to find the unvarying measure that I seek and that I lack?"

7. In "Encyclopédie," Diderot defines "poetics of the genre" in this way: "I am taking the term poetics in its most general sense, as a system of given rules one assumes must be followed in whatever genre in order to succeed" (p. 234).

8. The *Encyclopedia* thus faces the dilemma that modern continental philosophy has articulated for any "work" in history. (It is a dilemma that

I would maintain is an outgrowth of the dilemma of representation itself.) Descombes (*Modern French Philosophy*, p. 71) puts it like this: "Either the work is on the side of freedom, but then it remains a project that is opposed to the world as it is, or else it is real, it takes its place in the world, but then it passes over to the side of objective being [l'être en soi] and no longer has any human qualities." This is the dilemma that Diderot—if not resolves—then, at least, lives intensely and affirmatively in "Encyclopédie."

9. London: Routledge, 1973, trans. Henry Maas. Further page references will be given in the text.

10. "Prolepsis" is defined as follows: "Figure of grammar consisting in the use of an epithet in which either an anterior or a future states is depicted" (Henri Morier, *Dictionnaire de poétique et de rhétorique* [Paris: P.U.F., 1961]). I prefer the single term, rather than the superfluous reference to the somewhat less clearly defined term of "metalepsis."

11. On the problem of continuity versus contiguity in the encyclopedic order, see Jean Starobinski, "Remarques sur l'Encyclopédie," *Revue de Métaphysique et de Morale*, July-September, 1970, pp. 284–91.

12. See Jacques Derrida, "Hors livre," in *La Dissémination* (Paris: Seuil, 1972).

13. For a discussion of "utopia" in this text, see Christie Vance McDonald, "The Work of the Text: Diderot's 'Encyclopédie,' " *The Eighteenth Century: Theory and Interpretation* 21 (Spring 1980): 128–44. More generally, see Louis Marin's "Disneyland: A Degenerate Utopia," *Glyph I* (1977), pp. 50–66. Utopia, according to Marin, "expresses what is absolutely new, the 'possible as such'. . . . On the other hand, utopia cannot transcend the common and ordinary language of a period and of a place" (p. 53).

14. Derrida, "Hors livre," note 24, p. 47 and p. 51. Further page references are given in the text.

15. "The authority of the encyclopedic model, analogical unity of man and god, can act by very circuitous means, according to complex mediations. It is moreover a matter of a model and a normative concept: which does not exclude that in the practice of writing . . . some forces remain foreign or contrary to the encyclopedic model and throw it violently into question." (Derrida, "Hors livre," p. 54.)

16. In the *Réfutation d'Helvetius*, Diderot will refer to the mind as "this principal organ . . . this sensate mirror" (*O.E.*, p. 612).

17. Richard Rorty, *Philosophy and the Mirror of Nature* (Princeton, N.J.: Princeton University Press, 1979).

18. "The Mirror Stage as Formative of the Function of the I as Revealed in Psychoanalytic Experience," in *Ecrits*, trans. Alan Sheridan (New York: Norton, 1977), p. 2. Further page references are given in the text.

19. The "I" so constituted is "pregnant with the correspondences that unite the I with the statue in which man projects himself" (p. 2), which suggests several interesting extensions of the analysis into Diderot's essay on "Expression."

20. For an elaboration of "jouissance" as a general textual function in Diderot's writing, see my "Diderot and the Pleasure of the Other: Friends, Readers, Posterity," *Eighteenth Century Studies* 7 (Summer, 1978): 439–56.

CHAPTER TEN

1. Jack Undank, *Diderot: Inside, Outside, and In-Between* (Madison, Wisc.: Coda Press, 1979); and Elisabeth de Fontenay, *Diderot ou le Matérialisme enchanté* (Paris: Grasset, 1979), p. 212.

2. Here we must take note of Paul de Man's recent warnings about a too-easy claim to modernity in much contemporary critical discourse. See his "The Resistance to Theory" in *Yale French Studies* 63 (1982): 3–20.

3. Jacques Derrida, "La Clôture de la représentation," *L'Ecriture et la différence* (Paris: Seuil, 1967), p. 347.

4. For an excellent adumbration of an analysis that would prove very useful in such a project, see Jacques Michot, "Un concept frappé de suspicion: *l'Abbildung*," in *Revue des Sciences Humaines*, No. 154 (June, 1974), pp. 213–29.

5. Derrida, "La Clôture," pp. 348–49.

6. How often, though, have we seen the reverse labor: to discover the real itinerary of Jacques and his master (see Francis Pruner, *L'Unité secrète de Jacques le fataliste* [Paris: Minard, 1970]), to know the fidelity of Diderot's language to "things" (see J.-P. Séguin, *Diderot, le discours et les choses* [Paris: Klincksieck, 1978]), or to know whether Rameau's nephew really represents his historical namesake (Milton Seidon, "Jean-François Rameau and Diderot's Neveu," in *Diderot Studies I* [1949], pp. 143–91; or the classic in the genre, Rudolf Schlösser, *Rameaus Neffe* [Berlin: Dunckder, 1900]).

7. See, as examples, Aram Vartanian's *Diderot and Descartes* (Princeton, N.J.: Princeton University Press, 1953; Jerome Schwartz's *Diderot and Montaigne* (Geneva: Droz, 1966); Norman Laidlaw's *Elysian Encounter: Diderot and Gide* (Syracuse, N.Y.: Syracuse University Press, 1963); Alice Fredmen's *Diderot and Sterne* (New York: Columbia University Press, 1950).

8. Vincent Descombes, *Modern French Philosophy*, trans. L. Scott-Fox and J. M. Harding (Cambridge: Cambridge University Press, 1980), p. 38. Descombes, speaking of Kojève's influence in France as an interpreter of Hegel, also writes, "In introducing difference into identity and negativity into being, thus proclaiming the unity of opposites, the only purpose of the dialectic is to safeguard the copulative meaning of being. Difference is necessary in order for identity to preserve itself as the first if not the exclusive, meaning of being" (ibid.). If Diderot certainly stands as a prototype of this conceptual possibility, I am not sure that one could say of his writing that it sets out to "safeguard" anything. Its power comes from an extraordinary capacity to affirm and to risk, at the same time.

9. In the logic of Hegel, as Descombes presents it, "The concept is an identity. The other of this same [identity] which the concept is, is the thing of which it is the concept. By definition, the concept is different from the thing: but, if it were 'too different' it would no longer be the concept of this thing . . . which is to say that the concept, without the thing, would not be true (since it would be the concept of nothing, an imaginary representation)" (p. 54). Diderot has deconstructed in advance the exclusive criteria for falsification on which such a representational logic is based.

10. In his *Instructions à Catherine II*, Diderot uses the same image again. "Your majesty likes to think that she has a model in the heavens whose eyes are fixed upon her conduct, and which, seeing her walk with so much goodness, so much nobility, such grandeur and humanity, smiles upon her an shares in the pleasure of a spectacle that earth does not offer it very often" (quoted by Paul Vernière, *O. Ph.*, p. 541 n. 2).

11. See my "Diderot and the Pleasure of the Other," in *Eighteenth-Century Studies* 8 (Summer 1978): 439–56.

12. This is a god structurally homologous to the one that Descartes announces in the fourth part of the *Discourse de la méthode:* "Following this, reflecting upon the fact that I doubted and that, as a consequence, my being was not utterly perfect (for I saw clearly that it is a greater perfection to know than to doubt). I decided to search for the source from which I had learned to think of a thing more perfect than myself; and I readily knew that this ought to originate from some nature that was in effect more perfect [that is, from God]. . . . I observed that doubt, inconstancy, sorrow, and the like could not be in him, given the fact that I would have been happy to be exempt from them" (Trans. Donald A. Cress [Indianapolis: Hackett Publishing Company, 1980], pp. 18, 19).

13. Leo Spitzer, *Linguistics and Literary History* (Princeton, N.J.: Princeton University Press, 1948), p. 154 passim.

14. See my "Le Neveu de Rameau: 'Diary' of a Reading," in *MLN* 95 (French Edition, 1980): 995–1004. We badly need a full, psychoanalytic study of Diderot's relation to paternal structures, notably in his correspondence, in the *Père de famille* and related dramatic outlines, and of course, in *Le Neveu de Rameau*.

15. *Le Fils naturel, D.P.V.*, 4:81.

16. Elisabeth de Fontenay, *Diderot*, p. 180. See also Gilles Deleuze, *Différence et répétition* (Paris: P.U.F., 1972), p. 370.

17. *Rameau's Nephew*, trans. L. W. Tancock (Middlesex, England: Penguin Books, 1966), p. 34. (Further page references are given in the text.) I find it remarkable—and a telling indication of a cultural resistance to the undecidable status of the nephew—that one translation of this text offers the following rendering of this sentence: "No one can change so utterly" (trans. W. Jackson [London: Chapman and Hall, 1926], p. 4).

18. Hegel, *The Phenomenology of Mind*, trans. J. B. Baillie (New York: Harper Torchbooks, 1967), p. 543. See also Jean Hyppolite's qualifications in *Genèse et structure de la Phénoménologie de l'esprit de Hegel*: "[The Nephew] shows himself according to any defined aspect.

He is never what he is, always outside himself, and returning into himself when he is outside himself" ([Paris: Aubier-Montagne, 1946], p. 399). It must be said, of course, that Hegel's use of the Nephew as the emblem of spirit is itself a reduction of his undecidable status to a representational positivity. See de Fontenay's chapter entitled "Un Fond lyrique inaliénable," *Diderot*, pp. 236–43, and Deleuze, *Différence et répétition*, p. 344.

19. See Jean Fabre's footnote on Vertumnus in his edition of *Le Neveu de Rameau* (Geneva: Editions Droz, 1952), p. 111 n. 1.

20. Michel Foucault has described the Nephew as a "sovereign consciousness" of being and nothingness in a "twining circle" (*Folie et déraison: histoire de la folie à l'âge classique* [Paris: Plon, 1961], p. 421).

21. In his *Dostoevsky's Poetics*, Mikhail Bakhtin describes the carnivalesque tradition in literature in terms quite resonant with Diderot's metaphor for the nephew as a "speck of yeast." The "carnivalistic yeast," he writes, is the basis of "the carnival attitude [that] possesses an indestructible attitude, and the mighty, lifegiving power to transform." (trans. R. W. Rotsel [New York: Ardis, 1973], p. 88). Bakhtin explicitly includes *Le Neveu* in this tradition. In *Rabelais and His World* (trans. Helen Iswolsky [Cambridge: M.I.T. Press, 1968]), he also includes *Les Bijoux indiscrets* (p. 34) and *Jacques le fataliste* (p. 118) in the same tradition.

22. Thus the musical metaphor disdains the logic of non-contradiction upon which a word (*la parole*) is traditionally founded according to Julia Kristeva ("Poésie et négativité" in *Semiotike* [Paris: Seuil, 1969]), pp. 246–77). Kristeva has convincingly extended a very similar argument in an analysis of *Le Neveu* in "La Musique parlée, ou remarques sur la subjectivité dans la fiction à propos du *Neveu de Rameau*" (in *Langue et langages de Leibniz à l'Encyclopédie* [Paris: Union Générale des Editeurs, 1977], pp. 153–206).

23. Elizabeth Bruss notes in *Beautiful Theories* (Baltimore: Johns Hopkins University Press) p. 74: "It is only a slight step from such fictitious criticism to the 'critical fictions' and constructs of a theorist, which in their most extreme form may themselves be only ideal types— extrapolations and projections that have never actually been observed but that nevertheless help to classify the real. But in taking this additional step, and granting that theoretical constructs have a literary value too, one grants to reading that much more artfulness, acknowledging its powers and its burden to transform."

24. Fredric Jameson has articulated a resonant critique of Frankfurt School aesthetics: "What is unsatisfactory about the Frankfurt School position is not its negative and critical apparatus, but rather the positive value on which the latter depends, namely the valorization of traditional modernist high art and subversive 'autonomous aesthetic production' " ("Reification and Utopia in Mass Culture" in *Social Text*, No. 1 [Winter 1979], p. 133).

25. Elizabeth Bruss's formulation is precisely to the point here: "The problem for self-reflexive literature, then, is that having abandoned naïve imitation and 'aboutness,' it will be tempted to remain at this stage,

or even to substitute self-reference for the referent it has lost, becoming obsessively 'about itself . . . about the impossibility of its own existence.' Even if it refers only to itself, such works are ultimately no freer of the belief that they are copying in a pre-existent meaning than are conventional representations. Not bothering to construct rich or convincing illusions, its disillusionments will be petty and will therefore offer little insight into the nature of our faith and fantasies, however discourse manages to pique our curiosity and to arouse our credulity. Thus the impasse of contemporary art: on one side, a curiously falsehearted attempt to return to realistic representation (curious because what results is an 'imitation' of traditional representation), and on the other an equally phlegmatic avant-garde that has, in the words of Robert Scholes, 'failed to find viable, continuing solutions to the problem of linguistic limitations' " (*Beautiful Theories*, pp. 74–75). The quote from Scholes should not mislead. The limitations of language are not susceptible of being "resolved." Indeed, as the example of Saunderson or Mangogul shows us, language lives on its limitations, producing some of its most powerful and (sometimes) "felicitous" tropological effects from them. And what is more, as the same examples indicate, the problem of language's limitations is not one that we moderns face for the first time.

26. In "Resistance to Theory," *Yale French Studies*, no. 63 (1982), p. 12.

27. Ibid., p. 12. In the article in which this pasing comment is made, de Man goes on to discover similar difficulties in the medieval system of a trivium (concerning language's internal relations), and a quadrivium (concerning the non-verbal sciences). The issue thus becomes one of an agency capable of assuring the connection between the two—a problem that de Man sees underlying epistemology well into the eighteenth century (see pp. 13 ff). My argument in the present study has attempted to generalize the question of agency in such representational schemata, beyond the particular forms or expressions characteristic of a particular period.

28. Bruss has taken up this view, this attitude, with more persuasiveness than many on the Anglo-Saxon scene. Imported into the context of Diderot's writing—though not at all her topic—her language resonates loudly: "The literary devices that literary theory expose are thus allowed to do their own work and to achieve their own most characteristic effects, rather than being made futile from the start. The resulting analysis is bound to be more interesting, capable of greater depth and subtler illumination. As one piece of writing *penetrates the different native figures of another*, it strikes sparks in all directions rather than the steadily increasing pallor of images that mirror one another. In addition, theory avoids the bad faith of pretending to do the impossible, to catch itself in the act when in fact the act of scrutiny can never be the same as the act it scrutinizes, leaving *an eternal blind* spot that no discourse can overcome" (*Beautiful Theories*, p. 75; my emphasis).

POSTSCRIPT A TO CHAPTER FIVE

1. For a typical example, see Carol Blum, *Diderot: The Virtue of a Philosopher* (New York: Viking Press, 1974).

2. *A.-T.*, 5:213. Further page other references are given in the text.

3. "Representation and Its Discontents," in *Allegory and Representation*, ed. Stephen Greenblatt (Baltimore: Johns Hopkins University Press, 1981), p. 150. All further references are given in the text.

4. In the *Salon de 1767*, we read: "What a fine spectacle is the show of virtue put severely to the test. Assault by the most terrible forces does not displease us. In our thoughts we willingly identify with oppressed heroes. . . . Only one thing can draw us to the villain, and that is the grandeur of his views, the extent of his genius, the peril of his enterprise. In that case, if we forget his wickedness to throw in our lot with him, if we conspire against Venice with the Count of Bedman, it is again virtue that is subjugating us in another guise" (*A.-T.* 11:118).

5. There are many examples one could cite in Diderot that suggest such a conjugation of pain and pleasure, perhaps none so extraordinary as his letter to his mistress upon hearing of his father's death. See *Correspondence*, eds. G. Roth and J. Varloot (Paris: Minuit, 1956), 2:157–59.

POSTSCRIPT B TO CHAPTER FIVE

1. See, for example, "The Phaedo," 74c–75a, *Dialogues of Plato*, trans. B. Jowett (Oxford: Oxford University Press), Vol. 2.

2. Quoted by Derrida in "La Double Séance," in *La Dissémination* (Paris: Seuil, 1977), p. 216 n. 2. If we are perhaps less naïve about the status of such reversals in neoclassical thought, it is certainly due in large part to the work of Derrida. But his treatment of the texts has never pretended, in the case of Diderot, to be adequate to the task of placing him within that tradition.

POSTSCRIPT TO CHAPTER SEVEN

1. (Berkeley: University of California Press, 1980). Further page references are in the text.

2. Fried's work invites a serious correlation, comparison, or contrast with Foucault's analysis of Velasquez's "Las Meninas," in *Les Mots et les choses*, pp. 19–31.

3. See his chapter 2, pp. 71–105.

4. *Correspondance*, 4:57, as translated and quoted by Fried, pp. 147–48.

5. *O.E.*, p. 97.

INDEX

73, 84, 91, 170, 184 n. 16, 188 n. 5, 190 nn. 13, 16; 191 n. 26; 201 n. 14